MEDIA
MONOLITHS

Also published by Kogan Page

MEDIA
MONOLITHS

How great media brands thrive and survive

Mark Tungate

**KOGAN
PAGE**

London and Sterling, VA

For my mother and father, who taught me to read,
and never told me to turn off the TV

Publisher's note
Every possible effort has been made to ensure that the information contained in this book is accurate at the time of going to press, and the publisher and author cannot accept responsibility for any errors or omissions, however caused. No responsibility for loss or damage occasioned to any person acting, or refraining from action, as a result of the material in this publication can be accepted by the editor, the publisher or the author.

First published in Great Britain and the United States in 2004 by Kogan Page Limited

120 Pentonville Road
London N1 9JN
United Kingdom
www.kogan-page.co.uk

22883 Quicksilver Drive
Sterling VA 20166–2012
USA

© Mark Tungate, 2004

ISBN 0 7494 4108 9

British Library Cataloguing-in-Publication Data

A CIP record for this book is available from the British Library.

Library of Congress Cataloging-in-Publication Data

Tungate, Mark 1967-
   Media monoliths : how great media brands thrive and survive / Mark Tungate.
     p. cm.
   ISBN 0-7494-4108-9
   1. Mass media--Economic aspects. 2. Brand name products I. Title.
P96.E25T86 2004
338.4'730223--dc22
                 2004005769

Typeset by Saxon Graphics Ltd, Derby
Printed and bound in Great Britain by Scotprint

Contents

Acknowledgements

A lot of people need thanking for this book – not just those who spent hours recounting anecdotes and marketing strategies, but also the people who set up interviews, sent background material and sourced photographs. Obviously, my first word of thanks goes to everyone quoted in the book. Everyone else, I hope, is listed below. If I've forgotten you, feel free to call me up and I'll buy you a drink some time.

Nigel Pritchard and Claudia Coles at CNN, Rob Hooper and Polly Stevens at MTV, Anoushka Healy at *The Times*, Joanna Manning-Cooper at the *Financial Times*, Brigitte Trafford at *The Wall Street Journal*, Iliane Weiss and Arefe Shariatmadari at *Die Zeit*, Catherine J Mathis at *The New York Times*, Charlotte Gordon at the *International Herald Tribune*, Nathalie Sarazin at *Libération*, Emma Gilpin at *Time* magazine, Ellen Siskind at *National Geographic*, Antonia Camilleri at *Vogue* UK, Lorna Donohoe at *Playboy*, Kate Cooke at *The Economist*, Yvonne Diaz and Nancy Bobrowitz at Reuters, Georgie Whittaker at Bloomberg.

In addition, I'd like to thank people in various cities who offered accommodation, fed me, or found telephone numbers: Lisa in London, Kelly, Larry, and especially Claire in New York, Kimberly in Atlanta, Emanela and Elena in Milan.

And finally, thanks to all my friends in Paris, who encouraged me right from the beginning.

Introduction

'The biggest bazaar in the world'

It is a sultry, overcast day in downtown Manhattan, and I am looking for a very special store. I'm acting on a friend's casual tip-off: 'You're interested in the media, right? You have to see this place – I reckon it sells every single magazine that's published. It's on Broadway somewhere, near SoHo.'

I finally track it down – a narrow green-painted store on the corner of Broadway and Broome. A banner outside tells me that it is called Universal News & Café, and that it stocks no fewer than 7,000 magazines.

The store is very long and thin, with a counter running along one side and a few tables and chairs squished into the middle. People drink coffee and leaf through magazines that they have no intention of buying. It would be an entirely unremarkable place, were it not for the walls, which are lined from floor to ceiling with magazines. Lurid covers screech at me, their headlines promising to supply the latest info about sex, fashion, food, drink, music, movies, sport, business, vacations, men's health, women's health, going out, staying in, being single, being gay, falling in love, getting married, having a baby, getting a divorce, and retiring. And that doesn't include the specialist magazines aimed at everyone from archaeologists to zoologists.

For a second I am dizzy, and the store's garish walls seem to expand and contract like the prisms of a kaleidoscope. Then I balance myself, refocus, and begin searching for the magazines I habitually flick through: *GQ*, *The Face*, *National Geographic*, *Wallpaper*, *Time*, *The Economist* – my own little pantheon of brands. These are the publications that I trust, the ones that have kept me company through thousands of air miles, in hundreds of hotel rooms and cafés. I check out some of the other titles, but none of them really grab me. Of a choice of 7,000 magazines, I leave the store with the same four or five publications I always buy.

Back at my friend's apartment in Hoboken, I switch on the TV. The remote seems to give me access to well over 100 channels. As I zap rapidly through them, I find myself hesitating at those whose names I recognize: Discovery, HBO, CNBC, Fox, CNN… Finally I settle for MTV, another old friend, and the perfect accompaniment to drinking iced coffee and reading magazines.

By now you've got my point. The media market is just that: a bazaar, the biggest, noisiest and most crowded on the planet, with thousands of different vendors competing for your attention, urging you to look at their latest stuff. In a world where just one small shop in New York stocks 7,000 magazines, how can any of them hope to stand out?

WHAT'S IN A LIST?

As you may have gathered, this is no ordinary marketing book. For a start, I set out to write the kind of book that I might actually like to read. So I have deliberately avoided footnotes, statistics, and the sort of fussy graphs and charts that many branding experts use to add legitimacy to their claims. Besides, I am not one of those – I am a journalist, and my mission was to find out how other journalists (or rather, how other people who worked in the media) sold their products to the public.

In short, I set out to answer the question I asked a few sentences ago – along with a few others. Why do we remain loyal to certain newspapers and magazines? Why do we 'instinctively' turn to a narrow group of television channels when we have a choice of hundreds? And how has this elite group of media brands survived when so many others have expired?

During the course of my research, I visited newspaper offices and TV stations in London, Paris, Milan, Madrid, New York and Atlanta – and had telephone conversations with people around the globe. I felt it was important to capture the atmosphere of my journey, and to describe – or at least sketch – some of the places and people I came across in the media bazaar. After all, most marketing experts agree that the essence of a brand begins with its employees and their working environment. So I make no apologies if, from time to time, this book reads like a travelogue.

And what about the brands themselves – how did I choose them? Initially, it was quite simple. If you sat down one evening with a glass of wine and wrote a list of the 20 media brands you considered to be the most famous in the world, it would probably look a lot like mine.

After that, it was a case of tweaking the selection to fit the structure of the book. I wanted a good mixture of TV, magazine and newspaper brands. I did not want them all to be Anglo-Saxon. And I wanted to blend the highbrow with the populist – I liked the idea of writing about *The Economist* one minute and *Playboy* the next. Also, I wanted the brands to be internationally recognizable – I envisaged them as the kind of titles one might find on newsstands everywhere from Athens to Warsaw. (That's why I haven't included *The Sun* – a massive brand in the UK that has little presence, I would argue, outside its domestic market.) I dumped a couple of subjective choices in favour of those that would make more interesting case studies.

You'll have noticed that I did not include any radio or Internet brands. Radio stations were discarded because of their lack of global reach, at least in the commercial arena (although I have touched on the BBC World Service in the chapter about BBC World). And while I was interested in Internet brands like Amazon and Yahoo! I decided that the most interesting thing about the Web was the way the media monoliths had overcome their fear of it and adopted it as a marketing tool.

Once I was happy with my selection, I checked it with international media buyers, and compared it with the major readership and branding surveys. I was pleased to see that four of my choices (MTV, *Time*, Reuters and *The Wall Street Journal*) featured in Interbrand's annual survey of the world's most valuable brands. Ipsos-RSL's two important European readership surveys, the European Business Readership Survey (EBRS) and the Europe 2000 series, both confirmed that the names on my list were relevant. So did the European Media and Marketing Survey (EMS), conducted by Interview-NSS. The International Air Travellers Survey (IATS), carried out by the Inflight Marketing Bureau in Paris, also reassured me that I had chosen correctly.

Some readers will inevitably disagree with my choices, and a couple of media brands may even write to me asking why I missed them out. To the latter I can only apologize. And who knows? – maybe they'll let me write a sequel.

TRIALS AND PUBLIC RELATIONS

The list evolved during the writing process – and for reasons that are worth going into. For instance, I had originally included *Vanity Fair* and the *New Yorker*, because they are brands that I personally admire. But they are both part of the Condé Nast group, along with *Vogue*, so I was forced to choose one. It had to be *Vogue* – surely one of the ultimate media monoliths. While it was difficult to get information on *Vogue*, executives in London and Paris proved very helpful.

In general, it was noticeable that the largest and most successful media brands were also the most welcoming and efficient. CNN and MTV bent over backwards to help me. *The Times*, *The Wall Street Journal* and the *Financial Times* were also exemplary in their openness. Even *The Economist*, which I had previously imagined to be stuffy and unapproachable, was briskly cooperative. *The New York Times* and the *International Herald Tribune* were mired in internal politics for most of the research period, but finally came through with flying colours. (I had expected the family-owned concerns – such as Dow Jones and The New York Times Company – to be the most reticent, but this proved not to be the case.) Smaller titles like *Paris Match* and *Die Zeit* were much harder to crack, with public relations departments that seemed to have a brief to hinder rather than help.

All this is just the daily grind of research, but it brings me on to an important point. PR is a vital component of marketing, especially if you own a consumer product. And all of the 20 brands featured in this book are products, just like foodstuffs, cars and clothing. They owe their survival to the loyalty of their customers, to members of the public – to people like you and me.

The older media monoliths were confronted with this reality during the parallel rise of the Internet and satellite TV. Fragmenting audiences and falling circulation figures meant fewer advertisers and decreasing revenues. This trend was brought into sharp focus by the recession, a fissure that turned into a canyon after 11 September 2001. Suddenly, for the first time in decades, the media monoliths looked vulnerable. And then, just before I started writing this book, something else happened.

A HOSTILE CLIMATE

In May 2003, a 27-year-old journalist called Jayson Blair left *The New York Times* under a cloud. According to the paper's internal investigators, he had lifted material from rival newspapers and padded out his stories with hefty doses of invention. When he should have been on assignment in Maryland, Washington and Texas, among other places, he had been filing copy from his home in New York. (In other words, he had used good old-fashioned British tabloid journalism techniques.)

The New York Times was not impressed, and in an unprecedented display of self-laceration, it devoted two lengthy articles in its 11 May issue – including part of the front cover – to correcting facts and apologizing to its readers. Only a few days later, another *New York Times* writer was suspended after it was discovered that he had put his own name on a feature written by an intern. The newspaper seemed to implode with finger pointing and recrimination.

Some onlookers may have wondered why *The New York Times* made such a public meal of the Jayson Blair saga. After all, any journalist who has had any contact with the public knows that most people think the media make things up most of the time. A USA Today/Gallup poll published just after the Blair affair showed that only 36 per cent of respondents believed the media 'got their facts straight'. And that belief was not entirely linked to recent events – a similar poll published in December 2000 put the figure at 32 per cent.

Writing about the poll and the Blair witch-hunt, *Time* magazine columnist James Poniewozik pointed out: 'Collectively, we agonized: "Will the public ever trust us again?" "Don't sweat it," the public replied. "We didn't trust you in the first place."' ('Don't Blame It on Jayson Blair', *Time* magazine, 1 June 2003.)

Yet trust is now the single biggest issue concerning the media monoliths. Almost everyone I interviewed for this book brought it up in one form or another. Paul Hayes, general manager of *The Times*, was perhaps the most specific, when he said: 'If you lose the trust of your reader, you've had it. Everything else you do as a brand flows from that. If a reader thinks for one second that they can't trust what they are reading, the contract is broken.'

CNN's marketing slogan in the United States is 'The most trusted name in news'.

The media's paranoia about trust derives partially from consolidation. Although they are breaking themselves up to address fragmenting audiences, the media are controlled by an ever-shrinking number of conglomerates. While this has obvious business benefits – cross-media advertising packages, promotional synergies (hence a story about film studio Warner's *Matrix* trilogy makes the cover of *Time* magazine, owned by Time Warner) – it also leaves them open to accusations of corporate bias, greed and loss of integrity. The anti-globalization crowd have already had a go at the fast food and retail giants – how long can it be before they start attacking the media monoliths?

Actually, the offensive has already begun. In France in 2003, the newspaper *Le Monde* was accused of arrogance, corruption and political bias in a book called *La Face Cachée du Monde* (The Hidden Face of *Le Monde*, by Pierre Péan and Philippe Cohen). Although the paper ran a long article repudiating the claims, the rest of the French media – and quite a few members of the public – had great fun tearing chunks out of a cultural institution that had begun to look pompous and out of touch. (It also explains why *Libération* is the French newspaper featured in this book.)

The New York Times' handling of the Jayson Blair scandal was perhaps proof that the media monoliths know they are in the firing line. It was a pre-emptive strike, an admission of guilt that was also a step towards greater transparency. The media have begun to accept that they are, after all, accountable.

The other reason for the media monoliths' obsession with trust is their realization that, in an information-saturated world, it is one of the few things they have left to sell. When you're up against thousands of other magazines, for example, it helps if you have a pre-established connection with your customer – the kind of long and mutually respectful relationship that means they will keep coming back to your title, instead of picking up one of the many other fashion/food/skydiving publications on the same shelf. (They may even go to your Web site, buy your books, and wear your t-shirts too.)

If you let that customer down – by lying to them, or even worse, by patronizing them – you could lose them for good. All the brand equity in the world isn't going to help you if your customers no longer believe a word you say.

THE MEDIA BRANDING PARADOX

Media marketing directors understand the value of content, which is why an increasing number of them seek to influence it. As a journalist, I found the level of cooperation between marketing departments and editorial teams surprising, and occasionally disturbing. How much of a newspaper's content should be driven by commercial concerns, instead of by what is happening in the news?

During my research for this book, many newspapers and magazines admitted that they had begun tailoring their content to fit the 35- to 45-year-old readership group – which also happens to be the most important target market for advertisers. Any journalists who want to dispute my theory that the media are consumer goods should perhaps interview their own bosses.

Content is king, but it is not the entire realm. As the marketing director of a media brand you have three basic missions (apart from when your job interfaces with that of the advertising sales department): to retain the loyalty of your existing audience; to attract new readers or viewers; and to steer both groups in the direction of any profitable brand extensions you might have.

The catch is that all of these tasks can be self-defeating. Come on too strong with your marketing, and your existing audience might feel alienated by your ham-fisted seduction techniques. Play it too cool, and potential converts to your brand might not realize you are trying to woo them. And both parties may regard your brand extensions as tasteless and tacky, undermining the credibility of your core product.

Time and time again, the marketing directors and chief executives of famous media properties told me that they felt as if they were walking a tightrope – that they risked destroying years of brand heritage with a single bad advertisement or a cheaply branded product.

So what are they to do? Well, I'll provide a detailed roundup of their options at the end of the book. But until then, I think it's best if I let them explain their strategies in their own words.

AUTHOR'S NOTE: The statistics and job titles quoted in this book were correct at the time of writing (April–December 2003). Unless otherwise indicated in the text, all background and historical information was supplied by the media brands concerned.

PART 1

THE BROADCASTERS

1

CNN International

'It's always primetime somewhere'

There's no easy way of saying this, so I'll just spit it out: CNN is based in a shopping mall. To put it more accurately, the CNN offices and studios overlook a vast atrium at the core of a building called the CNN Center, an angular sand-coloured landmark in downtown Atlanta. The building also contains a sports arena in which I later watch an Atlanta Thrashers ice hockey game. But the ground floor of the atrium is lined with takeaway joints. A couple of CNN staffers told me that during the conflict in Iraq, they sometimes didn't leave the building for 48 hours. After all, they had plenty to eat.

As I wait for my first meeting at CNN, I sit at one of the café tables in the mall, tucking into a jet-lag breakfast of scrambled eggs and fried potatoes. (I could just have easily chosen a cheeseburger or 'chicken fingers', whatever they are.) High above me, two huge screens are showing CNN's international and US channels. Tony Blair is shaking hands with somebody on one, and George W Bush is addressing the press corps on the other. The walls of the atrium are lined with clocks telling me the time in all the major cities of the world. On the tiled floor beneath my feet is a giant map, studded with brass plaques indicating the locations of the CNN bureaux. Also within my line of sight are a CNN souvenir store and a sign promoting tours of the CNN studios.

Needless to say, I am delighted with all this. 'Now that's what you call marketing,' I think to myself. 'That's what you call a brand.'

CNN was one of the first channels to recognize that news is a product, and that it needs great packaging if it is to attract consumers. When you look at it that way, it makes perfect sense that the CNN Center is a shopping complex.

CNN has its critics – mainly those who fear American cultural imperialism, although they are missing the point – but there is no knocking its achievements. From its beginnings in 1980 as a single TV network with 25 staff, available to only 1.7 million homes, it has grown into a collection of 16 networks reaching more than 250 million households worldwide. Its international service alone (the main focus of this chapter) consists of two networks and five tailored 'feeds', covering more than 200 countries and territories.

Here at CNN's Atlanta headquarters, there are journalists from 50 different countries. Worldwide, CNN has 4,000 staff and 39 bureaux. Taking into account all its television networks, plus its Web, radio and mobile phone news services, CNN estimates that its brand now has the ability to reach a billion people across the globe. The company may have a healthy dose of Americana in its DNA – but it hasn't been a purely American product for some time now.

TURNER'S VISION

CNN does not belong to Ted Turner any more. The outspoken media mogul stepped down as vice-chairman of AOL Time Warner in January 2003. In subsequent interviews, he claimed that the poor performance of AOL Time Warner's share price had cost him seven or eight billion dollars ('How I lost $8 billion, by Ted Turner', *The Guardian*, 6 February 2003). It was a downbeat end to his 23-year adventure as the founder and figurehead of one of the ultimate media brands.

Turner had sold his television empire, Turner Broadcasting, to Time Warner in 1996, becoming the company's largest shareholder. When Time Warner and AOL decided to merge, Turner backed the decision. But later he came into conflict with the company's senior executives over its strategy. Nevertheless, when Turner resigned to pursue his 'socially responsible business efforts' (CNN/money, 29 January 2003, money.cnn.com), AOL Time Warner chief executive Richard Parsons said the company had been grateful for his 'vision and genius'. The description was not much of an exaggeration.

Robert Edward Turner III was born in Cincinnati, Ohio in 1938. He was only 24 when his father died in 1963, but he took on the ailing family business – a billboard company – and began to turn it around. He acquired a small Atlanta TV station in 1970 and used it as the foundation for his television company, Turner Broadcasting System. By the mid-1970s he was wealthy enough to buy the Atlanta Braves professional baseball team. A skilled yachtsman, he won the America's Cup in 1977 with his vessel *Courageous*.

Turner launched the Cable News Network on 1 June 1980. At the launch ceremony, the flag of the United Nations was raised alongside those of the United States and the state of Georgia, hinting at Turner's global ambitions. Quoted in a book called *CNN – Making News in the Global Market*, by Don M Flournoy and Robert K Stewart, Turner says that his worldwide yacht racing activities had given him a global perspective. 'The thing that made me think internationally was… sailboat racing. I went all over the world racing sailboats… [and] I realized how parochial most Americans are. We're such a big country and a wealthy country, and we think that the world – like the Romans did at the time of the Roman Empire – somehow circles around us, that we're the centre of the universe.'

According to Chris Cramer, president of CNN International Networks, Turner's vision lives on today. 'The brand promise as articulated by Ted Turner in 1979 remains unchanged. He was driven by the notion that existing broadcast networks did not serve viewers well enough, that they had similar narrow agendas and did not cover the world as it should be covered. His plan was that CNN should be a truly international news channel, spanning the globe.'

It was some time before Turner was able to achieve this ambition. His plan, in any case, was a radical one for the period. Turner had realized that by using satellites to deliver CNN to cable operators across the USA, he could reach consumers without having to create a traditional network of local broadcasters. But at that time, as Flournoy and Stewart's book points out, 'only about 20 per cent of US television households could receive cable television, and [Turner's] new 24-hour news channel reached only 1.7 million of those households – far fewer than were needed to make a profit'.

The book describes how CNN lost money hand over fist for its first few years, with Turner spending as much as US$70 million to keep it afloat. However, this did not stop him launching a second channel,

CNN Headline News – which provided quick news updates, as opposed to CNN's broader analysis – in 1981.

By the mid-80s things were changing. New cable operators were coming on to the scene, and the wider variety of channels was attracting more viewers. Satellite was enabling the media to go global, so Turner combined the CNN and Headline News signals and put them on an international satellite, creating CNN International in 1985. That same year, CNN posted a profit for the first time.

THE CNN EFFECT

The milestones came thick and fast after that. In 1987, CNN launched the first global newscast, *CNN World Report*, providing unedited, uncensored news reports from broadcasters in 100 countries. Turner had always felt that the world's TV viewers needed an unbiased news report. Interviewed for Flournoy and Stewart's book in 1996, he says with chilling prescience: 'Nobody ever gave the Palestinians or the Arab side a voice. Not here in the United States anyway. They didn't have a voice. The most angry people in the world are those that don't get listened to.'

By 1989, CNN operating profit had reached US$100 million. It served 50 million US households and was available 24 hours a day in Europe, the Middle East and South East Asia.

And then, in 1991, the Gulf War began. CNN reported exclusively live from Baghdad on the first night of the air attacks on Iraq. Its pictures were picked up and retransmitted by terrestrial TV channels around the globe – complete with the telltale CNN logo in the corner of the screen. This was probably the single most significant event in CNN's rise to global recognition. The network's coverage of the war created what became known as 'the CNN effect', which now has people switching on the channel or logging on to its Web site whenever a major news event occurs, confident that they'll find the latest news. The company itself says its trademark across all its platforms is 'breaking news'. CNN's rise to prominence was acknowledged by *Time* magazine in January 1992, when it made Ted Turner its Man of the Year.

The remarkable achievements continued. CNN had doubled its operating profit level to US$200 million by 1993. It embarked on a significant expansion in the Asia-Pacific region, opening its regional production centre in Hong Kong two years later. It also launched its Web site, CNN.com, as the only site with a 24-hour full-time staff, providing constantly updated news augmented by video, sound clips, still photographs, maps and text.

Turner himself hit the headlines even harder than usual in 1997 when he donated US$1 billion to the United Nations. UN secretary general Kofi Annan called him a 'world citizen extraordinaire'.

He certainly seemed to have a talent for making friends. That same year, CNN received permission from Fidel Castro to set up a bureau in Cuba – the first American news organization to be allowed into the country for 30 years. But Turner knew the Cuban president personally, having first visited the country a decade earlier. And Castro was a fan of CNN – he had a satellite dish and felt that it was important to keep track of world events.

Also in 1997, CNN set up a Spanish-language network, CNN en Español, for the Latin American market. At the same time, CNN International began tailored regional programming, eventually splitting into five different feeds (for viewers in Europe, Asia-Pacific, South Asia, Latin America and North America). Turner's dream of a global news service had become a reality.

The fact that CNN was now part of Time Warner did not slow its progress, with the creation of CNN+ in Spain and CNN Turk in Istanbul in 1999. By the end of Turner's reign, CNN had 11 different networks.

Turner's departure may not have occurred under the happiest of circumstances, but he can be proud of the incredible brand he created. One CNN employee told me that Turner's motto is: 'Lead, follow, or get out of the way.' Turner has taken the third option as far as CNN is concerned, but he is still there in spirit.

INTERNATIONAL VERSUS AMERICAN

While CNN is a global, all-encompassing brand, its various strands have their own distinct identities. CNN/US and CNN International (CNNI), for example, have developed radically different approaches to the same task. In a bid to compete with the blaring, strident Fox News, CNN/US appears to have adopted a more populist stance, with slick presenters, urgent editing and an information-filled screen. For a news network, CNN/US is unusually bright and cuddly (during my visit to Atlanta, the morning show devoted a large chunk of airtime to the fact that one of its anchors was leaving).

CNN International, on the other hand, is a more sober affair, recalling the BBC. There are fewer American accents. The tone of the news coverage is restrained rather than dramatic. This disparity was at its most obvious during the conflict in Iraq, when CNN/US was accused of presenting an Americanized, perhaps even sanitized view of the conflict – while CNNI was praised for showing both sides, unblinkingly depicting Iraqi casualties and American wounded. (The two channels even have different slogans – CNN/US is 'The most trusted name in news', while CNNI has opted for 'Be the first to know'.)

Even the US press noticed the difference, when CNNI took over the slot usually reserved for CNN's 24-hour financial channel, CNN*fn*, for a month. 'The best cable-news alternative to Fox isn't CNN, it's CNN International, the branch of CNN the rest of the world sees,' noted *LA Weekly* ('How American is it? Fox News vs. CNN International', *LA Weekly*, May 2–8 2003). And *The Wall Street Journal* observed: 'Viewers outside the US now see a far more global view of the current conflict... frequently reflecting the opposition to American policy felt by much of the world.' ('CNN Gives US, World Two Distinct Views', *The Wall Street Journal*, 14 April 2003.)

Chris Cramer, president of CNNI Networks (and a Brit), is aware and even proud of this distinction. 'CNN should be one church with different sermons,' he says. 'We all aspire to editorial integrity and strive to be comprehensive, fair, accurate, and impartial. That's the basic mission. No matter how big we are, or how many networks or Web sites we have, in no matter what language, that's the beating heart of CNN.'

But Cramer points out that expatriate Americans make up only 1.5 per cent of CNNI's audience, so its approach is naturally different to that of its US counterpart. During the conflict in Iraq, most Americans wanted to know how their troops were doing. But CNNI had a duty to acknowledge that many people around the rest of the world didn't think they should be there in the first place.

In fact, CNNI's regional strategy sprang from changing attitudes to the CNN brand after the first Gulf War. 'When I first arrived at CNN in 1995, there was a vague suspicion that we were living off the laurels of the Gulf War. But times had changed, and we couldn't guarantee that people would automatically switch to us. We were beginning to lose relevance, so we decided to get closer to our audiences.'

Like BBC World, CNNI has worked hard to 'de-nationalize' its brand identity. Many of its viewers speak English as a second language, so it studiously avoids American slang. Its anchors are multicultural. 'We are not an Atlanta channel that strives to be international, but an international channel that happens to be based in Atlanta – an important distinction,' Cramer says. 'The fact is, we could be based anywhere. Our dilemma is that our intelligent, educated target audience know that we are based in America, and expect us to provide the very best coverage of American news. So we have to over-serve them with that, while not stooping to Americana.'

Cramer is certain that CNNI has achieved this balance – if only because he was highly critical of the network's approach in the past. 'When I got here in 1996, we looked extremely American. I'm exaggerating a little, but it was all big hair, white teeth, and coverage that focused on bombs, bullets and ballots. It was brash and aggressive. We adjusted all that – not to disguise the fact that we are an American channel, but to meet the expectations of a very sophisticated international audience.'

He stresses that CNNI's viewers are 'movers and shakers' (although he hates the term) – well-travelled business types who demand certain standards. Although CNN provides a sprinkling of what might be referred to as 'entertainment programming' – a quick glance at the schedule reveals *The Music Room*, *World Sport*, *Design 360* and *Larry King Live* – its content is overwhelmingly news-based. As CNNI is a 24-hour global channel, it doesn't have the luxury of being able to fill the airwaves with fodder when nobody is looking. Several people at CNN headquarters told me: 'For us, it's always primetime somewhere.'

This demand for constantly updated reports puts a lot of pressure on the channel – and its journalists. Some critics claim that in the constant battle for spectacular visuals, news channels are pushing their reporters closer to the action, and into more danger. Cramer says CNNI's strategy is the reverse – to provide the technology that allows journalists to report from conflict situations, without putting their lives at risk.

'The use of appropriate technology to aid the gathering and telling of stories is very high on my agenda,' he says. 'After Iraq, nobody had to ask the troops, "What did you do in the war?" – because you could see what they were doing. That emphasized how far technology had come. On the other hand, we're fully aware that there are people in some parts of the world who view journalists as legitimate targets. But because it is becoming more portable, technology actually reduces the number of people we have to put in harm's way.'

In any case, he emphasizes that CNNI is not in the business of sensationalism. 'One of the dangers you face as a broadcaster is to assume there is more profit to be made in pursuing a tabloid agenda. That's a pressure that CNNI has been under for some considerable time, and which it has resisted. And we've done it without making boring television. I think that's a great achievement.'

ADDING LOCAL FLAVOUR

Like MTV – in many ways its adolescent cousin – CNN will continue to chase local audiences and advertising dollars by launching regional and non-English channels. One of its most successful projects so far is CNN en Español. This is primarily aimed at viewers in Latin America, although it has a growing audience of ethnic Spanish speakers in the United States. (It has even found an audience in Portuguese-speaking Brazil.) Launched in 1997, the channel reaches 13 million households and sources news from nine different bureaux, including those based in Havana, Buenos Aires, Mexico City and Miami.

It also has its own unique identity within the CNN family. Caroline Rittenberry, vice-president of communications for Turner's Latin American arm, explains: 'We stand for the same core values as CNN International – accuracy, trustworthiness, experience and so on – and we have the same affluent, well-travelled audience. This helped a lot when we were launching CNN en Español, because people knew and welcomed the brand. But we quickly realized that we could not use CNNI as a crutch, as if to say, "It's the same – but in Spanish!"'

Because the English language channel was also available in the Latin region, audience research showed that viewers were becoming confused. CNN addressed this by splitting the marketing strategy in two, with the international channel concentrating on pan-regional and English language magazines, and CNN Español taking a local approach.

'It worked because Español has a different feel to the international network,' Rittenberry says. 'The audience tends to skew younger, and we also have more female viewers – it's about 50–50 for us, as opposed to about 70 per cent male for CNNI. The channel has a warmer feel about it – the set is more colourful, there is more interaction between the anchors. But the main factor is local relevance. CNNI gives you a global perspective, but Español shows its viewers how international news affects them. It's a bridge between Latin America and the rest of the world.'

Rittenberry confirms that with the emergence of digital TV, there is a chance that CNN could break down its pan-regional offering further. 'We already have a separate feed in Mexico, and we are looking at other options. But you have to bear in mind that advertising revenues are still pretty small in Latin American markets. We get most of our revenue from distribution.'

Even so, it is clear that CNN will keep on expanding, subtly adjusting its brand to suit local audiences.

BRANDING ON THE AIR

As with any TV product, CNN's marketing strategy begins on its own airtime. Both CNN/US and CNN International place a great deal of emphasis on on-air promotions.

Scot Safon, who is responsible for marketing to US audiences, says: 'What we say to people while they're watching our networks is critically important. It's obviously the best moment to send them a brand message. And as about 80 million people come to us during the course of a month, it's an extraordinary opportunity. There's probably no one [in the US] who doesn't see CNN at one time or another.'

Creating on-air promotions is a craft in its own right. The director of on-air promotion for CNN International is Cathy Cleary, whose job covers 'signposting' – telling the audience what shows are on, when – as well as more general messages designed to fix the CNNI brand in the minds of consumers.

Cleary says: 'Sometimes our brand promotions refer to specific programmes, but more often they focus on the fact that CNN is *the* place to come for news. Its key attributes are speed, breadth, accuracy and experience. The experience factor is important – we often play on the experience of our journalists, which also gives the branding a human element. But all these elements work together to back up our positioning as a knowledge provider. This is summed up by the phrase "Be the first to know", which is supported both on and off air.'

Cleary adds that CNNI works hard to ensure that its message is consistent through every element of its marketing, from screen to poster to press. 'And most of the time we succeed – although it's not easy. Marketing works best when you have a simple message, but CNN is a diverse and complex product. We aren't a generic, easily defined entity.'

CNN also has an advantage in that it can run branding promotions on its fellow Turner channels – which include Turner Classic Movies, drama channel TNT, the general-interest TBS Superstation, and even Cartoon Network (the latter is often used for branding initiatives in Latin America, where it is the most popular channel across the entire region, in all age groups).

The danger with on-air promotions is that the audience might feel bombarded with branding, something Cleary obviously wants to avoid. 'We try to provide a mixture of messages that help the viewers navigate their way through our programmes, while also reinforcing our identity.' Branding also incorporates set design, music, graphics, and the general on-air 'look' of the channel. At CNNI, this responsibility falls to Mark Wright, the broadcaster's creative director. Wright says people in his position are usually so skilled at their jobs that viewers barely notice the branding.

'But they'd sure notice if you took it away,' he points out. 'One day, just as an experiment, I'd like to take five minutes of television and pull all the promotions and the music and the graphics out of it. I'd have it start off black, and then cut to the presenter talking. Just how interesting do you think that would that be?'

The logo is another classic element of branding, and CNN arguably has one of the best-known marks in the world. This remains consistent across all the broadcaster's networks.

'The CNN logo has stood the test of time,' Wright says. 'I think it's right up there with Nike and Coca-Cola in terms of recognition. We were right not to change it. The number one component for successful branding is consistency.'

THE CHALLENGE OF MULTIMEDIA

Consistency is something that Scot Safon thinks about a lot. As senior vice-president of marketing and promotion for CNN in the USA, his communication brief covers no fewer than four different TV networks (CNN/US, CNN Headline News, CNN*fn* and CNN Airport Network), three branded Web sites (CNN.com and sites covering sport and finance), content distribution services, and the mobile phone service CNN to Go.

'Because the competitive situation is different for each product, of course you've got to have different messages,' he says. 'The challenge is to make sure those messages don't conflict with the global brand promise.'

This is easier than it sounds. For Safon, CNN's gradual shift from broadcaster to multimedia news provider makes perfect sense. 'To my mind the global position of CNN is that it is responsible for your first level of understanding of a news event. By that I mean it's the first time you hear about a news event, or the first time you've been given enough information to grasp its impact. That's basically what we provide, on a 24-hour basis. And now we're able to take that promise and fulfil it using different media.'

The multimedia strategy makes even more sense in the light of the fact that CNN no longer has the monopoly on 24-hour TV news. 'When Ted Turner first started the channel, he said that he hadn't done any market research – he created it for himself. But what he really did was recognize that there were a lot of people out there like him, who could really use a 24-hour news channel. And for the first 10 or 12 years, he was the only one providing it. That is no longer the case.'

CNN has first-mover advantage, but that can easily be eroded by time and competition. 'We can't stand still – we have to take our leadership position in the field of news on demand, and translate it to other media. That's why, as a marketer, I can be proud of the fact that CNN.com is now a leader in its category. I'm proud of the fact that 2.5 million people have signed up for CNN's breaking news e-mail alerts. I view those as just as much a part of our mission as TV.'

Even in these new fields, CNN has competition – notably from MSNBC, the joint venture between Microsoft and broadcaster NBC. Safon says: 'That's exactly where our leadership position helps us, because if a telecommunications provider wants to offer breaking news as part of its mobile phone service, it's always going to choose CNN. We mean "news" to people. Once you have great brand equity, you can do a lot with it.'

ENOUGH – BUT NOT TOO MUCH

Cross-media branding and on-air promotion have not lessened the need for traditional marketing techniques. For CNNI, this means choosing the right vehicles to reach its target audience of affluent professionals. Sally Perry, vice-president of marketing for Europe, Middle East and Africa, comments: 'Marketing is not just a question of promoting your brand, but of promoting it in the right way. It has to fit our values – we tick off everything we do against our specific brand world.'

CNNI advertises in upmarket publications such as *The Wall Street Journal*, the *International Herald Tribune*, *The Economist*, *Time* and *Fortune*. Posters are used tactically, being placed only where the target group is likely to see them. Radio is also used with restraint, normally to promote specific programmes.

The network also uses more creative methods of spreading the word. For instance, CNN International recently embarked on a partnership with the London Business School to help the faculty raise its profile. Ads created by CNN featured three of the school's eminent professors – Elroy Dimson, Lynda Gratton and Sumantra Ghoshal – delivering thought-provoking solutions to the challenges facing global business. The spots ran across CNN's European and Middle Eastern feed. The broadcaster also sponsored the school's London Media Summit.

A more long-standing relationship is with Time Warner stable mate *Time* magazine and researcher Taylor Nelson Sofres (TNS). Each month, TNS conducts a poll on a topical issue among CNN viewers and *Time* readers. The results are published in a press release and are often widely quoted in other media.

'These surveys frequently make headlines,' says Perry. 'This kind of public relations initiative is extremely important, as it goes way beyond traditional marketing, and puts us at the heart of political debate.'

But how much marketing is too much? Although CNNI received a stack of positive press for its coverage of the Iraq conflict, it did not use any of the quotes in marketing initiatives. CNNI president Chris Cramer says he felt this would have flirted with bad taste.

In fact, Cramer is wary of marketing overload. 'Although I am absolutely guilty of using the word myself, I am uncomfortable with the notion that news is a product,' he admits. 'I accept that some people regard news as a commodity, and that we have to show the audience that our commodity is better than the others – but I'd like to think our service speaks for itself to a large extent.'

The brand in brief

Media brand: CNN

Founded: 1980

Owner: Time Warner

Viewers: 250 million households worldwide (Source: CNN)

Key marketing strategies: On-air promotion, cross-media branding, TV, print, posters, sponsorship

Brand extensions: There are more than 30 CNN branded products covering TV, the Internet, radio and mobile phone services

Web site: CNN.com (plus 11 local language and specialist subject sites)

2

BBC World

'The BBC brand is seen as inspirational – it has the ability to reach out and touch lives across the world'

When you emerge from White City tube station on the Central Line, there are two signs. One points to BBC Television Centre (turn left), while the other points to BBC Worldwide (turn right). The BBC is to this little corner of London what Nokia is to the whole of Helsinki: every second building seems to be connected with the organization in some way, and the area has a bustling sense of importance that is out of step with its bland, rain-spattered suburban architecture.

While BBC Television Centre is a city in itself, a honeycomb of offices, studios and editing suites, BBC World's sales and marketing arm is based in a more modest redbrick building a stone's throw away from a noisy flyover. In its foyer, the receptionist's cheery Englishness and the little shop selling newspapers and chocolate bars remind one of a railway station waiting room.

BBC World is something of an unsung hero in the pantheon of BBC brands. It would be easy to write an entire book – or even two – about the British Broadcasting Corporation, but BBC World is arguably its biggest marketing challenge, as well as one of its most youthful services. In international terms, it represents the future.

BUT FIRST, SOME HISTORY

However, it would be inadvisable to write about BBC World without first putting it into the context of this massive corporation – a leviathan among media brands.

Every such brand begins with a visionary, and the name to remember here is John Reith. In the 1920s, Reith imagined a broadcasting company that would fall somewhere between the heavily commercial, wildly unregulated radio stations of the United States, and the inflexible, state-controlled system of the Soviet Union. One of the first to spot the mass appeal of radio, he said that the BBC was created to 'bring the best of everything to the greatest number of homes'.

The British Broadcasting Company was founded on 18 October 1922 by a group of leading wireless manufacturers, including Marconi. Daily broadcasting began in Marconi's studio on The Strand, London, on 14 November that same year. Reith, a Scottish engineer, was appointed general manager. The service was funded by the Post Office licence fee, a 10-shilling (50 pence) charge to be paid by each viewer, ensuring that the BBC would not be financially dependent on either the government or advertising revenue.

In its early days, the BBC broadcast plays, debates and variety programmes, as well as popular and classical music. News broadcasts were made after 7 pm to avoid affecting newspaper sales. The power of radio became apparent in 1924 when King George V addressed the public from the British Empire Exhibition at Wembley. The speech was relayed to loudspeakers outside major department stores, and the swollen crowds blocked the traffic.

Listening at home was a little more complicated, requiring a 'cat's whisker' – a fine wire – which made contact with a crystal, sending a weak signal to a pair of earphones. More sophisticated valve devices soon replaced the 'crystal set', and by the 1930s listeners were tuning in on extravagant Bakelite sets with sweeping art deco lines. Radio had proved even more popular than Reith had predicted, with the number of licences surpassing two and a quarter million by 1926. Twelve years later, the figure stood at eight and a half million, and 98 per cent of the country's population could tune in.

Meanwhile, the BBC was evolving. In 1927 the British Broadcasting Company became the British Broadcasting Corporation, and John Reith was knighted for his role in the radio revolution. The BBC was granted its first Royal Charter, defining its objectives, powers and obligations. Under the charter, the BBC is answerable to the BBC Board of Governors, a group of trustees acting for the public interest and tasked with ensuring that the organization is accountable, while maintaining its independence. The governors are officially appointed by the Queen-in-council (the Privy Council) on the recommendation of the prime minister.

The current Royal Charter runs until 2006. Its renewal looks set to be a hotly debated issue, following the clash between the BBC and Prime Minister Tony Blair over the war in Iraq. In 2003 a BBC news report suggested that the government had 'sexed up' intelligence reports about Iraq's firepower in order to justify entering the conflict. This provoked waves of claim and counter-claim and led to the subsequent suicide of one of the BBC's sources, weapons expert Dr David Kelly, and the high-profile Hutton Inquiry. It is feared that the government would like to tamper with the Royal Charter, or even scrap the licence fee. (Under the Royal Charter, the BBC obtains permission to charge a licence fee from the relevant government minister. Originally it was the Postmaster General, later the Home Secretary – today it is the Secretary of State for Culture, Media and Sport.)

THE 'BEEB' TAKES SHAPE

The first iteration of the modern BBC took shape in 1932, when the organization left its home at Savoy Hill for Broadcasting House in Portland Place. Now a London landmark, the art deco building resembled a radio set built on the scale of an ocean liner. Also that year, the BBC began broadcasting its Empire Service, which later evolved into the famous World Service – foreshadowing the creation, many years later, of BBC World. The first foreign-language service was Arabic, introduced in 1938.

Meanwhile, television was going through a slow and difficult birth. John Logie Baird had demonstrated his invention back in 1925, and there had been experimental transmissions from a studio in Broadcasting House as early as 1932. The first regular service was broadcast from Alexandra Palace, perched high on a North London hill, in 1936. But the tentative rays could only reach 20,000 homes in the surrounding area, and viewers had to stump up the price of a car for a tiny, flickering, television set. Even Sir John Reith, for once behind the times, was not impressed.

Undaunted, the BBC forged on, broadcasting live events such as the Coronation procession of King George VI on 12 May 1937, the tennis championships at Wimbledon in 1938, and the following year's FA Cup Final football match. It also covered the ominous countdown to war.

On 1 September 1939, a Mickey Mouse cartoon was being shown when the BBC TV service abruptly blacked out. There were fears that enemy aircraft could use the powerful television transmitters as navigation aids. BBC television remained off the air until 7 June 1946, when it proudly flickered back into life with the same cartoon. (Although Mickey Mouse is an American character, the defiant spirit of the broadcast seems entirely British.)

It was left to radio to fly the flag, and it was arguably during the war that the BBC became fully established as an accurate, trustworthy, highly regarded – and even cherished – broadcasting brand. These were the days of Winston Churchill's powerful orations, and the sugary escapist songs of Vera Lynn, 'the forces' sweetheart'. Overseas, the BBC became a powerful tool for boosting morale and passing on intelligence – notably through General de Gaulle's broadcasts to occupied France. By the end of the war, the BBC was broadcasting in 40 languages, and even the Nazis' dark wizard of propaganda, Josef Goebbels, was forced to admit that the corporation had won 'the intellectual invasion of Europe'.

TV COMES OF AGE

Television in the United Kingdom came into its own on a single day – 2 June 1953, the date of the Coronation of Queen Elizabeth II at Westminster Abbey. Even today, many British parents and grandparents remember enormous TV sets being hefted into their homes a few days before the event. These bulbous pieces of furniture had to be switched on several minutes before the programme began in order to 'warm up', eventually producing grainy monochrome images. By 1954 there were over 3 million combined sound and vision licences in the UK.

Over the next three and a half decades, the BBC expanded and modernized. BBC Television Centre opened in June 1960, and a second TV channel was launched in 1964. The moon landings, the first colour images, classic TV shows like *Monty Python's Flying Circus* and current affairs programme *Panorama* flickered past the nation's rapt gaze. Prince Charles married Lady Diana Spencer, a televisual event akin to the Coronation years before. The BBC raised the standard of news reporting as its foreign correspondents gazed unwaveringly into living rooms from Beirut, the Falklands, Tiananmen Square, Romania, Ethiopia... When the Berlin Wall fell, Britons saw it live on the BBC.

The end of the 1980s saw a change in the way the BBC did business. In order to supplement the licence fee, the corporation had for some time been developing a range of commercial activities, producing videotapes, records, books and magazines under the BBC brand – as well as selling its programmes around the world. These strands were brought together under a single entity called BBC Enterprises, which later became BBC Worldwide. This was to become the parent of BBC World, the BBC's first genuinely global TV news service.

BBC World was launched in 1995, slap bang in the middle of an era of extraordinary change for the BBC. The organization was now entering the digital age, and was determined to take advantage of the opportunities that a multi-channel future presented. Innovations included BBC News 24, a round-the-clock news channel funded by the licence fee for UK viewers, launched in 1997, and the niche entertainment and drama channel BBC Choice, aimed at the 25–34-year-old demographic. This later evolved into BBC Three.

In June 2002, a consortium made up of the BBC, BSkyB and Crown Castle, a transmitter company, was awarded a licence to broadcast digital terrestrial television free to British homes. Freeview, as the new digital network was called, was launched on 30 October 2002 and included no fewer than eight BBC TV channels, as well as its interactive and radio services.

The future of interactive television is open to debate, but the BBC is pushing ahead with its services. At the push of a handset button, digital viewers call up different camera angles, background information, and links to related material available from the BBC on the Web. On-screen text provides information on forthcoming programmes, as well as news and weather reports.

The ongoing power of the BBC brand is demonstrated by its Web presence. The corporation says that its online service BBCi (originally known as BBC Online) reached over 36 per cent of all Internet users aged 15 and over in the United Kingdom in 2002. The corporation further claims that its Web service is the most visited content site in Europe, with over 660 million page views logged monthly. BBC News and BBC Sport are the most popular sections, followed by the BBC World Service and BBC Radio.

But it is perhaps BBC Worldwide that has benefited most from the strength of the brand. By 2002 the corporation's commercial arm had raked in over £100 million through brand extensions, licensing and the sale of programmes and formats like *The Teletubbies* and *The Weakest Link*. It had also become the largest UK-based provider of international television channels, with BBC World, BBC Prime and BBC America reaching a total of 450 million homes across the planet.

However, at the end of 2002, BBC World left the fold. It became a limited company in its own right, and joined the newly created Global News Division, which also embraced the World Service and bbcnews.com. The move was seen as an acknowledgement that BBC World had come of age.

BUILDING ON BRAND EQUITY

I am sitting at a boardroom table with Jane Gorard, BBC World's director of marketing, and Carolyn Gibson, its regional sales director for Europe, the Middle East and Africa. Outside, the sky is the colour of a pigeon's wing – London weather. But in here, we're about to travel the globe.

It may be hard to believe, but until the 1990s the BBC did not have a coherent international showcase for its TV news reporting. While radio listeners across the planet had revered the World Service for decades, millions of English-speakers outside the United Kingdom came up empty when they searched cable and satellite channels for the best of British television journalism.

Not that BBC World appeared overnight. It sprang out of a channel called BBC World Service Television, launched in 1991. That channel was itself a revamped version of a service called BBC TV Europe, which had been providing Europeans with light entertainment programming since 1987. BBC World Service Television included the additional but crucial element of international news. The service was initially available only to Europeans, but in 1991 it expanded to Asia and the Middle East, branching out to South Africa at the end of 1992. In 1995 the decision was taken to split the service into two separate channels, BBC World and BBC Prime. The latter would concentrate on entertainment, while BBC World would be the corporation's global news and information channel. By 2003 it was reaching 270 million homes across 200 countries and territories.

Carolyn Gibson has been involved in airtime sales for BBC World since 1994. At that time, the responsibility for selling space on the channel was held by external ad sales representatives – IP Networks in Europe and Star TV in Asia.

Gibson recalls: 'When the channel was launched the aspiration, as it remains today, was to showcase the best of BBC journalism globally. Looking at the size of the operation, and the infrastructure it had, it was a logical step. While CNN had forged the way, we clearly had the resources to do the same thing.'

All of which begs the obvious question: why didn't the BBC commit itself to a global TV news service much earlier? In fact a BBC committee began investigating the possibility of launching an international TV news service as early as 1987 – but the government turned down a request for an extension of the grant-in-aid that it gave to BBC World Service Radio. The pressure was then on to find a commercial solution, which turned out to be BBC World Service Television, the extended BBC TV Europe and the effective 'parent' of BBC World.

Jane Gorard, the channel's marketing director, takes up the story. 'From the mid-1990s through to 2000 there was an explosion not only of media, but of the audience's desire for more global information. It was a period when people were travelling more, when they were acquiring stocks and shares, and when businesses expanded across borders. There was a hunger, both from a business and a personal point of view, for more information about countries and companies.'

The simple fact of the matter was that CNN had shown there was a market for international TV news, and the BBC saw no reason why it shouldn't grab a slice of the action. By 1998, BBC World had grown its distribution and audiences to a critical mass and it was becoming an increasingly effective marketing tool for international advertisers. The decision was taken to move airtime sales in-house. This was also when a dedicated marketing role was created – until then, advertising reps had been responsible not only for selling space, but also for promoting the brand. The assumption, not unjustified, was that the BBC's brand positioning was already clear enough.

Gorard explains: 'The change of approach was provoked by the channel's evolution. Rather than being an international service right from the start, we expanded progressively across the world. But when you find yourself reaching right around the planet, and you are not in control – totally – of the consistency of the brand image, you put yourself in a vulnerable position. This was the thinking not only for bringing advertising in-house, but also for addressing our marketing strategy.'

As Gorard points out, even for a brand like the BBC, it is not easy to maintain a consistent image when you are dealing with viewers and advertisers across a vast range of different cultures. 'It comes back to the familiar question: can you have a global product with local relevance? The answer is yes, you can – but the brand image must be controlled from a central point. Think of all the things that happen at what might be called a "street" level: local newspaper advertisements; programme guides in hotels that take the channel; presentations by local sales people. All these strands must express a single, coherent brand identity, worldwide.'

As far as international media brands go, BBC World's identity is a familiar one. A heavyweight blend of news, current affairs and finance, it is aimed at a core target of international business decision makers. It fits into an elite group of media (including CNN International, the *Financial Times*, *The Wall Street Journal* and *Time* magazine) whose audience are equally likely to be their advertisers.

Gorard says: 'Our viewers are typically senior people working for multinational companies, often with strategic responsibility. They travel all the time, so they have to keep in touch with international news and what's going on in the markets, particularly any crises or unexpected blips that might affect their businesses.'

She stresses that BBC World is not the channel of UK expatriates – who tend to tune in to BBC Prime to keep up with their favourite soap operas. BBC World viewers are cosmopolitan globetrotters, whose birthplace is as irrelevant as their country of residence, and for whom English is probably only one of a number of languages at their disposal.

The channel's key brand attributes gel with this idea of an elite viewer. Says Gorard: 'People turn to us for accuracy and impartiality, and because we are a trusted source of information. They know that we work with a professionalism and rigor that ensures reliability. We have the image of being unallied with any outside influence or partnership. We invest more in news than any other organization, we have people on the ground for any given event, and we are likely to be closer to the story and understand it better. As far as the BBC as a whole is concerned, this has been the case for many years. The beauty of this for us is that although we are a young, commercial venture, we can draw on that heritage and those resources.'

Moreover, Carolyn Gibson believes that the BBC name adds certain indefinable ingredients to the mix. 'It's not just about staid information provision, but about a certain "BBC touch". I think the brand is seen as inspirational – it has the ability to reach out and touch lives across the world. That comes not only from the sheer size and professionalism of the organization, but also its ethos.'

The clash in the summer of 2003 between the BBC and the British government over Iraq appears to have done little to alter this perception. 'If anything, it showed how impartial we are,' points out Gorard. 'We had a fantastic response to our coverage of the conflict in Iraq, and a number of surveys suggested that we were the most trusted source of news during that period. From a marketing point of view, all the things that I have been saying in our promotional material, or in public relations activity during meetings with journalists, have been totally underlined by these events. Occasionally, overseas viewers assume that the BBC is in some way owned or controlled by the British government. The Iraq controversy definitely reassured them that this is not the case.'

BBC World's greatest rival is undoubtedly CNN, and the channels compete head-to-head for viewers in a number of markets. The BBC's biggest obstacle is in the United States, where its service is shown on a bulletin basis on public service television, a poor substitute for CNN's full-time channel. CNN also has first-mover advantage, and in distribution terms it can bring to bear the full weight of Turner Broadcasting, offering broadcasting platforms a bouquet of channels rather than a single news service.

But the BBC may have a wild card in its favour – the factor of 'Britishness'. Says Gorard: 'I'm always hesitant to use that as a brand attribute, because we are an international channel, but you can't ignore the fact that we are, indeed, British. Interestingly, different markets lean towards different sources for their news. In certain markets – the

Philippines, for example – there is a tendency to look towards American media, and they feel comfortable with CNN. In India, however, our British heritage is a definite advantage. But you'll find that like us, CNN is trying to blur its identity. Both of us almost want to become rootless, without boundaries, and accessible to all.'

A BENIGN INFLUENCE

So how does a totally unbiased viewer from Prague, for instance, differentiate between the two channels? After all, as Carolyn Gibson points out, once a viewer has chosen a station he or she tends to remain loyal to it, and is unlikely to flip between CNN International and BBC World on a whim. The channel's basic ingredients are therefore vitally important from a promotional point of view. So it is no surprise to learn that both the marketing and airtime sales teams have an influence on content.

Gibson confirms: 'Given the imperative, when selling advertising and sponsorship, to be accountable to our clients, the airtime sales team have been highly focused on audience research. This data has helped to shape our views on programming that will better serve the needs of our audiences, but at the same time provide our advertisers with a highly targeted environment for their commercial messages. For instance, our data shows that frequent travellers are a hugely important part of our audience, and it is exactly this knowledge that helped us to launch *Fast Track* – a weekly show about the business of travel. This not only serves our audiences, but also provides a backdrop for tourist boards, airlines and hotel chains that utilize international television as an efficient way of reaching their core target audiences.'

The sales team also works closely with the BBC's creative services unit and with programme producers during the commissioning process for short programmes and event-driven slots.

Although this approach might seem unnervingly commercial to those in the UK who know the BBC in its public service guise, Gibson does not feel that it undermines the brand in any way. 'Its initial purpose is to better serve our audience – although it obviously benefits advertising sales, as it gives brands access to desirable target groups in the right environment, and marketing, because it provides additional hooks with which to pull in viewers.'

The channel's commercial concerns affected its structure right from the start. It was clear that a rolling 24-hour news service, with bulletin after bulletin, would not work. The channel needed a varied schedule of programming – so while each hour begins with the news, viewers can also tune in to programmes about science, culture and sport.

Jane Gorard explains: 'What we call the "front" half an hour is purely editorial. We monitor that on a daily basis, because it may affect promotional material if there is a change of presenter, for instance. Similarly, the editorial team may talk to us for ideas about how to tweak or refresh the look of the output. But mainly it's a case of them doing what they do in an extremely professional manner, and us expressing that in our promotional material.'

The 'back' half of the hour is a different, story, however. 'Basically the rule of thumb is that if you watch the back half an hour, you need to come away feeling that you have learnt something – that you have been enlightened. And that is the area where we can to a certain extent have an influence, by helping to develop programmes that address a certain need or opportunity for the channel.'

One example concerned *Question Time*, a current affairs debate show format commissioned by BBC World for the Indian market. The programme was extremely popular in India, but it had also generated a certain amount of controversy. Gibson explains: 'Audience research uncovered a debate about why the Indian edition was being shown in Pakistan, which considers itself a separate market. As a result of this, we decided to launch a Pakistan-specific edition. It was exactly the same format as the Indian version, only with a Pakistani production company, presenter and audience, and it covered issues appropriate to the market. The programme served not only to reinforce our editorial values of balance and impartiality, but it also meant that we were in a new market, with all the commercial benefits that entailed. It was so successful that we followed up with a Pakistan edition of another popular show, *Face To Face*.'

In common with CNN International, BBC World has also adapted its on-screen look to reflect marketing concerns. Gorard says: 'Although [the advertising and marketing departments] have not had a direct influence on the visual appearance of the channel, there is a general realization that it is a vitally important factor. Compared to five years ago, the channel looks very different. Part of that was because the BBC rebranded across all its channels, adopting warmer, brighter colours and a more down-to-earth approach. It wanted to get away from the distance and formality that were the negative elements of its brand image. We took that on board, and our whole on-screen look has changed – right down to the fact that we now have more women presenters, and they seem younger and less "BBC-ish", with all the formality that that implies. When marketing any kind of media, it is important to appear welcoming, because you want to establish a relationship with your audience.'

This idea of 'establishing relationships' also had a bearing on the creation of BBC World's new umbrella organization, the Global News Division. In bringing together the various strands of its international news operations, the BBC acknowledged that while perceptions of its brand remain consistent all over the world, people experience it in different ways.

Gorard explains: 'When there is a big news story, the BBC is the first port of call for a great deal of people. But their methods of access vary. If they want something in their local language, they may turn on the radio and listen to the World Service. If they are at work, they may go to the Web site. And if they're at home, in an airport or at a hotel, they can watch BBC World.'

GLOBAL TACTICS

Reminding people around the globe that this service is available is another matter, however. Responsibility for the marketing campaigns that give potential BBC World consumers a vital nudge falls to a third important member of the team – head of marketing Seema Kotecha.

'While we tend to think of our audience as international business decision markers, or IBDMs,' Kotecha explains, 'one of our recent audience surveys narrowed them down even further into a category we call "reformers". These are people intelligent enough to make up their own minds about current affairs, and who are not looking for any kind of spin. They require a lack of bias, a medium that gives them both sides of the story – which is what the BBC provides. They are the main target group for all our marketing initiatives; hence our tagline, created in 2002: "Demand a broader view".'

The interesting thing about this niche group is that, while one might imagine them to be roughly the same all over the world, their attitudes to the BBC brand vary from market to market – often based on their exposure to it during their youth. In India, for example, where the BBC is revered, BBC World has a very loyal audience. In other parts of Asia and Latin America, viewers are slightly more reticent. So marketing varies from sweeping global campaigns to tightly focused local initiatives.

'We use a mixture of outdoor, international print media, and on-air promotions, both on BBC World itself and on other channels that appeal to our target market, such as Eurosport and National Geographic,' says Kotecha. To keep costs down, slots on these other channels are 'bartered' – exchanged for either an equal number of slots on BBC World, or advertising space to the same value.

But the most recent campaign at the time of writing was an outdoor promotion, with six posters stressing BBC World's lack of bias. Each one showed a single picture of a news event, and provided three different interpretations of its meaning. The message, clearly, was that the BBC covers every viewpoint. 'We ran the campaign in airports, as our target audience are naturally frequent travellers,' says Kotecha.

The channel's technology-savvy target audience is also allowing it to develop some innovative digital marketing techniques. It often uses India as a test bed for these projects, as it did when it launched the general knowledge quiz show *University Challenge* there. To promote the show, BBC World teamed up with Yahoo! to create a microsite on the Internet search engine's home page. This took the form of a competition, with contestants being urged to answer a general knowledge question every day. Daily and weekly winners were then entered into a prize draw, giving them a chance to win a scooter or a DVD player. Kotecha says: 'This time the campaign was aimed not at our core target group, but at students – the BBC World audience of the future.'

BBC World is also experimenting with SMS (mobile phone text messages) as a way of interacting with this younger audience – competitors were encouraged to send their answers via SMS during the *University Challenge* promotion.

Meanwhile, back in Europe, the broadcaster has created a weekly e-mail newsletter containing programme news and details of its schedule, which it sends to BBC World viewers on request. 'In Germany we supported the launch of the newsletter with banner advertising on Web sites, and got five times as many subscribers as elsewhere,' reveals Kotecha. 'I believe digital marketing is going to be an increasingly popular tool for media brands.'

The newsletter supports Kotecha's current goal, which is to express the fact that BBC World broadcasts a wide variety of programmes and is not just a rolling 24-hour news service.

Kotecha says: 'It's very important for us to explain exactly what the channel offers. The BBC is such a big organization that potential viewers might not understand exactly what our brand does. We accept that this can be confusing, but at the same time we gain a great deal by being part of the BBC heritage.'

For the many people who have already got the message, it must be reassuring to know that, wherever in the world they may be, they can always get their news from the BBC.

The brand in brief

Media brand: BBC World

Founded: 1995

Owner: BBC World Ltd

Audience: 274 million homes in 200 countries and territories; 940,000 hotel rooms (Sources: PAX, EMS, Europe 2003)

Key marketing strategies: Print, outdoor, TV and digital media advertising, carefully tailored content based on extensive research

Brand extensions: N/A

Web site: BBCworld.com

3

MTV

'We have an approach that crosses borders: youth, energy, a passion for music, and a certain amount of irreverence'

'Okay, let's get in our places – tall ones at the back, please, you know who you are.'

On the set of MTV's daily live show, *TRL*, there is a sense of controlled panic. The pop star Pink is about to perform her latest single, and excited pre-teens and early adolescents are being herded into a telegenic crowd around her. A camera on a massive boom, like the arm of giant robot, sweeps over the circular stage. Floor managers bustle about with clipboards and head-mikes. The ad break is almost over and, standing in the wings, I can see the monitor counting down.

'Twenty seconds!'

Pink sits on a stool in the middle of all this chaos, a relaxed smile on her face. Her image is supposedly rebellious, but she looks scrubbed and healthy, with an explosion of blonde hair and generous curves shoved into too-tight clothing. Beside her, the show's presenter – a chirpy, good-looking Londoner called Dave Berry – checks his microphone and ambles into position.

I'm standing next to Michelle, the PR person from MTV, and a reporter from the *News of the World*. We are definitely off-camera, among the scaffolding and the thick black cables that writhe across the scuffed floor. The reporter looks nervous, and a second later I find out why. A young woman dashes up to Michelle, saying: 'The photographer needs to get here right now, or it isn't going to happen.'

Michelle shrugs. 'I've left loads of messages on his mobile. There's nothing we can do.'

Hearing this, the *News of the World* reporter looks pained: the pictures were destined for his article. Michelle tells me that MTV always provides its own photographer for star guests, and retains full control over the images. Then the man in question appears, looking apologetic, with only a second to spare.

An invisible cue indicates that we're live, and the crowd controller bounds on to the stage, waving his hands and jumping up and down to conjure screams and applause from the audience. But the kids need little prompting, and the noise is deafening. Berry's introduction is all but drowned out. As Pink goes into her song, I glance between the monitor and reality. Once again I'm struck by how small and temporary the set looks – a pool of light in the centre of a giant metal box – compared to the glamorous image that appears on the screen. Even the screaming fans are not 'real', as such – MTV sources them from a specialist company called Audience Store. The other fans are outside, in the October drizzle, waiting for a glimpse of Pink when she leaves the studio.

All this is happening in Camden Town, London – but we could be on the other side of the Atlantic. The format of *TRL* (it stands for Total Request Live) was borrowed from the United States and retooled for British audiences. This is a valid metaphor for MTV itself, which began broadcasting in the USA in 1981, and is now available in localized forms across most of the planet. Interbrand's annual survey of the world's 100 most valuable brands put MTV at number 46 in 2003 – the highest media brand in the survey – with a value of US$6.28 billion, up 3 per cent on the previous year.

Reaching 400 million households in 166 countries via 42 different channels, MTV is quite simply the only global music television brand.

GETTING READY TO ROCK

Of course, there were plenty of people who didn't think it would work.

MTV was established by a small group of enthusiasts at an organization called Warner Amex Satellite Entertainment Company (WASEC), a joint cable TV venture between Warner Communications and

American Express. One of the inspirations for the channel was Mike Nesmith, a former member of the 1960s band The Monkees, who had been making pioneering pop videos for his solo recordings and for other artists. WASEC's vice-president and CEO John Lack approached Nesmith and asked him to make a test version of MTV, which was shown on children's channel Nickelodeon. Although viewers were receptive to the idea, Nesmith eventually decided that he did not want to be involved in 'a channel full of commercials for records'. ('Birth of an MTV nation', *Vanity Fair*, November 2000.)

But Lack was convinced that music television had a future. He managed to persuade WASEC's conservative owners that, as record companies usually provided promotional videos for free, the channel would be cheap to run.

Then he surrounded himself with like-minded people, including Tom Freston, now chairman of MTV Networks. Freston was hired as the channel's regional marketing director.

'I had been involved in marketing before, but I had sort of dropped out,' Freston recalls. 'I had been working at an advertising agency, and when they assigned me to a toilet paper account, I knew it wasn't for me. I travelled around the world, and fell in love with Asia. For a while I had a clothing business in Afghanistan, but I realized that I didn't want to stay there all my life. A wise decision, as it turned out.'

Back in the States, Freston was scanning the music industry trade journal *Billboard* when he read about 'this unnamed music channel' that was looking for enthusiastic people. He applied right away. 'I had always been a music aficionado of the highest order, and the idea of a music channel just knocked me out. I thought it was a total winner. Videos were just starting to get screened in downtown clubs in New York – although they really began in Europe, because it was the way bands would promote themselves over there.'

One of the biggest obstacles was selling the idea to cable operators. 'As usual with something totally innovative, nobody saw the need for music television,' says Freston. 'It didn't help that none of the people we were talking to were in our target demographic. The cable operators were mostly engineers who were into sports. They were terrified of the idea of rock music TV. Only a few them agreed to carry us.'

Even the record companies hesitated at first, being naturally wary of providing content for free. 'Of course Warner owned the company, and some of the others played along to get us going. And then when we launched, all the artists would be watching and ringing their record companies and saying, "How come I'm not on this thing?"'

Freston knew from the start that MTV would succeed if it became a brand. 'Television had never really had brands before – people watched programmes rather than channels. But our format was borrowed from radio, with videos playing the role of records. We had to create a sense of cohesion, a flowing link between all these videos, so that the audience would identify with the channel and stay with it.'

A key part of this brand identity was the MTV logo, which was deliberately designed to look edgy and raw, like graffiti sprayed on a wall. 'We paid about a thousand dollars to a small company called Manhattan Design,' says Freston. 'The logo they came up with was primitive, which was exactly what we wanted, because our idea was to make the channel cartoon-like, not slick or corporate. Then we showed it to our advertising agency, Ogilvy & Mather, and they absolutely hated it. But we kept it, and they lost the account. I still see the guy occasionally, and he just grins at me ruefully.'

The logo was established in the opening moments of the channel, which featured doctored footage of the moon landing, with Neil Armstrong planting an MTV flag. The first video, with famous appropriateness, was *Video Killed The Radio Star* by The Buggles. It was 1 August 1981, and MTV was on the air.

'I WANT MY MTV'

With the press dubious and advertisers indifferent, MTV knew it needed to do some serious brand building. As it was difficult to gauge audience reactions from the channel's New York headquarters, Tom Freston and a colleague were despatched to the heartland of America.

'At the time, you couldn't even get MTV in Manhattan. The idea was to go to the places where cable systems were actually carrying the channel, and find out if it was working,' Freston explains. 'We walked into this hotel in Tulsa, Oklahoma, and when the bellhop discovered who we were, he went crazy. And it was the same everywhere we went – everyone was into MTV. They all wanted buttons with our logo on.'

Even better, record store owners said that MTV was having a dramatic effect on sales, and were prepared to be quoted for a marketing campaign. Gradually, advertisers grew enthusiastic, and record companies began sending more videos. Artists with an eye for the new medium of video, like Billy Idol and Adam and the Ants, suddenly found that MTV was making their careers. An element of competition crept in, and rock videos became bigger, glitzier, sexier and more expensive. This later led to the blockbuster vehicles created for the likes of Duran Duran, Michael Jackson and Madonna.

Meanwhile, MTV had found a way of putting pressure on cable operators to carry the channel. The whole thinking behind the brand was that it belonged to its viewers – it was 'their' MTV, something their parents and teachers couldn't identify with. So the broadcaster shot a series of ads featuring rock stars saying 'I want my MTV!' and screened them on mainstream channels in areas that didn't have the service. After an ad blitz costing US$2 million, cable operators across the USA were deluged with calls from kids demanding MTV. Even Manhattan Cable, which had refused to take the channel unless the price was right, finally relented.

Says Freston: 'We would target a city and run the ads constantly for a couple of weeks, and by the time we were finished nearly every cable operator was carrying MTV. It worked perfectly.'

But with the success of the music television format and the rising cost of videos, the channel's identity slowly began to change, becoming less brash and more honed – less 'rock and roll', and more popular entertainment. In 1984 MTV Networks became a publicly traded company, with Warner Amex retaining a controlling share. Another sign that the channel had now entered the big time came in the form of the first MTV Music Video Awards, staged in September 1984 at Radio City Music Hall in New York. A glittering extravaganza featuring, among other things, Madonna and a giant wedding cake, it set the scene for an annual event that has become a brand in its own right.

The following year, American Express sold its stake in the company to Warner, which in turn began negotiating to sell MTV to Viacom (owner of CBS and Paramount Pictures, among other leading media brands). After a short-lived attempt at a management buy-out, the deal went through. The relationship between the music video channel – which retained something of its original rebellious identity – and its new corporate owner was turbulent, until media mogul Sumner Redstone took control of Viacom two years later. Redstone had made his fortune from running a huge US cinema chain, and had an instinctive grasp of youth culture.

Now chairman and CEO of Viacom, Redstone recalls: 'When I acquired Viacom in 1987, the banks thought MTV was a fad and told me to sell it. My gut told me they were dead wrong, so we not only kept it, but that same year we launched our first international channel.'

FIRST EUROPE, THEN THE WORLD

MTV Europe went on air on 1 August 1987 – marking the start of the brand's long evolution from a purely American product into the 42 tailored channels that are available across the world today. Brent Hansen, president and chief executive of MTV Networks Europe, admits that catering to the diverse tastes of a pan-European audience was not easy.

'The channel was aimed at young people with mobility, rather than any specific nation, so it had to have an international flavour,' he says. 'The only problem with that was that occasionally you ended up with a Scandinavian blonde talking about Italian music in English to a German audience.'

Even at the time, MTV was aware that it would have to regionalize. Hansen explains: 'We didn't want to be a one-stop shop, but the cost of launching channel after channel in different countries in analogue was clearly prohibitive, so we had to get the brand out there first. The name of the game with MTV Europe was to grow European distribution, which would provide revenue for further regionalization. It also helped us to build an advertising base.'

In order to spread the news that MTV was now available to European audiences, the broadcaster sponsored local artists and events, and helped international stars bring their tours to Europe. It also created the MTV Europe Music Awards.

'While the channel was supposedly aimed at people who thought of themselves as international, there was a slight danger that it might come to be seen as patronizing,' says Hansen, an easy-going New Zealander. 'I've always been sensitive to that, coming from a small country next to a somewhat larger one. I felt that after a period of time we could end up providing something that, no matter how interesting and exotic it might seem, was largely irrelevant to our viewers' lifestyles. To be relevant, you have to be part of daily life.'

Technology made this possible in 1994, when MTV went digital, enabling it to compress its signal and provide targeted 'feeds' to different parts of Europe. Initially this meant local advertising slots, but the plan was to give each country's music fans their own MTV channels, with presenters who spoke their own language, and local artists alongside the usual array of global superstars. Regular 'network moments' like the music awards would sustain the overall MTV brand.

'There were signs that local broadcasters were beginning to tread on our toes. But because we were MTV, we knew we could provide more creative programming, we could have a more dangerous edge, and finally we had access to international artists that other channels didn't. The biggest marketing tool for MTV has always been the channel itself.'

In 1997, spurred on by competition from a home-grown German music channel called Viva, MTV launched its German language service, MTV Central. This was quickly followed by the UK and Ireland and Italian services, and later by launches in Scandinavia, France, Spain, the Netherlands, Romania, Poland and Portugal. (Other territories are still covered by a generic MTV Europe channel.)

Hansen's boss at the time of MTV's European expansion was Bill Roedy, now president of MTV Networks International. Since then, Roedy has helped the channel expand into Asia, Australia, Canada, Latin America and Russia with a mixture of regional and localized channels. A former US army officer and Vietnam veteran, he plots the brand's expansion like a military campaign. In markets where he couldn't get cable access, he negotiated to put MTV on air as a national frequency. He says his model, which he developed at the US movie channel HBO, is 'aggressive, creative, relentless distribution'.

'I'll get MTV out there any way I can, even if I have to offer it free and unencrypted. There's no better branding strategy than that. When I first went to Europe, I knew that we had to go local. After all, Europe was where the music video originated, and it was clear there were whole creative scenes that we were missing out on. Since then, everybody has adopted the same strategy – you know, "think global, act local" – but we were doing it before it was cool.'

As well as making pots of money for Viacom, this strategy has delighted audiences and given local stars international exposure. The

Colombian singer Shakira was virtually unknown outside Latin America until she performed live for MTV Unplugged – and subsequently sold millions of CDs. And two teenage Russian girls collectively named Tatu became an overnight sensation across Europe in 2003 thanks to MTV.

'Sometimes I can't believe how truly global MTV has become, compared to how it started,' says Roedy. 'I once met the Chinese leader Jiang Zemin, and the first words out of his mouth were, "Oh, MTV". He knew exactly what the brand was all about.'

MTV made its debut in China in 1995 and was the first foreign-owned broadcaster permitted to enter the country's then nascent cable TV market. The channel's managing director, Yifei Lei, says: 'A lot of cable stations in China are still really grateful for what we have done. We not only opened up the market, but we also showed local operators what could be achieved. The high standards of programming you see here today owe a lot to MTV.'

Yifei says the MTV brand values translate relatively smoothly to China. 'The only difference is a lack of rebellion. There is nothing particularly cool about being anti-society or anti-family in China – young people here respect their elders. MTV China is friendly and irreverent rather than rebellious. But apart from that, Chinese teenagers are surprisingly bold and outspoken, and have become more so over the past 10 years. I believe MTV targets a sort of global tribe. Teenagers in China have more in common with teenagers in New York than teenagers in New York have with their parents.'

MTV China is something of a flagship for the brand internationally, as it illustrates how well the concept crosses borders. The channel's content is 30 per cent Chinese, 30 per cent Hong Kong and Taiwan, and 40 per cent international. Local stars include the boy band Yu.chun and Tibetan singer Han Hong. The channel even plays an educational role, in an MTV kind of way. A cult show called MTV English takes key Chinese phrases and translates them directly into English – and vice versa – with often-hilarious results. The show has sparked a cultural phenomenon known as 'Chinglish'.

Yifei confirms that the channel works closely with the Chinese government to 'build trust'. She says: 'There is an emphasis on reciprocity, and we have a commitment to using the MTV name to export Chinese culture. For instance, we arranged for a philharmonic orchestra playing traditional Chinese folk instruments to appear at the Lincoln Center in New York. The audience loved them, by the way.'

As in other markets, MTV China has also given international brands access to young consumers. The channel has sponsorship deals with a number of multinationals, including Procter & Gamble, Intel, Samsung, Motorola and Nokia. Yifei says Intel is particularly pleased with its sponsorship of MTV's Super Talent Search, in which viewers are challenged to produce pop videos on their computers, using Intel's Flash technology. The winning video is screened on the channel.

Supportive advertisers, enthusiastic audiences and a cunning marketing strategy have allowed MTV to spread unhindered across the globe. Bill Roedy states proudly that 8 out of 10 MTV viewers are now outside the United States, and that less than 1 per cent of its 2,000 employees are American.

'We're not in the business of exporting American culture. Instead, we have an approach that crosses borders: youth, energy, a passion for music, and a certain amount of irreverence. But that formula can resonate in different ways in different markets. In Taiwan it's very edgy and in your face, in India it's Bollywood and colourful, in Brazil it's vibrant and sexy, and in China there is more of an accent on family values. All of our channels are locally run, and they are free to interpret the brand any way they choose.'

Nobody seems to think this constant tweaking could eventually damage the integrity of the brand. 'It's like the MTV logo,' says Brent Hansen. 'The shape always stays the same, but over the years we've had a lot of fun with it – put a lot of things in the same box.'

Tom Freston is more emphatic. 'There are certain limits to what you can do. After all, it's not as if anyone is going to take MTV Italy and turn it into a classical music channel.'

OZZY AND COMPANY

But it's not just the MTV brand that has evolved – the content has changed too. Long gone are the days when MTV was about being hypnotized by back-to-back music videos. Over the years, the offering has matured into a more familiar broadcast format, with interviews, documentaries, live broadcasts and a whole string of hit shows – from cartoon duo *Beavis & Butthead* in the 1990s to the more recent phenomenon of *The Osbournes*, a real-life soap documenting rock star Ozzy Osbourne's madcap domestic set-up. Properties like these have also provided licensing and merchandizing opportunities, from which MTV now draws as much as 20 per cent of its revenues.

Chairman Tom Freston says the move towards more 'conventional' programming began as early as 1987. 'At that time I was general manager, and we were facing a ratings slump. It looked like the novelty of back-to-back videos was wearing off, so we had to look around for ways to rejuvenate the channel. We didn't have enough money to pay writers or hire stars, so we came up with the idea of putting a bunch of young people in a loft and filming them. The series was called *The Real World*. We had basically invented reality TV – although at the beginning it was purely a financial consideration.'

Freston says that while MTV's contents have developed, 'the package is still the same'. He explains: 'It's about music culture first and pop culture second. But it's also about being leading edge. We're always trying to reinvent ourselves.'

Brent Hansen of MTV Europe wholeheartedly agrees. 'Over the years we've affected and changed mainstream television, while always staying one step ahead of it. We often sell our programmes to traditional broadcasters. This emphasizes our cutting-edge content and provides another marketing opportunity for the MTV brand.'

MTV is committed to developing even more original content. In early 2003 it announced that it would increase its investment in new programming by 20 per cent. In Europe it launched something called The Greenhouse, a pan-European 'development lab' that will commission programme formats and develop co-productions for use across the whole of the network. In the United States, a reality show called *Newlyweds: Nick & Jessica* has been one of the channel's biggest hits to date. Another reality series called *Viva La Bam* will follow the life of skateboard star Bam Margera.

NEW FRONTIERS

MTV has no intention of putting the brakes on its evolution. The company's latest buzz-phrase is 'the 360 degree MTV experience' – which involves providing music and 'youth lifestyle entertainment' across as many platforms as possible: not just TV, but also online, via broadband and on mobile phones.

At the time of writing, MTV has no fewer than 27 localized Web sites, enabling users around the world to download music and videos. In May 2003 MTV Networks Europe bought 50 per cent of French videogames channel Game One in partnership with French media company Atari. And the growth in popularity of mobile phone SMS or 'text messaging' in Europe has allowed the company to become increasingly interactive, with viewers submitting votes for their favourite artists by text to a show called *Videoclash*. Not only that, but the MTV mobile phone service gives users access to music, quizzes, pop trivia, gig guides and programme listings.

Traditional media remains important too, and MTV regularly releases branded books, CDs and DVDs linked to its content. For some time, it has had a partnership with sister Viacom company Paramount Pictures to develop movies for its target group.

Despite this proliferation of services, there is no indication that MTV intends to distance itself from the music that has been its bread and butter for so long. In Europe alone, recent developments have included a winter live rock event, Winterjam, and a summer dance party called Isle of MTV. Even more heartening is the 'Night With...' strand, featuring an artist performing live across the network. Those who've taken part so far include Bruce Springsteen, Mariah Carey and Moby.

In addition, digital technology is enabling the company to target even smaller audience niches. While it continues to regionalize, it has also begun to home in on pop culture's disparate tribes, launching specialist dance, rock and rap stations. MTV Networks International president Bill Roedy says: 'In the UK alone we have nine channels, and there is no reason why we shouldn't continue to expand. That's the beauty of digital – it allows you to reach specific demographic groups.'

THE FLIPSIDE OF PROFIT

It would be easy – a little too easy – to portray MTV as a sort of musical McDonald's, munching its way relentlessly across the globe.

But while the brand is undeniably omniscient, it does strive to put something back into youth culture.

Says Bill Roedy: 'When you're as big as we are, some people will see you as an organization that is purely out for profit – that takes without giving. But we do a lot of pro-social work showing that we don't take any of this for granted.'

Roedy is being modest – he is personally committed to improving HIV and AIDS education, and became an ambassador for UNAIDS in 1998. Under his leadership, MTV has screened AIDS-related documentaries and public service broadcasts internationally through its Staying Alive initiative, making them available to other broadcasters at no cost. In November 2003 MTV once again joined forces with Nelson Mandela – who had appeared in two earlier broadcasts about AIDS and human rights issues – for the 46664 campaign, which aimed to raise awareness of HIV and AIDS in Africa. (The figure 46664 was Mandela's ID number during the 18 years that he was a political prisoner.) A concert featuring an array of international superstars was staged on World AIDS Day, 1 December, and now looks likely to become an annual event.

Such grandiose projects strike a chord with audiences and are good for the brand's profile, but MTV seems to pay attention to its internal policies, too. Many MTV employees told me off the record that they were impressed by the training and advancement opportunities at the company. It appears to have a genuinely inclusive culture, as one gay member of staff confirms. 'They're pretty happy for you to be who you are. In fact, they encourage you to be as individualistic as possible,' he says.

Brent Hansen of MTV Networks Europe comments: 'Our policy with staff is like our policy with the channels. We give them a slot, tell them the basics, and let them interpret it any way they like. We want them to bring their own personality in – there isn't a cookie-cutter "MTV person".'

Hansen admits that he gets a little irritated by the McDonald's analogy. 'Our critics sometimes portray us as a kind of soulless monolith, but I like to think of the company as a selection of small tribes. Once an organization gets bigger than about 125 people, it becomes difficult to control, so we tend to break things down into small, virtually self-contained units.'

A CULTURAL PHENOMENON

One thing is for sure – MTV is not going away. Although we're constantly told that the world is growing older, there were 2.7 billion people between the ages of 10 and 34 in 2000, and by 2010 there will be 2.8 billion. The number of TV sets around the world is rising, and satellite technology has broadened access to the medium.

Bill Roedy says: 'Even I'm surprised by the kind of places you can see MTV. It is literally everywhere. I was in the Amazonian rain forest recently and at one point I was shown inside this hut. Sure enough, there were a bunch of people sitting around a TV set, watching MTV.'

Both audiences and advertisers love the brand. Viacom says MTV is the number one global TV operation in terms of revenue and distribution, and it has been the corporation's fastest-growing unit for the past three years. Viacom chairman and CEO Sumner Redstone comments: 'MTV is a cultural and business phenomenon. It is a true generational brand that can be seen in some 385 million households around the world. It is a remarkable growth machine that has not only been incredibly profitable, but among the most important Viacom assets.'

MTV Networks says that income from advertising internationally rose 50 per cent in 2003. Localization has given it access to smaller domestic brands, while allowing multinationals to either 'cherry pick' markets that interest them, or run massive international campaigns. For global youth brands, MTV is the perfect vehicle.

So what is it that makes MTV so universally appealing? What are the core brand characteristics that have enabled it to get so big? Brent Hansen of MTV Networks Europe thinks he knows.

'For me, it's like a club – a club that young, active, intelligent people opt into as part of their experience of youth culture. We don't treat viewers like couch potatoes – in fact we inspire them to go and see a band, buy a CD, go to a movie. We treat our viewers as participators in the musical environment, not just spectators. That's why it's a stamp of credibility for an artist to appear on MTV. We're not observing youth culture from on high – we are right at the heart of it.'

The brand in brief

Media brand: MTV

Owner: Viacom

Viewers: 400 million households in 166 countries (Source: MTV)

Key marketing strategies: Localization, 'aggressive, creative, relentless' distribution, on-air self-promotion, exporting brand to new technological platforms, high-profile concerts and events, syndicated content

Brand extensions: CDs, DVDs, movies (in partnership with Paramount Pictures), books, merchandizing and licensing of TV properties

Web site: MTV.com (plus country-specific sites)

PART 2

THE NEWSPAPERS

4

The Times

'Changing the chemistry without blowing up the lab'

I would have preferred to stroll down Fleet Street on my way to *The Times*. The two names – both brands, in a sense – are linked in my mind with the glory days of British journalism, when cynical hacks still propped up the bar at El Vino's, swapping salacious gossip and tales of foreign assignments. But these images are founded on an unreliable blend of myth and imagination, and the reality was probably quite different.

In any case, all the newspapers are gone from Fleet Street. The very last news organization located there, Reuters, moved out in 2003. The others went much earlier, a migration precipitated by the owner of *The Times*, Rupert Murdoch. In 1986, he embarked on an unpopular but long overdue modernization of the newspaper industry, building a new printing plant in Wapping and moving *The Times* and his other newspapers there. A bitter dispute with the print unions over the introduction of new technology led to demonstrations and violent clashes with the police. The security measures put in place to ensure the continued distribution of Murdoch's newspapers earned the area the nickname Fortress Wapping.

Seventeen years later, on a sunny weekday morning, Wapping is calm to the point of torpor. A rather drab district, nestled in a curve of the Thames, it is an odd mixture of light industrial units, council housing, and old warehouses converted into shops and luxury apartments. At the bottom of Pennington Street, just beyond Tobacco Dock, lies the glass frontage of *The Times* building.

I arrive at the newspaper at a pivotal moment in its history. Rival media have been eyeing its ongoing modernization sceptically, and pounced upon the launch of a tabloid edition for readers in London as another sign that *The Times* was gambling with its heritage.

But however much it has changed, there is still a certain thrill to be had in visiting this legendary newspaper. As its current editor Robert Thomson says: 'Many papers around the world share our name, but only one is identified by those two words – *The Times*.'

TIMES PAST

According to its archive, *The Times* was the very first newspaper to use the name. It was founded on 1 January 1785 as *The Daily Universal Register*. The name was changed to *The Times or The Daily Universal Register* at the beginning of 1788. Later that year, it dropped the unwieldy appendage and became simply *The Times*.

Appropriately enough, the newspaper was launched as a marketing device. A printer named John Walter started the publication to adver-tise a revolutionary typesetting process called logography. The method utilized pre-cast blocks of whole words and common letter groups, as opposed to the single letters that had been used before. The theory was that this would speed up the composition process. In prac-tice, it proved just as time-consuming as the older method, and was quickly abandoned.

But when Rupert Murdoch introduced new printing technology in the mid-1980s, he was inadvertently continuing a long tradition of innovation. In 1814 *The Times* became the first newspaper to be printed by steam, using a Koenig and Bauer press. Before that, newspapers were printed meticulously by hand. When John Walter II saw a demon-stration of the Koenig press, he realized that it would enable him to increase the paper's print-run – at that time limited to just 4,500 – and give him the flexibility to accept late-breaking news.

Other advances followed throughout the 19th century. The invention of the Walter Press in the 1860s allowed printing on both sides of the paper at once, speeding up production even further. And having been an early adopter of delivery by train – as opposed to mail or express horse-drawn coach – *The Times* became the first English newspaper to be delivered to Paris on the day of printing, arriving by rail at 1.30 pm on 11 December 1849.

It was also during this period that *The Times* earned its famous nick-name, 'The Thunderer'. This is often thought to have derived from a leader on the Reform Bill written by editor Thomas Barnes in 1831, who urged readers to 'thunder for reform'. Not so, according to the paper's online archive.

In 1830, the newspaper ran a leader questioning the circumstances surrounding the death of one Lord Graves. Graves had been found lying in his bedroom in a pool of blood, his throat slashed. The inquest recorded a verdict of suicide, but *The Times* felt this was questionable. Graves was the subject of scandalous rumours involving his wife and the Duke of Cumberland. Evidence later emerged that seemed to remove any suspicion of foul play, and a second *Times* leader admitted that the paper had 'thundered out' its original article in hasty indigna-tion. A rival newspaper, the *Morning Herald*, took the opportunity to chide *The Times* – 'otherwise [known as] The Thunderer, but more commonly called "The Blunderer"'. Whatever the source of the nick-name, it stuck – and enhanced the image of *The Times* as a weighty, authoritative publication.

This is just as well, because over the years *The Times* has been rather adept at building on its brand. It launched the first *Times Atlas* in 1895 – a tradition that continues to the present day – and the first edition of what became *The Times Literary Supplement* in 1902. In 1932 it even created its own typeface, Times New Roman. This was originally designed to improve the legibility of the newspaper, but was later adopted by Penguin Books for its paperbacks. It is now one of the most widely used typefaces in the world.

In the era of digital communications, *The Times* brand still has marketing clout. At the beginning of 2002, following in the footsteps of *The Wall Street Journal* and the *Financial Times*, the newspaper began charging users to access parts of its Web site for the first time.

Another thread running through the history of *The Times* is its series of charismatic and colourful owners. The first John Walter began his career as a coal merchant, later becoming an underwriter at Lloyds – where he lost a fortune when a hurricane tore through shipping off the coast of Jamaica, resulting in a torrent of insurance claims. Walter went into the printing business in 1784, convinced of the potential of logography. Although the new typesetting method was not the money-spinner he had envisaged, his newspaper brought in considerable advertising revenue. With its metamorphosis into *The Times* in 1788, it became populist and gossipy, often printing controversial stories about the public figures of the day.

The paper regained a more serious demeanour under John Walter II, who inherited *The Times* from his father in 1803. It strongly supported the call for political reform, which would give more people the vote and challenge the Tories' overwhelming majority in Parliament. The Reform Act was passed in 1832.

The Walter family owned *The Times* until 1908, when it was sold to newspaper magnate Lord Northcliffe (although the Walters retained a minority interest until 1966). Another fascinating character, Northcliffe (born Alfred Charles William Harmsworth) had started out as a freelance journalist, later founding a series of popular newspapers – including the *Daily Mail* in 1896 and the *Daily Mirror* in 1903. In the early 1900s *The Times* was going through a rough patch, losing money and readers. Northcliffe re-equipped its outdated printing plant and slashed its price from three pence to two, and then to one. By the outbreak of the First World War, its circulation had risen to 278,000 from 38,000 at the start of the decade.

After Northcliffe's death in 1921, the newspaper was sold to John Jacob Astor, the youngest son of Lord Astor and the great-great grandson of the American fur trader turned multimillionaire. It remained in the family's hands until the mid-1960s, when it entered another of its moribund periods. Circulation was down to 228,000, advertising revenues were low, and the future looked uncertain. There was even talk of merging *The Times* with the *Financial Times*. Roy Thomson, the First Baron Thomson of Fleet, stepped in to save the newspaper in 1965.

Hardly less impressive than his predecessors, Thomson was the son of a Toronto barber who – in a more contemporary version of the strategy adopted by John Walter two centuries earlier – had opened a radio station in order to sell more radios. The business grew into a media empire with interests in Canada, the United States and the United Kingdom. Kenneth Thomson succeeded his father in 1976 and *The Times* remained part of the Thomson group until 1981. In February that year, it passed into the hands of a certain Mr Murdoch.

CHANGING TIMES

Born in Melbourne, Australia in 1931, Rupert Murdoch studied at Oxford and inherited *The Adelaide News* from his father, Sir Kenneth Murdoch, in 1952. The paper's unprecedented success under his control eventually enabled him to acquire further titles in Australia and later the *News of the World* and *The Sun* in London. He bought *The Times* in 1981, when the paper was once again losing readers and advertising revenue.

In his determination to modernize, Murdoch wrenched the entire British newspaper industry out of the dark ages. Fleet Street presses were antiquated – some dating back to the 1930s – and conditions for those who worked with them were cramped, filthy and dangerous. Historians and media commentators agree that the move to Wapping, however painful it may have been at the time, was inevitable.

Despite the rapid modernization that came with the Murdoch era, in the early 1990s *The Times* found itself in a no-man's land in the British newspaper landscape. The conservative *Daily Telegraph* was the leading quality newspaper, with a circulation of around 1 million, while *The Times* and its other rivals, *The Guardian* and *The Independent*, languished morosely several hundred thousand sales below.

Clive Milner, the managing director of *The Times*, remembers this period well. 'It was a classic marketing dilemma. There was *The Telegraph* with about a million [sales], and the also-rans with between three and four hundred thousand. We were very keen to break out of that group, but there were problems with our image.'

The newspaper was perceived as being read mainly by wealthy middle-aged men. It was 'the top people's paper' – the notice board of the establishment. The challenge was to make the paper seem more accessible, while hanging on to positive core values like quality, accuracy and authority. 'Our intention was not only to close the gap with *The Telegraph*, but also to win over the 25- to 44-year-old market, the key target group for advertisers. Our first solution was to get into some pretty aggressive pricing.'

In 1993 the paper's price was cut from 45 pence to 30 pence, falling again to 20 pence in 1994. Milner says: 'Our critics said that you couldn't bring new readers to a paper simply by making it cheaper. But we went ahead anyway, because we felt that if we could get people to buy the paper, we could win them over with our content. Then we could gradually put up the price again.'

As the strategy took hold, *The Times* worked hard to adjust its content. Its already highly regarded coverage of general news, politics and business was made sharper and more concise. More sport was introduced. A greater effort was made to appeal to women. In 1996 the paper drew readers' attention to these changes with an advertising campaign using the slogan 'Changing Times'.

The strategy worked. Milner says: 'Between 1993 and 1998 we raised our circulation from 17 per cent of the market to 31 per cent. And advertising went up three-fold.'

At the time of writing, the newspaper has a circulation of more than 600,000 – still below *The Telegraph* but with a comfortable lead over *The Guardian* and *The Independent*. And it costs 50 pence.

WHAT'S IMPORTANT

During its drive to pull in younger readers and boost sales, *The Times* faced accusations that it was 'dumbing down' – abandoning solid reporting and analysis in favour of blatant commercialism. The launch of a tabloid version for readers in London in late 2003 added new fuel to these claims.

George Brock, the managing editor of *The Times*, believes it is naïve to expect a newspaper, even a venerated one, to stand still. 'All news-papers are permanently trying to change the chemistry without blowing up the lab. A newspaper must adapt to the mood of society and the preferences of its readers.'

And despite all the flak, the paper has successfully retained some of its more positive traditional values. At the beginning of the 21st century, the words *The Times* stand for many of the same things as they did at the end of the 19th.

Managing director Clive Milner says: '*The Times* is an iconic brand, it's a world brand, and more importantly it's a trusted brand. Integrity is an essential part of our reputation. We are in the business of fantastic journalism – the best journalism that we can afford, and we have a lot of firepower in that direction.'

The two themes that crop up the most during conversations with exec-utives at *The Times* are its status as Britain's 'paper of record' – almost an ambassador in newsprint – and its independent voice. Politically, it is being positioned as neutral.

'This is not an easy position to take from a marketing point of view,' observes Milner. 'You can be very clear about being a left-wing paper or a right-wing paper. But when you are a paper of record, a paper of integrity, a paper that represents and interprets a spectrum of views – try explaining all that in a simple marketing proposition. That's not to say it can't be done, but it does present something of a challenge.'

In 2002 *The Times* launched a TV advertising campaign called 'What's Important'. It used metaphors to demonstrate the hidden layers of meaning behind apparently simple images. One execution, called 'The Bottle', showed how that single object could symbolize everything from alcoholism and rioting to the launch of a ship.

Says Milner: 'The campaign addressed the problem of every educated person today, which is information overload. When you are cash rich, time poor, bombarded with different media but want to know what's going on, how do you decide what's important? The clear message was that we can show you.'

The second goal was a familiar one, which was to re-establish *The Times* as a contemporary, accessible newspaper. 'There was still a danger that some readers might view us as impenetrable, inaccessible, or part of the establishment,' says Milner. 'We wanted to make them think again.'

The Times may no longer wish to be linked to the British establishment – but it certainly represents Britain, at least in overseas markets. When Hollywood wants to depict London, a shot of somebody reading *The Times* does not take long to appear. Milner offers sound reasons for the brand's international reach.

'You only have to look at the global tentacles of power and influence – multinational business, the Foreign Office. The people who work for these organizations have limited time, so while they want to keep up with events in the United Kingdom, their choice of reading is very select. It's not unreasonable to assume that a fair percentage of them have *The Times* sitting on their desks.'

Managing editor George Brock says the paper's inherent 'Britishness' can be amusing as well as frustrating. 'Even today, well after the end of the Cold War, there are some foreign states who think that *The Times* is a mouthpiece for the British government. But there's no denying the newspaper has global reach and influence. For instance, 60 per cent of our Web site users live outside the United Kingdom.'

THE BURBERRY OF NEWSPAPERS

One man fully embroiled in the paper's marketing strategy is Paul Hayes, its general manager. Indeed, his light-hearted yet incisive approach seems to capture the contemporary image of *The Times*.

'We certainly strive to make people understand that this is now a very modern newspaper,' he says. 'Even our editorial stance has evolved to mirror British society. Thanks to the Blair revolution, Britain today is a much more centrist society, politically speaking. And as "the paper of record", we have a duty to reflect that. So we don't have a doctrine on a story. We give you the news and we give you analysis and depth, but we don't spin it.'

This is in contrast to *The Guardian* and *The Daily Telegraph*, which make no secret of their respective left-wing and right-wing positions. But isn't there a danger that *The Times* could get stranded somewhere in the middle?

Hayes says: 'Of course, our critics could say we don't stand for anything. But I think we stand for reliability. The paper that got the biggest uplift after September 11 was *The Times*. On September 12 our circulation went up by 50 per cent, and stayed there for a very long time. People come back to *The Times* whenever there is a crisis or a period of uncertainty.'

His thoughts are echoed by managing editor George Brock. 'Because people nowadays receive so much news information, what matters very greatly is the ability to distil, select and explain. What people trust is our judgement. Journalists tend to use words like context and analysis, but what we actually provide is "meaning" – what does this event mean?'

Hayes wholeheartedly agrees. 'That's where newspapers win, every time. You can turn on the TV and see what's happened – "Oh look, tanks just rolled into Baghdad" – but to find out what that event actually means to Iraq, to the Middle East, or to you as an individual, you turn to the newspaper you trust.'

This reflex harks back to the traditional image of *The Times* as solid and reliable. But the paper wants to have its cake and eat it too – the tabloid version and new(ish) pullout sections like the lifestyle supplement *T2* are clearly aimed at wooing younger, hipper readers. Hayes is greatly amused when I suggest the newspaper is trying to 'do a Burberry' – take a classic British brand and retool it for the Kate Moss generation.

'We don't deny our heritage and it's very important to us,' he says. 'But we're no longer the newspaper of the pinstriped, bowler-hatted gentleman. He doesn't exist anymore. So we have to focus on other elements of our heritage – such as quality and independent thinking.'

Advertising campaigns like 'What's Important' clearly project this message. But how many readers can they actually bring in? After all, even Hayes admits that newspaper marketing is one of the toughest briefs around. 'Newspaper reading is a very engrained habit, and it's difficult to get readers to change. They are very lethargic. It's a bit like being a bank. Once you've got your customer, you really have to upset them to make them move.'

He says advertising is largely designed to reinforce the brand to existing readers – 'this is a good product, this is why you are reading it' – as well as convincing irregular readers to buy the paper more often. 'Imagine if we got every four day a week reader to become a five or six day a week reader? Our fortunes would be transformed.'

In order to ensure that it is on the right track, the paper monitors its readers' opinions very closely. It has a panel of 2,000 readers which it surveys every month to determine what they think of its contents. Says Hayes: 'Working here in our little world it's very easy to forget about the people out there. We have customers and we should listen to them.'

For this reason, *The Times* is careful to ensure that all its marketing strategies reflect its status as a 'quality' product. 'A year or so ago there was a trend for giving away CDs with newspapers,' says Hayes. 'Your local newsagent began to look like a Virgin Megastore. Only last week, one newspaper was giving away a CD called *20 Great Love Songs of the 1970s*... I mean, please.'

Instead, as part of its drive to improve readership of its Saturday edition – once the lowest circulation day of the week for British papers, but now a major battleground in the sales war – *The Times* introduced a free DVD called *Film First*. This includes clips and trailers of forthcoming movies, and reviews by respected film critics. It also slotted in nicely with the newspaper's sponsorship of the annual London Film Festival.

'It reflects the fact that our readers today are predominantly young and urban. We really have succeeded in capturing that prime ABC1 25- to 44-year-old market. The advantage is not only that this is a key constituency for advertisers, but also that our readers aren't going to start dying off. That sounds cynical but it is a genuine problem for long-established quality newspaper brands.'

One thing everybody agrees on is that the paper's connection with Rupert Murdoch – a figure often maligned by the media products he does not own – has had little impact on *The Times* brand.

Paul Hayes says: 'Some readers probably don't know who owns the paper, and the others don't care. It has become fashionable to criticize Murdoch, mainly in our rival newspapers, but it's way out of proportion. He's a powerful guy, but he's not George W Bush. At the end of the day, people envy his success.'

Clive Milner agrees. 'There is probably a tiny section of the British public who will not buy a Murdoch paper, but that has not limited our ambitions. There have been claims [of editorial interference], but Rupert Murdoch sits in New York at the head of a vast corporation, and he certainly does not have the time to pick up the phone to our editor every five minutes.'

FUTURE TIMES

The current editor of *The Times* is Robert Thomson, an Australian. Thomson's colleagues say that as the first non-British editor of the paper, he is not hamstrung by old-fashioned notions about *The Times*, and has helped it move forward.

Thomson himself comments: 'I have a duty to make sure the newspaper is relevant and modern, but at the same time I am aware that it has a history few can match. It's a huge responsibility.'

He respects the fact that the newspaper still has loyal older customers alongside its new readers. 'You can't just leave them behind in the modernization process, just as you can't progress without a sense of continuity. I am determined to maintain the traditions for which this paper is noted – for instance, accuracy, wit and fine writing.'

A couple of editors were wary of being interviewed for this book, feeling that marketing and branding should not be the concern of journalists. Thomson was not among them. He says: 'While they are not directly involved in marketing, journalists are very conscious of their role in the market. This is a commercial operation and we want it to be successful. And that success is related to how your product is perceived.'

But he would certainly not let tawdry marketing initiatives undermine the brand. 'Any marketing we do has to be relevant – hence our sponsorship of the London Film Festival, for example. It's part of a gradual brand-building process. You can buy readers with cheap promotions, but it's a temporary phenomenon. It's better to coax them to become engaged with the product, and earn their respect.'

General manager Paul Hayes backs up this opinion. 'You can't bribe a reader to pick up the newspaper. At the end of the day, they base their decision on the content. For all the bravado of advertising and marketing people, it boils down to what the journalists produce. The marketing director of an FMCG product also gets involved in R&D. But you can't create a great newspaper by focus group. Fortunately, our journalists produce an excellent product.'

Hayes states that while *The Times* has a commercially aware editor 'commercial people don't hold the editorial pen'. The newspaper has even turned down commercial propositions that its rivals might accept, he adds. 'There are some very aggressive advertising and PR agencies who tell us that their clients will sponsor a special section, but only if they get editorial control. We won't do that. We will only agree to sponsorship if it brings something extra to our readers. And the resulting pages must be as of high a quality as the rest of the newspaper.'

Once again, it's about protecting the integrity of the content. Over the past decade content has become more precious than ever, because newspapers have realized that, in a multimedia environment, it is their only commodity. Readers do not buy newspapers any more – they buy media brands.

Hayes: 'These days we absolutely understand that it's the content that is important, not the delivery. Customers should be able to consume content how, when and where they want. We have a very successful Web presence that provides not only a traditional site, but also an exact replica of the newspaper in electronic form, if that's the way you want it.'

The days are perhaps not far off when *The Times* will no longer position itself as a newspaper, but as a content provider.

'There was a time not so long ago when mobile phone companies went around hiring journalists and saying, "We are the new publishers",' says Hayes. 'But that didn't work because they didn't have the resources, they didn't understand the publishing business, and they didn't have the brands. So now they do deals with us to use our content.'

Managing director Clive Milner agrees that in a multimedia world, the brand is everything. 'We can tailor products to suit our readers – if they want to access our content on paper, online, on their mobile phone or on their PDA, so be it. But they won't bother unless they care about the brand.'

But do readers – who aren't all marketing directors, let's face it – really think of newspapers as brands? Does my father, hunched over his toast in the morning with his copy of *The Times*, enjoy the paper because of its brand values? Or because it has good telly reviews?

Times managing editor George Brock has a theory about this. 'A newspaper is considered by a very large amount of people to be a statement about who they are. They may not consider it to be a brand, but they are thinking about it in brand terms.'

So what statement are people making when they read *The Times*? Editor Robert Thomson says: 'I think our readers understand very clearly that they have invested in a quality product that also reflects modern Britain.'

The brand in brief

Media brand: The Times

Founded: 1785

Owner: News International

Circulation: 638,797 (Source: Audit Bureau of Circulations)

Key marketing strategies: TV and print advertising, sponsorship, promotions, cross-media branding, extensive modernization

Brand extensions: Books

Web site: timesonline.co.uk

5

Financial Times

*'This is a business newspaper, and if we allow
ourselves to become distracted from that idea,
then we are in big trouble'*

The most important branding initiative in the history of the *Financial Times* was put into effect on 2 January 1893. On that day, the newspaper turned pink. According to David Kynaston's (1988) exhaustive study of the paper, *The Financial Times – A Centenary History*, the public announcement of the move was bland and to the point. 'In order to provide outward features which will distinguish the *Financial Times* from other journals… a new heading and distinctive features will be introduced, and the paper will be slightly tinted.'

History does not identify the marketing genius responsible for this momentous change, although the paper's proprietor Douglas MacRae must at least have signed off the idea. There was already another pink paper at the time – the *Sporting Times*, known as 'the pink 'un'' – but adding a rosy hue to a financial journal was a bold move. It had the added advantage of saving money, because pink paper was cheaper. As Kynaston points out: 'It was a marketing decision that over the years must have been responsible for selling many millions of extra copies of the paper.'

More than 110 years later, I'm thinking about this as I enter the *FT*'s headquarters beside the Thames. The paper is on the wrong side of the river these days, just across Southwark Bridge from The City. But it is still within walking distance of its old post-war base at Bracken House, in the lee of St Paul's. Brendan Bracken was one of the most influential figures in the history of the paper, transforming the publication by merging it with a rival title in 1945. Today his sculpted likeness glares out at the *FT*'s black marble-clad lobby, among stock prices streaming past on LED screens.

I wonder what Bracken would have made of the modern *FT*. Apart from the familiar pink glow it bears little resemblance to the product he knew. With a clean, uncluttered design that makes it accessible even to financially inept types like myself, it blends general news, lifestyle and culture with business coverage. On the day I arrive, it has just launched a sports page. 'Do readers want sport in the *FT*?' sniffs the media page of the *Evening Standard* (30 April 2003).

The answer may well be 'yes'. Editor Andrew Gowers has surmised that the wheeler-dealers who read the *FT* don't have time to wade through stacks of newsprint, and prefer to get all the day's news from one source. So the *Financial Times*, while still concentrating on business, now gives them a heads-up on everything else too.

None of this is revolutionary, but the *FT* has a history of subtle, incremental change. In fact, the conversion to pink more than a century ago is still its most radical departure – unless, of course, you count the great merger.

A TALE OF TWO PAPERS

The modern *Financial Times* was a cross-pollination of two newspapers with equally colourful roots. The brand that was lost in the 1945 merger, the *Financial News*, was older by four years and equally respectable, although printed on pallid paper.

The *Financial News* was started in 1884 by Harry Marks, an adventurer who had cut short his education at 15 to head for New Orleans, in the hope that he could get a job with some friends of his father. After knocking about there for a couple of years he moved on to Texas, where he held jobs as a mule team driver and a sewing machine salesman. Inventing some journalistic experience, he got a job on the *San Antonio Express*, rising to become editor of the *San Antonio Daily Press*. He was still only 18 when he settled in New York, where he became editor of the *Daily Mining News* in 1880. A year later he started a special edition of the paper called the *Financial and Mining News*.

With that experience behind him, it didn't take Marks long to find investors when he returned to London in 1883 to launch an English version of the *Financial and Mining News* (shortened to the *Financial News* in July 1884). The only newspaper of its kind at the time, it quickly became noted for its comprehensive coverage and punchy American prose style.

The paper's success bred imitators, among them the *London Financial Guide*, which changed its name to the *Financial Times* on 13 February 1888. The chairman of the *FT* was a roguish-sounding figure called Horatio Bottomley, the son of a tailor's cutter from Bethnal Green. He ran a series of local newspapers, and had recently gone into partnership with Douglas MacRae, the owner of a large printing works. Together they promoted the *Financial Times* as 'the friend of the Honest Financier and the Respectable Broker'.

Bottomley turned out to be somewhat less than respectable. He left the newspaper soon after its launch, convinced that there were bigger profits to be made elsewhere, and became embroiled in a series of increasingly nefarious schemes. He was finally convicted of fraud in 1922. David Kynaston's book contains the following succulent exchange, which took place when a friend visited Bottomley in prison:

'Ah, Bottomley, sewing?'

'No,' said Bottomley. 'Reaping.'

As for Douglas Gordon MacRae, the real founder of the *FT*, he took the paper from strength to strength, weathering the stock exchange depression of the early 1890s and introducing innovations like Linotype machines and, of course, the famous tinted paper.

The *Financial Times* and the *Financial News* would be direct rivals for decades. Even in those early days, both papers showed a flair for self-promotion. The *FT* may have had its pink pages, but the *FN* had age on its side, and it underlined this for its 20th anniversary in January 1904. On top of its normal 8 pages, it ran a 40-page supplement devoted to an analysis of world finance, and threw a lavish party at the Carlton Hotel. (One of the guests was Sir Arthur Conan Doyle, the creator of Sherlock Holmes.)

In the early 1900s the papers were already scrapping over international readers, with the *Financial Times* claiming to be read in clubs throughout 'Siberia, China and the East', while the *Financial News* launched a continental edition, published in Paris from 1907 to 1914.

In 1919 the Berry brothers, owners of *The Sunday Times* and later *The Daily Telegraph*, acquired the *Financial Times*. At around the same time, following the death of Harry Marks, one John Jarvis become proprietor of the *Financial News* – but at that stage the paper was battered and ailing after the First World War. It limped on through the early 1920s, and was put up for sale again in 1928. It attracted the attention of Brendan Bracken, a young entrepreneur who had recently founded a magazine called *The Banker* on behalf of the publishers Eyre & Spottiswoode. Bracken persuaded his company's board to buy the *Financial News*, and became the paper's chairman.

The determined and by all accounts brilliant Bracken tugged the *Financial News* back into the fight. But he had inherited the paper on the brink of a recession, and by the mid-1930s it was already clear that there was not enough room in the market for two financial titles.

The war years inevitably hit the papers hard – symbolized by the fact that many issues of the *Financial Times* could not be printed on its optimistically pink paper. Although both titles survived, there was a gradual acceptance that a single strong newspaper would be better than two weakened ones. Negotiations began between Bracken and his opposite number Lord Camrose (formerly Sir William Berry). The merger took place in 1945, and on 1 October that year a new paper appeared, still pink, but combining the best of the *FT* with the most compelling features of the *Financial News*. Brendan Bracken, once again, was made chairman.

The foundations of the modern *Financial Times* were now in place.

THE *FT* AS A SINGLE BRAND

As we've seen, the *Financial Times* has always had good marketing brains behind it, and the post-war years were no different. David Kynaston highlights the work of Sidney Henschel, the paper's remarkable advertising director during that period. He writes: 'After the war Henschel had quickly discerned the importance of the new advertising agencies… [He began] writing regular letters to the media directors of every agency in the country telling them what the *FT* was doing in the way of its coverage, industrial and otherwise, and what it was proposing to do in the future.'

The paper's managing director Lord Drogheda was equally aware of the importance of public relations. According to Kynaston, when the

BBC decided to drop the *FT*'s share price index, Drogheda talked the corporation into changing its mind. And he was not above using his connections among the business elite to secure advertising for the paper.

The 1950s were golden years for advertising and art direction, and the *Financial Times* played a small role in that revolution. It hired cutting-edge graphic designer Abram Games to design a poster for the newspaper. Games came up with a simple graphic device involving a 'walking newspaper' dressed in pinstriped trousers and holding a rolled-up umbrella and a briefcase. The 'Games man' became the newspaper's mascot for almost 20 years.

But marketing can only complement editorial, and the newspaper made huge leaps in that sphere thanks to Gordon Newton, who became editor in 1949 and remained in the post until his retirement in 1972. Straight talking and decisive, yet open to ideas that might previously have been considered out of character for the *Financial Times*, he is regarded as one of the most influential editors in the history of the paper.

In 1953 the *Financial Times* celebrated its 20,000th issue with an 80-page survey of the British economy. It also added the words 'industry, commerce and public affairs' to its masthead, reflecting the increased scope of the newspaper. And in 1957, another step on the road to the modern *FT* was taken when the Pearson group acquired the paper.

Brendan Bracken died the following year, at the age of only 57. As a tribute to him, the newspaper's new headquarters near St Paul's were named Bracken House.

The 1960s dawned with the introduction of two new sections that seem to capture the mood of the times – the Technical (now Technology) page, and How To Spend It in the Saturday edition. In 1961, the *Financial Times* had an average readership of 132,000, hinting that it already appealed to a far wider audience than its pinstriped City image suggested. One of the most intriguing events of the decade was the short-lived prospect that the *FT* might buy *The Times* – then suffering from falling circulation – and merge the two papers. But the speculation was ended when Roy Thomson snapped up 'The Thunderer' in 1966 (see Chapter 4).

There were more marketing innovations in the early 1970s. The famous 'Games man' was regretfully retired, and a new slogan was introduced to target European readers: 'Europe's business newspaper'. Although not widely used in Britain, a large poster bearing the message was run at Heathrow airport. Around the same time, the *FT* ran full-page advertisements in *The Daily Telegraph*, *The Guardian*, the *Daily Mail* and the *Daily Express*, promoting itself as 'complementary' to these titles.

The 1970s ended as the 1980s were to continue – with internationalization. A European edition began printing in Frankfurt in 1979, anticipating the launch of *The Wall Street Journal Europe*. The US-based *WSJ* was the *FT*'s clear rival in terms of international readers and advertisers. In the years to come, the *FT* would tackle this challenge head-on by setting up printing and distribution operations all over the world. It began printing in New York in 1985 and by the end of the 1990s had established sites covering most of the USA, Europe and Asia. The strategy culminated in the launch of *FT Deutschland* in 2000. This was an entirely new, German-language product, which addressed the largest economy in Europe on its own terms while utilizing the *FT*'s brand heritage. It would later have an impact on the design of the British paper.

Meanwhile, the 1980s saw another key marketing initiative. In 1981, the advertising agency Ogilvy & Mather devised the slogan 'No *FT*, no comment'. Hugely influential in both its TV and poster executions – which suggested that you risked being left out if you didn't read the *FT* – the campaign helped the newspaper's circulation climb past the 250,000 mark.

In 1989, the *FT* left Bracken House and moved to its current location at One Southwark Bridge. This set the scene for further modernization, including the launch of a glossy magazine version of How To Spend It in 1994, and the debut the following year of the Web site FT.com. By the beginning of the 21st century, the *Financial Times* was a truly global newspaper, with more readers overseas than in the UK, and a circulation of more than 450,000 worldwide.

BUSINESS AND BEYOND

The current editor of the *Financial Times*, Andrew Gowers, knows the newspaper's brand values inside out. That's because in March 1999 Gowers was appointed to edit the *FT*'s German-language venture, *FT Deutschland*, launched in partnership with the German publisher Gruner + Jahr.

He comments: 'The experience forced me to think about the essence of the brand, because I was given the chance to bring it to life in a totally different form, without overturning the standards set by the original product.'

To this day, Gowers has a sheet of paper on his office wall listing some of the values he associates with the *FT*: words like concise, credible, analytical and international.

'The German experience was an exciting one because I had a clean slate,' he says. 'But at the same time I knew it was essential that we adhered to the *FT*'s long-established standards of rigorous and incisive business coverage, otherwise we would have been committing a crime against the brand.'

The resulting product is more compact than its British big brother, with an easier-to-navigate format using boxes, breakouts and signposts that pull the reader in to articles. 'It looks extremely attractive, especially when you compare it to the dense print-heavy look of our competition in Germany,' says Gowers. 'As a result, we achieved a slightly younger readership than the paper in the UK. And by 2003 we had a respectable circulation of 93,000.'

When he was appointed editor of the *Financial Times* in July 2001, Gowers was 'in the strange position of being an insider-outsider'. He was excited about bringing some of the innovative spirit of *FT Deutschland* to the *Financial Times*, but he did not want to change the newspaper overnight.

'It would not have been wise to come rushing in saying, "Right, everything's going to be different." As well as insulting the existing product, it would have put the staff under unnecessary intellectual strain,' he points out. 'My approach was to let people know that I loved the paper and that they were doing a fantastic job, but that there were some new things I wanted to introduce.'

One of Gowers' goals was to encourage a more holistic approach to the *FT*'s online and offline offerings. 'At the height of the dotcom boom there was talk of taking FT.com and turning it into a separate entity. While it is indisputable that a great newspaper needs to be present on the Web, it should be integrated into the brand, not bolted on and certainly not floated off.'

Like many journalists, Gowers believes the Internet has given newspapers the freedom to become more analytical, and less focused on providing the bare facts. 'There is absolutely no point in repeating information that is available for free elsewhere. Our job is to add depth.'

With this in mind, Gowers has set up a small team of investigative journalists, working separately from the rest of the editorial staff, who provide a daily probe into topical events or skulduggery they have uncovered for the first time. All this seems to fit in with the *FT* ethos – but what about the coverage of arts, lifestyle and sport?

'It is clear that our readers are interested in subjects beyond business, and in fact we have had a small but respected arts section since the 1950s. Secondly, it is obvious that today there is a huge correlation between business and sport,' Gowers points out.

The newspaper was given a light redesign in 2003, and these days it is an extremely comprehensive product. Business readers can feast on regular special reports covering specific markets, as well as a fund management supplement called *FTfm*. Meanwhile, the weekend edition, published on Saturday, covers everything from fashion to holidays, and *How to Spend It* has become increasingly glossy.

But Gowers stresses that by making the paper broader and more accessible, he has not abandoned its original purpose. 'We don't want to turn the pink paper into a white general interest paper. This is a business newspaper, and if we allow ourselves to become distracted from that idea for one second, then we are in big trouble.'

PAINTING THE MAP PINK

Olivier Fleurot, the chief executive officer of the *Financial Times*, is a Frenchman. He joined the newspaper from *Les Echos* – the French business paper owned by *FT* parent Pearson – where he had risen to chief executive after joining the title 10 years earlier in a marketing role. All this is a rather long-winded way of saying that Fleurot is the face of the new, global *Financial Times*, and that he understands the importance of branding.

'Our international expansion only began in 1979, when we started printing in Frankfurt, which really wasn't that long ago,' he points out. 'I believe that up until that point we were still a very British paper, associated with the City and playing a specialized role. Now if you ask a banker in Milan for a list of European newspapers, he will certainly mention the *FT*. We are still a British paper, but now we have a European, and indeed international, voice.'

The paper's global expansion paralleled its internal evolution into a broader, more complete product – no longer aimed entirely at number-crunching finance geeks, but at anybody with an interest in business. This positioning is given particular emphasis in the UK, where in 1999 the newspaper launched an advertising campaign around the theme 'And you thought we only covered business'. (This retained the now classic 'No *FT*, no comment' line.)

Fleurot says the *FT*'s new approach can be understood simply by adopting the psychology of a typical executive. 'What do they want when they arrive at work? Of course they need to know all the business news, but they also need to know the result of the match between Manchester United and Real Madrid, or that a fantastic exhibition has started at the Tate Modern. Their boss and their clients may be talking about that. And if we don't give them all this information, they will go elsewhere for it.'

The change was broadly designed to capture younger readers – a vital target market for a paper with a traditionally older (and ageing) readership. The message that the *FT* had changed took a little while to get through, however. 'Our research in the UK showed that younger people who had not actually read the paper assumed that it was dry, boring, and only for people working in the City. But interestingly, when we asked them to read the paper for a week, and then went back to them for their reactions, they were astounded.'

But Fleurot accepts that the newspaper's traditional 'serious finance' image enables it to gain readers in overseas markets. 'Of course, that perception gives us strength. In Hong Kong or Tokyo, or even in places where we don't have a particularly high circulation, everybody knows what we stand for. When we introduce ourselves to someone, they say: "Oh – the *FT*!" They know that we are a serious and authoritative newspaper.'

In fact, the newspaper's positioning varies from market to market. In the UK, it is being pushed as a broader product – the 'beyond business' idea – while overseas it is promoted as a source of international business news, and a complement to domestic titles. There are different editions of the *Financial Times* for the UK, continental Europe, the United States and Asia, 'with FT.com as a fifth edition,' adds Fleurot. Although 85 per cent of the content is the same, the international editors choose their subjects from a central 'pool' of news, and tailor the paper to suit their markets. (*FT Deutschland* is a separate paper with its own staff.)

In the United Kingdom, there has been a pressing reason to expand the paper's readership beyond the financial community – the economy. Fleurot says: 'There has always been a strong correlation between the stock market and the *Financial Times*. When the markets fall, we suffer. I think about 30,000 people have been made redundant in the City. We decided we couldn't just wait around for the markets to pick up.'

Additionally, Fleurot believes the United Kingdom is the most competitive newspaper market in the world. 'You have to keep moving ahead, adding new things, keeping the paper in people's minds, and backing it up with promotion. Otherwise you lose ground.'

HOW TO BRAND IT

Gordon Willoughby, marketing and content sales director, is the man responsible for promoting the *FT*'s brand globally. 'At heart we are a global brand – we cover international business, and only 30 per cent of our readership is in the United Kingdom,' he says. 'But like any other expanding multinational business, we are at different stages of brand development around the world.'

The basic brand profile is clear, however. 'The *FT* is a niche brand, aimed at a global elite. At its core is the product – the editorial content. What that means is integrity, accuracy and impartiality. And of course what all these things add up to is trust. In the UK, we are second only to the BBC in terms of trust. Our readers see us as an ally. They could succeed on their own, but we give them a helping hand.'

Willoughby adds that the wild card of 'Britishness', while apparently a disadvantage for an aspiring global brand, actually helps the *FT* in its quest. 'It's a bit of a two-edged sword, but it works if we play up the positive side of "Britishness". In journalistic terms, British journalism is seen as rigorous, combative, robust, and challenging.'

Given the dominating voice of the United States in global affairs, the *FT*'s British heritage also gives it a unique selling point. 'In the US, we are seen as providing an acceptably European view of business, while in Europe we're seen as an Anglo-Saxon voice that is not red in tooth and claw American capitalism.'

Bearing this in mind, marketing messages have to be adjusted around the world. In the United Kingdom, the *FT* can get away with more ironic and subtle messages, because it is, as Willoughby puts it, 'part of the warp and weft of society'. 'That's the global versus local challenge: achieving a consistent tone of voice for the brand while expressing it in different ways.'

The *FT*'s advertising tone of voice, according to Willoughby, is 'confident but not arrogant, intelligent but not intellectual, and witty but not sarcastic'. Promotional campaigns need to capture all this – while at the same time delivering the key message of revitalization and renewal, without alienating loyal readers.

Two campaigns highlight the different strategies the paper has adopted. In the UK, it launched a campaign using the slogan 'New *FT*, new comment'. Obviously, this appealed to UK audiences' familiarity with the paper's old slogan. Other print and poster executions used word games that would not have worked overseas: 'Pink is now perkier'; 'Success reads success'; 'Ltd insight, not limited insight'; and 'If at first you don't succeed, maybe you're reading the wrong paper'. There was also a promotion offering readers a 30 per cent reduction at Thomas Pink, retailer of fine British shirts. ('Get into something smarter', ran the text.)

Willoughby says: 'For me the campaign had a certain lightness of touch that communicated the fact that yes, we are a business newspaper and yes, we are intellectually rigorous – but that does not make us boring. Because we are an iconic brand in the UK, even people who don't read us have very strong ideas of who we are, and so we have to challenge them.'

In contrast, a European press and poster campaign that ran at the same time used a much more visual (and basic) message. It showed sportsmen protecting themselves with pink *FT* paper – a boxer bandaging his hands before putting on his gloves, a football player strapping on a pink newsprint shin pad. The baseline was: 'Win at business.'

The campaign was placed at what the *FT* terms 'international media spots' such as airports and railway stations. 'One of our strategies for communication is to recognize that we have an international audience, and because it is a very disparate audience – there just aren't many of them – we have to reach them at cluster points.'

There is a sound psychological reason for choosing airports, too. 'Without wanting to insist too much that the medium is the message, it makes sense that as a global brand we should advertise at an airport, because people are behaving "globally" at that moment. We're saying,

"Business is international, and you've proved that because you're just about to get on a plane to go to a meeting."'

The international campaigns feature the FT.com address prominently, reflecting the manner in which the Web has helped media brands expand overseas. (The *FT* has also launched a Chinese language Web site to support its Asian issue.) Willoughby says the Internet has also changed the nature of the paper's readership.

'I think it has helped us attract younger readers, and also female readers. FT.com is known to be a very useful source of information, and it acts as an entry point for the brand. And then of course we hope that they will move on to the newspaper. Young people find the Web a less threatening environment.'

The *Financial Times*, threatening? Willoughby explains: 'I think people who don't know the paper find it daunting. It's a bit like when you get your first proper job and you're given business cards. It's exciting and a bit weird – you feel strange using them at first. But after a while, it seems totally natural. I think the *FT* is like that for some people.'

In common with other upmarket media brands, there is something clubby about reading the *Financial Times*. Says Willoughby: 'The paper can become totemic. The pink works well in that respect, because it makes the paper highly visible when it peeks out of your briefcase. People know it says something about them. It's not an exclusive club, but it takes a bit of time and effort to become a member.'

The brand in brief

Media brand: Financial Times

Founded: 1888

Owner: Pearson plc

Circulation: 455,491 (Source: ABC)

Key marketing strategies: Press, poster, TV and radio advertising, promotions

Brand extensions: Research service, books, annual reports, conferences, mobile phone and PDA service

Web site: FT.com

6

The Wall Street Journal

'Whether a reader trusts you or not depends on how often
you get things right'

In the covered walkway that leads to the headquarters of Dow Jones in New York, I stop to look out of the window. Below me is a gaping hole – a crater, to be exact. Its bottom is dusty and grey, and trucks and bulldozers bustle about in it like neurotic ants, as if its sheer scale intimidates them. Despite all the media coverage, it is still unclear what they are building here. For now it remains an eerie non-landmark, a phantom memorial with a search engine name: Ground Zero.

Dow Jones & Co. and its most famous brand, *The Wall Street Journal*, are based just across the street from Ground Zero, in a building called the World Financial Center. When the Twin Towers fell, they almost took the *Journal* with them. Except that they didn't. What happened instead was that, despite the fact that its offices had been half-demolished and evacuated, that some of its staff were still missing, and that the others had reconvened in a makeshift site in New Jersey – despite all that, the paper managed to bring out an edition the next day, and deliver it to 1.6 million subscribers.

It was one the best examples of cool-headed teamwork in the history of journalism, and it justly won the newspaper a Pulitzer Prize. A lot of papers have boasted about their coverage of 9/11, but compared to the *Journal*'s performance, their claims sound hollow.

The *Journal* was well aware of this at the time. In the days that followed the attacks, the paper's public relations people contacted media journalists to talk about its achievement. For the *Journal*, the fact that it had provided outstanding coverage of an historic news event under intolerably harsh circumstances also became a promotional tool.

When I arrive at the *Journal*, its employees have only recently moved back into their old home, and it still has a shiny, fresh-paint feel about it. There is a sense that the paper is trying to regain its momentum after a punishing couple of years. Following the attacks on the Twin Towers, there was the kidnapping and murder of *Journal* reporter Daniel Pearl in Pakistan. And apart from these heavy psychological blows, there were the economic ones – in 2002, Dow Jones's revenues declined 12 per cent to US$1.6 billion, according to its annual report. Matters were looking healthier in 2003, but only after a brutal cost-cutting drive and the shedding of about 16 per cent of the workforce over two years.

As if all this were not enough, there is speculation that the paper might be sold. A single family has controlled Dow Jones for decades, but *The New York Times*, *The Washington Post* and Rupert Murdoch's News Corp are all said to be eyeing the company with interest. However, according to an article in *The New Yorker* ('Family Business', 3 November 2003), the Bancroft family isn't interested in selling, for the moment.

The newspaper itself betrays no outward sign of these tensions. In April 2002 it got its first redesign since 1942, the culmination of a long-term investment programme that had seen the number of pages increase from 80 to 96. This enabled the *Journal* to divide into five easily identifiable sections – including the new Personal Journal, which introduced tips on personal finance, health, and lifestyle, among other subjects. The pages became more spacious and colourful. The revamp also tripled the paper's capacity for carrying lucrative colour advertising. Today's *Wall Street Journal* is still far from lightweight, but it looks considerably less austere than in the past.

DOW, JONES AND BERGSTRESSER

The business came first. In 1882 three young reporters called Charles Dow, Edward Jones and Charles Bergstresser started a small news agency in a basement office near the New York Stock Exchange. Dow Jones & Company produced handwritten newsletters, nicknamed 'flimsies', that contained up-to-date nuggets of financial news and were delivered by messenger to subscribers in the Wall Street area.

The business prospered and by 1889 it had 50 staff. The company then decided to turn its 'Customer's Afternoon Newsletter' into a newspaper called *The Wall Street Journal*. The first issue on 8 July 1889 was only four pages long and cost two cents.

Although the *Journal* quickly found an audience, its founders realized that the usefulness of financial news depended on the swiftness of its delivery. So they started the Dow Jones News Service, supplying information by telegraph. The paper and the wire service grew in parallel, and today Dow Jones Newswires delivers real-time financial news to almost 400,000 financial professionals worldwide.

After the death of Charles Dow in 1902, the company was sold to the journalist Clarence W Barron, who had been hired several years before as the news service's 'out of town' correspondent. At that time the *Journal*'s circulation was around 7,000, but under Barron's leadership it swelled to more than 18,000. He invested in modern presses and additional editorial staff, and by the end of the 1920s he was printing 50,000 copies of the paper a day. (He also founded *Barron's*, another Dow Jones publication, in 1921.)

When Barron died, in 1928, his stepdaughters Jane and Martha inherited the company and his son-in-law Hugh Bancroft took over the running of the business. But Bancroft's tenure lasted only five years before he succumbed to depression and committed suicide at the age of 54. Although the Bancroft family retained ownership of Dow Jones, the editor of *The Wall Street Journal*, Bernard Kilgore, came to the fore as the driving force behind the company. He was made chief executive in 1945. Kilgore is acknowledged to have been 'the architect of the paper as it is today' ('Our History', dowjones.com).

Throughout the 1950s, Kilgore expanded the *Journal*'s coverage to embrace every aspect of business, economics and consumer affairs, as well as general news that was likely to have an impact on business. This enabled the newspaper to reach outside the financial community, and by the 1960s circulation had topped 1 million.

The 1970s was a period of expansion for Dow Jones. It founded the weekly *Far Eastern Economic Review*, and launched *The Asian Wall Street Journal*. Back home, it acquired local newspaper group Ottaway.

There was a boom in the money-hungry 1980s, when the circulation of *The Wall Street Journal* briefly touched 3 million. In 1988 it launched *The Wall Street Journal Europe*, based in Brussels. This was also the period in which Dow Jones acquired an electronic financial data delivery system called Telerate – a product it was later forced to sell in the face of competition from Bloomberg and Reuters.

Since the early 1990s, Dow Jones has expanded its media offering. It moved into television with the launch of Asia Business News in 1993 and European Business News in 1995. This evolved into CNBC, the joint venture TV operation with NBC. In 1999 it joined forces with Reuters (rather ironically) to launch Factiva, a Web-based global news and information service. So far, this has fared much better than Telerate.

But the company has not lost interest in print. Other publications include the magazine *SmartMoney* (published with Hearst), the Latin American business magazine *AméricaEconomía*, and a newspaper called *Vedomosti* in Russia. In 1999 it did a deal with the German Holtzbrinck group to swap stakes in *The Wall Street Journal Europe* and *Handelsblatt*, Germany's leading financial paper. This was seen as a move to establish a stronger footing in Germany with the arrival of the *Financial Times*, which was poised to launch *FT Deutschland*.

Generally, Dow Jones has been smart about extending *The Wall Street Journal* brand. In 1999 it launched *The Wall Street Journal Sunday*, a supplement that initially appeared in 10 local newspapers in the USA. By 2003 it was carried by 78 newspapers across the country, with a circulation of more than 10 million. And since 1994 the paper has run *The Wall Street Journal Special Editions* – branded pages that now appear in 12 different languages in 38 newspapers around the world.

THE FRANCHISE THEORY

But *The Wall Street Journal*'s real stroke of genius in the last decade was the decision in 1996 to make its Web site a subscription-only service. This was a radical policy at the time – and is still fairly unfashionable today, when many publications continue to offer online content for free, and newspapers like *The Times* and the *FT* have only just begun edging towards the full subscription model. They will have trouble catching up with WSJ.com, though, which is now the biggest subscription site on the Web with some 700,000 subscribers.

The man who made the decision was Peter Kann, the chairman and chief executive officer of Dow Jones & Company, who is brushing aside my apologies of lateness and answering my fuzzy jet-lagged questions as we sit in his office at the World Financial Center.

'To me it didn't make sense to give away information in a new distribution channel that we charged for in an existing one,' he explains. 'If we have something of significant value in print form, then it's illogical not to charge for it online.'

Kann is a long-standing advocate of the theory that a product with an established reputation for accuracy and trustworthiness can transfer seamlessly on to different media platforms. When he was based in Hong Kong during the 1970s, covering Asia for *The Wall Street Journal*, he pushed for the launch of an Asian edition. *The Asian Wall Street Journal* made its debut in 1976, with Kann as the editor and publisher.

'I prefer the word "franchise" to "brand",' he says. 'The US edition of *The Wall Street Journal* is the core product of much larger franchise, which we have very successfully expanded across geographic and technical boundaries.'

Citing products like *SmartMoney* and CNBC, as well as the foreign language supplements, Kann suggests that the newspaper has extended its brand 'more aggressively and more innovatively than any other publication'. He believes that the *Financial Times*, *The Washington Post* and *The New York Times* still have a long way to go.

'These are all fine publications – but they are still more publications than franchises. The reason we've been able to grow in this way is not necessarily because we're smarter or more innovative, which maybe we are, but because our content has a high degree of essentiality. It appeals to a specific community which is not limited geographically and which is increasingly interested in receiving information from a single trusted source.'

For Kann, as for so many media executives, it all comes back to trust. A brand like *The Wall Street Journal* can raise its head above the landslide of information battering today's business executives because it is familiar to them, and they believe in it.

'You can get information from a whole lot of sources, but how much credibility do they have? The fact that there are hundreds of Web sites and trade magazines out there is almost helpful to us, because what our readers increasingly rely on us for is judgement. They want us to select the most important and relevant stories. And you're not going to leave that to someone you don't trust.'

Kann points out that Dow Jones Newswires delivers some 8,000 pieces of information every 24 hours. 'That's an impossible amount to digest. So you need someone to sift it, to analyse it and to put it into context. And that's something we do particularly well.'

In order to maintain this reservoir of trust, *The Wall Street Journal* has certain guidelines – not using anonymous sources, for instance, and clearly marking the division between news and opinion within the paper. But Kann points out that there is a certain amount of serendipity too. 'Whether a reader trusts you or not depends to an extent on how often you get things right,' he says. 'When we make certain predictions about the economy, it helps that we're often proved correct.'

He adds out that the burden of trust weighs even more heavily on *The Wall Street Journal* than on other publications, because its readers base crucial decisions on its contents. 'If you mess up sports coverage, nobody is particularly hurt by it. But if you mess up your coverage of what's going on in the stock market, it has an impact.'

An article in *Fortune* magazine shortly after our interview backed this view. In its review of the most powerful people in business, it gave an honorary mention to Paul Steiger, the *Journal*'s editor. 'As editor of *The Wall Street Journal* – the paper that posts the agenda for American business – Steiger can move markets and strike fear into the hearts of CEOs everywhere.' ('Zeitgeisters', *Fortune*, 11 August 2003.)

Steiger himself chuckles at this, but confirms: 'It's fair to say that the newspaper has a tremendous influence, and it's a responsibility we take extremely seriously.'

Facts are checked and double checked before a story is released, and Steiger says he would rather wait for a day than release an item that might lack balance or a last vital piece of information. 'There's no written code, but there are certainly principles that we adhere to.'

Because Kann believes its task is to join the dots rather than spitting out factoids, he prefers to call *The Wall Street Journal* a 'publication' instead of a newspaper. 'In its physical appearance it is a newspaper, but in what it does for its readers it's also in some sense a magazine.'

And who are *The Wall Street Journal*'s 2 million daily readers? Surely not all of them are sweating over a terminal in some frenetic trading environment?

Kann says: 'There was a time when you could define the reader in a predictably narrow sense as a US business man – I stress "man" because they were all male back then – who worked for a Fortune 500 company as vice-president or above. But that's changed in a whole lot of ways. Now I would say that the audience is any global business person who wants to keep up with current trends and events in that field.'

The paper has changed along with its readers. Although the redesign in 2002 was almost laughably subtle (media journalists at the unveiling said that they couldn't tell the difference), it reflected a gradual shift away from financial news, and towards more general news viewed through the prism of business. Kann points out that the success of any media franchise depends on the continuing relevance of its core product.

'We have to keep moving. We need to reflect the changing patterns of business behaviour and activity, and keep up with or preferably ahead of the interests of our audience.'

This does not mean introducing sports, society or entertainment sections – an idea of which Kann seems particularly dismissive – but redefining what 'business' means. 'To give an example, we realized 20 years ago or so that technology was going to transform business. So we expanded our technology coverage.'

The paper also noted the thinning of middle management and the rise of service industries like marketing and consulting, so it beefed up its coverage of those sectors accordingly. When it spotted a trend towards personal investing, it boosted its personal finance coverage.

'Most media franchises serve a community, and the secret of success is to respond to that community's needs,' sums up Kann.

Joining us in Kann's office is Dick Tofel, the *Journal*'s assistant publisher. He points out that the newspaper's respected position in the marketplace is aided by the existence of Dow Jones Newswires.

'We are the only business newspaper that also provides a real-time financial news service. That's a huge advantage in terms of differentiation. It also helped us a great deal when it came to charging for our online content. While many newspaper sites closely resemble one another, ours remains distinct. After all, we were in the real time news business even before we were in the newspaper business.'

MARKETING WITH DIGNITY

The Wall Street Journal believes in marketing – but not in selling out. Peter Kann makes it very clear that he dislikes obvious promotional activity.

'We won't sell with gimmicks. If you look at how most print products attract the attention of the public, it's usually by saying: "Here, take this cell phone and we'll also give you a 13-week subscription to our newspaper." We prefer to emphasize the value that our product provides. We do some introductory offers, but by and large we sell our products at full price because we believe that the value proposition is fair. That's what really led us to be so innovative on the Web.'

The Wall Street Journal's longevity is such that it has no need to explain itself to its target audience – everybody knows basically what it does. In TV shows and movies, it is used as a symbol to signify 'business' in the same way that *The Times* indicates 'British'. The paper has played minor roles in films ranging from *Some Like It Hot* in 1959 to *American Beauty* in 1999.

Kann continues: 'What we have to do, however, is elaborate on the benefits that the product provides. And of course, when we make any significant changes to the publication, we advertise to promote these and to assure our core audience that the changes were beneficial.'

Kann is referring to the paper's redesign in 2002. The print advertising campaign for this event was a minor classic, in that it lightly mocked *The Wall Street Journal*'s serious image, while assuring loyal readers that their favourite paper was not going to be ruined. The ads showed redesigned front pages mocked up to resemble *Cosmopolitan*, *Rolling Stone*, a custom car magazine and a comic book. 'Rejected,' said the one-word caption under each.

While the campaign cleverly manipulated perceptions of the *Journal*, it also highlighted the paper's stolidity. *The Wall Street Journal* has no intention of messing around with its heritage in order to capture a few younger readers. (It still retains its most charming stylistic quirk – the tiny pointillist portraits of people in the news that are hand-drawn by the art department.) However, Kann accepts that an illustrious past does not necessarily guarantee survival.

'Long-standing brands don't survive on their own – they survive by remaining contemporary and by continuing to provide value. When it comes to trust, a long-standing track record obviously helps. But I think it's quite possible to establish a successful media brand within a decade. CNBC [founded in 1989] is a well-established media brand on television. Bloomberg is less than 20 years old.'

Taking a brand into a market where it is less well known is a similar experience, as *The Wall Street Journal* discovered when it expanded into Asia and later Europe. Assistant publisher Dick Tofel points out that in places where the paper does not carry its fame like a calling card, there is a distinct correlation between marketing and brand awareness.

'In the United States, we need no introduction. In Asia, we have almost reached that position. And in Europe, we are much better known than we were five years ago. And that is a result of the fact that we have pumped more resources into marketing in Europe in the past five years.'

Even so, the newspaper remains primarily a US product, with a circulation in its home market of 1.8 million (discounting online subscribers), compared to 100,769 for the European edition and 84,467 for *The Asian Wall Street Journal*. Virtually unchallenged in its home market, it is competing with an increasingly aggressive *Financial Times* in both Europe and Asia. But with the aftermath of September 11 behind it, and painful cost-cutting measures now out of the way, *The Wall Street Journal* should be able to concentrate on reporting economic conditions, rather than having to adapt to them.

The brand in brief

Media brand: The Wall Street Journal

Founded: 1889

Owner: Dow Jones & Company

Circulation: 2,661,650 (Source: Wall Street *Journal*/ABC)

Key marketing strategies: TV, print and radio advertising, expansion across media

Brand extensions: Europe and Asia editions, branded supplements in local and overseas newspapers, edition for schools, magazine, books, radio and television properties

Web site: WSJ.com

7

International Herald Tribune

'Our readers are prepared to pay for the kind of journalism we do, and they feel an incredible amount of loyalty towards us'

It seems fitting that the *International Herald Tribune* is based just off avenue Charles de Gaulle, a wide traffic-screeching highway on the wrong side of the Arc de Triomphe. From this vantage point the *IHT* sits between two worlds – glancing nostalgically back at the old Paris of bistros and leafy boulevards, and looking optimistically ahead at the gleaming skyscrapers of La Défense, the ultra-modern business district that looms on the horizon.

The *IHT* is an oddity. A global newspaper located in Paris, owned by Americans but with a European heritage, it manages to be quaint and sophisticated at the same time. Once it was the local newspaper for Anglo-Saxons in Paris. Now it is the international newspaper for English-speakers everywhere, and you can hardly tell it is based in Paris at all.

The newspaper's reception area reflects this duality. Modern and antiseptic, it also contains a gothic three-foot-high bronze sculpture of an owl, whose staring electronic eyes blink on and off. I've been here before, and every time I want to ask: 'So what's with the owl?' But somehow the question gets shuffled away among other, more businesslike concerns.

This time I learn that James Gordon Bennett Jr, the newspaper's rakish founder, believed that owls brought him good luck. There are conflicting stories about how he came to adopt the creature as his symbol, but the most convincing is that his father – the owner of the original *New York Herald* – once said to him: 'Young man, your future depends upon night work on the *Herald*, and eternal vigilance.'

In recent years the *IHT* could have done with a character like Bennett to spice up its brand identity. During the 1990s the paper seemed to become staid and corporate, apparently stuck between the conflicting concerns of its two owners – *The Washington Post* and *The New York Times* – while serving the purposes of neither.

But all that has changed. On 1 January 2003 *The New York Times* acquired full ownership of the *International Herald Tribune* from *The Washington Post*, paying US\$65 million for its 50 per cent share. The *Times* promised expansion and investment, the long-overdue introduction of colour – and bigger marketing budgets.

Richard Wooldridge, president and chief operating officer of the *IHT*, is delighted by this development. 'I feel we've entered a new era,' he says. 'I've always been enthusiastic about the *IHT*, but this is an incredibly exciting time for the paper.'

It almost sounds like the good old days.

ROGUE AND VISIONARY

Appropriately enough, it was an owl that summoned the Paris edition of the *New York Herald* into life. Legend has it that James Gordon Bennett Jr was standing on the balcony of his Paris apartment late one night, contemplating the idea of launching a European version of his paper, when an owl hooted. It was the only encouragement Bennett needed.

The newspaper appeared without preamble on 4 October 1887. It was four pages long and copies had been distributed to newsstands in the most elegant *quartiers* of the city, as well as all the best hotels. As Bennett had predicted, his target readers were delighted with the paper. According to Charles L Robertson's (1987) excellent book, *The International Herald Tribune – The First Hundred Years* (the contents of which forms the backbone of this short history), one of them even took the trouble of writing to him to ask why the publication had not been given more of a fanfare.

In one of the offhand remarks that disguised Bennett's true marketing genius, he replied: 'We do not... believe in buncombe articles about "long felt needs" and telling what one intends to do, and what not to do. A good newspaper speaks for itself.'

Bennett's pep talk to his editorial staff shortly before the paper came out sounds equally suicidal by modern marketing standards. 'I want you fellows to remember that I am the only reader of this paper. I am the only one to be pleased. If I want it to be turned upside down, it must be turned upside down. I consider a dead dog in the rue du Louvre more interesting than a devastating flood in China. I want one feature article a day. If I say the feature is to be Black Beetles, Black Beetles it's going to be.'

Although Bennett was a much shrewder businessman than he sometimes appeared, he was as oddball as his newspaper. By the time he launched the Paris edition of the *Herald*, he had already been in self-imposed exile for 10 years, having obstinately refused to return to his native America.

He was the son of James Gordon Bennett, who had founded the *New York Herald* in 1835. As a result of the paper's success, Bennett Senior became enormously rich. But the New York of the 19th century was a brutish place, and in 1841 Bennett's wife was forced to stand by while he was almost beaten to death by a corrupt politician's henchmen. Mrs Bennett escaped to the more genteel surroundings of Paris, taking James Jr and his sister Jeanette with her.

With his combination of a French upbringing and American self-confidence, not to mention a hefty dose of spoilt decadence, the young James grew up to be a dashing rogue with an eye for the ladies. Back in New York – while ostensibly being groomed to take over the *Herald* – he spent a lot of his time drinking, scrapping, and chasing women.

Even after the death of his father, Bennett Jr failed to mend his reckless ways. The final straw came when he arrived drunk at his own engagement party and urinated into the fireplace. He was escorted off the premises, protesting and incoherent. Bennett failed to apologize the next morning and the incident swelled into a scandal. Soon he found himself barred from fashionable gatherings and his favourite New York clubs. Incensed, he left for Paris – vowing never to return.

Bennett continued his flamboyant lifestyle in France, while somehow managing to run his late father's paper remotely. Out of necessity he founded a new transatlantic cable company, breaking the Western Union monopoly and creating cheaper rates. This enabled reporters to cable more European news to the American publication. It had the secondary effect of allowing Bennett to launch the Paris edition, which for years would be stitched together out of material cabled from the USA.

But there was another element at play, too. Bennett had noted the growth of a 'cosmopolitan class'. This was not the old aristocracy, but a new consumer group that had grown rich on industrialization, and was now spreading into Europe's elegant cities and resorts via steamships and railways. The fact that Bennett spotted this niche so early proves that an innate business sense lurked behind the dissolute playboy façade. Even today, executives at the *IHT* often describe its target readers as 'the global class'.

IHT president Richard Wooldridge confirms: 'Bennett was way ahead of his time. There's no doubt that his spirit of internationalism and innovation is what we still strive for while editing, producing and selling the newspaper today.'

A PAPER FOR COSMOPOLITANS

The growth of the *Herald*'s Paris edition owed much to Bennett's pioneering use of promotional techniques. For instance, he offered free copies of the paper to English governesses. As these women usually worked in rich households, it was an ideal way of getting the paper in front of his target readership.

Bennett also arranged for branded newssheets to be delivered to incoming steamships at Le Havre. Starved of news during the week-long Atlantic crossing, passengers snapped up the special editions, and remembered the name of the newspaper that had produced them. Bennett later had this service extended to Boulogne, Southampton and Liverpool.

Recognizing that the cosmopolitan class were a self-regarding bunch, he launched a 'Traveller's Guide', listing the names of those who were arriving on the steamers. In a similar manner, Bennett encouraged amateur correspondents to send travel features from fashionable resorts across Europe. These made the paper popular with restaurants and hotels in places like Trouville, Aix and Lucerne, providing advertising sales leads and ultimately enabling Bennett to expand the paper's distribution.

The headquarters of the *Herald* were spread out across Paris, but Bennett ensured that there was a large public reception and classified advertising office on avenue de l'Opéra, with a gleaming frontage that was little more than a publicity hoarding. The couriers who scuttled between the newspaper's various outposts wore olive green uniforms emblazoned with a golden owl.

Bennett's commitment to new technology, faster newsgathering and rapid distribution foreshadowed some of the strategies utilized by later media moguls. His was the first European newspaper to use Linotype machines – doing away with the need to compose pages by hand. He installed gleaming new American printing presses. He introduced full-colour advertising supplements and cartoons. He backed Marconi's wireless experiments, and later used radio to receive news of First World War shipping movements. He was an early adopter of the automobile, and commissioned a driver in a powerful red Mercedes sports car to deliver a pile of newspapers to Trouville each morning during the summer season. He quickly replaced the horse-drawn vans that had been used to distribute the paper in Paris with modern trucks.

All this investment meant that the Paris *Herald* was not hugely profitable during Bennett's lifetime. It also soaked up a great deal of his personal wealth. However, it was in good enough shape to limp through the early days of the First World War, even though it was once forced to shrink to a single page. And then, in 1917, American troops began pouring into Europe. Circulation soared to over 300,000. Even the launch of a rival newspaper, the Paris edition of the *Chicago Tribune*, had little impact on the *Herald*'s success. By the time the war was over, many young Americans had had a taste of life in Paris, and the scene was set for the *Herald*'s golden age.

In one crucial respect, however, the newspaper would never be the same again. James Gordon Bennett died at his villa in Beaulieu-sur-Mer on 15 May 1918, at the age of 77. By his side was the woman he had married four years earlier – Maud Bennett, the former Baroness de Reuter.

FROM PEAK TO TROUGH

At the start of the 1920s, the *Herald* was under new ownership, having been snapped up by the rival *New York Sun*. This had little effect on the Paris edition, apart from the fact that former *Sun* reporter Laurence Hills was sent over as editor – a post he was to hold until 1940.

Everybody knows about Paris in the 20s: Hemingway, Fitzgerald, Gertrude Stein, Henry Miller and the rest of them, not to mention the jazz and booze-fuelled explosion of art and creativity on the Left Bank. Interestingly, the *Herald* tended to focus on the less bohemian Right Bank crowd, leaving the artier stuff to the *Chicago Tribune*, which had by now launched a Paris edition.

The *Herald* believed its role was to provide comprehensive world news for wealthy, sophisticated Americans in Paris – the kind of people Fitzgerald wrote about. And there seemed to be droves of them. Charles L Robertson writes that 'the 20,000 or so resident Americans were augmented by a continuous flow of tourists, celebrities, clothes buyers, and transient high society…'. Circulation was high and ads fattened the newspaper.

The *Herald* even managed to secure the scoop of the decade, when reporter Ralph Barnes got an exclusive interview with Charles Lindbergh, who touched down near Paris after the first solo flight across the Atlantic in May 1927. At the time the fêted flyer was hiding in the US embassy to avoid being mobbed by admirers. Perhaps inspired by this incident, the paper kept up its reputation for innovation by becoming the first newspaper to be distributed by aeroplane. In 1928, it began flying copies to London in time for breakfast.

But the good times couldn't last forever, and the 1929 Wall Street Crash marked another change in the newspaper's fortunes. The depression hit hard, and although the Paris *Herald* survived, the 1930s were not a happy period. In 1934 the title changed hands again, and it was merged with the *Tribune* to become *The New York Herald Tribune*, a brand name it retained until 1966.

As the rumblings of European conflict grew louder, editor Laurence Hills preached an appeasement policy, until being forced to change his mind almost on the eve of the Second World War. When the Germans began to close in on Paris, the paper's staff started to pack up and go home. Finally, on 12 June 1940, the last edition appeared – printed on one side of a single sheet of paper.

THE CHANGING BRAND

The first post-liberation *New York Herald Tribune* celebrated by reprinting its most famous letter to the editor, sent in by 'Old Philadelphia Lady' in 1899. 'I am anxious to find out the way to figure the temperature from Centigrade to Fahrenheit and vice versa,' it began. James Gordon Bennett, who wanted everyone to convert to centigrade, had reprinted the letter hundreds of times, turning it into one of those editorial in-jokes that journalists love. The letter's reappearance on 22 December 1944 was accompanied by the proud message: 'The mailbag is now open!'

Over the next decade, the *New York Herald Tribune* re-established itself as the newspaper for Americans in Paris – the last time it was to play that role before evolving into a genuinely international publication. The 1950s seemed almost as much fun as the 20s, thanks to characters like the reporter and columnist Art Buchwald, whose wisecracking prose style was to make him a journalistic legend.

A key marketing stunt of this period was the creation of the Golden Girls – a team of beautiful students who would stalk the boulevards selling the newspaper, wearing sweaters with the paper's masthead splashed across their chests. The newspaper got perhaps its best piece of free publicity of all time when French actress Jean Seberg played one of the girls in Jean-Luc Godard's movie *A Bout de Souffle* (Breathless). The paper's current president Richard Wooldridge has a still from the film hanging in his office.

In 1959 John Hay Whitney, a wealthy American who was at that time US ambassador to Britain, acquired the *New York Herald Tribune* – and, of course, its European edition. Throughout the 1960s Hay helped the Paris paper fight off new competition from an international edition of *The New York Times*, also based in the French capital. In 1966 he did a deal with *The Washington Post* to ensure further investment in the *Herald*. Ironically, the partners decided to keep the Paris-based venture, while closing its ailing parent in New York.

The contemporary newspaper was effectively born when *The New York Times* surrendered, merging its international edition with the *Washington Post–Herald Tribune* venture. (Whitney eventually sold his stake in 1991, making the *Post* and the *Times* equal co-owners.)

On 22 May 1967 the first edition of the *International Herald Tribune* appeared. Not everyone was impressed by the new brand name. According to Robertson's book, Art Buchwald joked: '*International Herald Tribune*? By the time you've finished pronouncing it you've missed your plane!'

INTERNATIONAL AT LAST

On a warm evening in May 2001, the *International Herald Tribune* took over an enormous ballroom in the Senate – one of the grandest buildings in Paris – to bid farewell to Walter Wells, the newspaper's managing editor, who was retiring after 21 years of service. There were many moving speeches and a lot of backslapping, as well as a clubby, American atmosphere hinting that 'The World's Daily Newspaper' had not entirely abandoned its origins as a little piece of the United States in Paris.

A couple of years later, Wells was back again. *The Washington Post* had been bought out, and a line under the *IHT* masthead proudly affirmed: 'Published by THE NEW YORK TIMES.' The newspaper had wanted to get its hands on the Paris title for decades, and now it had succeeded. Wells had been reinstalled as a respected and experienced pair of hands. Michael Golden, vice-chairman and senior vice-president of *The New York Times*, was named publisher of the *International Herald Tribune*. He would report directly to Arthur Sulzberger Jr, chairman of the New York Times Company, and Janet Robinson, the company's senior vice-president for newspaper operations. The *International Herald Tribune* was about to go through yet another metamorphosis.

Not that the paper had been standing still since the 1960s. Drawing on the resources of its parents, it had continued to strengthen its reputation as an objective provider of international news. In the 1970s, the paper renewed its tradition of investing in the latest technology. In 1974, it pioneered the electronic transmission of facsimile pages from one country to another, with the opening of a printing site near London. A second site was opened in Zurich in 1977.

A year later, it became one of the most technologically advanced newspapers in Europe by installing a fully computerized typesetting system. And in September 1980, the paper began to transmit pages by satellite from Paris to Hong Kong – making it the first daily newspaper to be electronically sent from one continent to another, simultaneously available to readers on opposite sides of the world.

The paper is now printed at 26 different print sites and distributed to 186 countries across four continents. Parochialism is a thing of the past, and today American readers make up only a third of the paper's total readership.

'There is no arguing with the fact that this is a truly international brand,' says Richard Wooldridge. 'I think the situation in our office mirrors our position as a newspaper. More than 25 different nationalities work here. We have a lot of Americans – because our heritage is American, and always will be – but also French, British, Swiss, and numerous others. Just walking around the building, you can hear three or four different languages being spoken. The product itself reflects this sense of global community.'

In the recent past, the newspaper has had very little money to spend on marketing, so it has had to stand on its own merits. In any case, Wooldridge believes that 'the product is always going to be our most efficient marketing device'. During the 1990s, the *International Herald Tribune* embarked on a unique distribution and branding initiative that proves his point.

PROMOTION THROUGH PARTNERSHIP

In 1997, the *IHT* joined forces with a newspaper in Israel called *Ha'aretz*. It was something of an experiment – the idea being to produce a co-branded newspaper offering a combination of local and international news, in English. 'When we started we thought the idea had great potential, but we weren't entirely sure it would work,' admits Wooldridge. 'In fact it was wildly successful, both with readers and to a certain extent with local advertisers. So we decided to carry on.'

Following on from the deal with *Ha'aretz*, the *IHT* now produces co-branded English language supplements with *Kathimerini* in Greece, *Frankfurter Allgemeine Zeitung* in Germany, *El País* in Spain, *JoongAng Ilbo* in Korea, the *Daily Star* in Lebanon and the *Asahi*

Shimbun in Japan. Projects in Italy and the Netherlands have been abandoned owing to low advertising figures, but the *IHT* continues to expand the strategy into other markets. Wooldridge says: 'We never thought it would be hugely profitable, and in some places it has been a struggle – hence our decision to close the versions in Italy and the Netherlands – but there is a strong tactical incentive to continue.'

The partnerships work well for a number of reasons. Firstly, they gain exposure for the *IHT* brand, partly doing away with the need for expensive international marketing campaigns. Secondly, they allow local newspapers to attract additional non-native readers, such as expatriates, meaning that there is no shortage of potential partners. And thirdly, they are aimed perfectly at the international business travellers who are now the main target readership of the *IHT*.

Says Wooldridge: 'Basically, you get a distillation of these great newspapers, in English, together with the best of the *IHT*. The concept was considered quite revolutionary at the beginning, but it has really taken off. Now we get continual approaches from newspapers all around the world asking if we will partner with them. This is good because it enables us to pick and choose. The *IHT* must make sure its products are of the highest quality, and we will only do partnerships with leading newspapers. We've actually refused to do deals with certain papers on the basis that they weren't right for our brand.'

In a slight twist on the strategy, copies of the *IHT* distributed in Asia carry a four-page section called 'Business Asia by Bloomberg'. It contains business news and analysis put together by *IHT* staff in Hong Kong, from material provided by the Bloomberg news wire. Asia is a crucial growth area for the *IHT*, where circulation has grown from 43,000 in 1997 to nearly 90,000 today.

'We came together naturally,' says Wooldridge, referring to the Bloomberg deal. 'They are growing their brand in Asia in a big way, and we wanted to beef up our Asian business coverage. As Bloomberg has more than 200 business correspondents across the region, it made perfect sense to join forces.'

A THREE-LETTER BRAND

Other marketing initiatives, although less innovative than the partnership strategy, have been designed to position the *IHT* as the newspaper for 'the global class'. In 1994, the newspaper adopted a new subtitle, 'The World's Daily Newspaper'. It also began to use the colour yellow in its direct marketing, advertising, and other communications. (This may have been a nod to the long-gone Golden Girls, whose yellow sweaters had disappeared from the Champs-Elysées and other major thoroughfares in the early 1970s.)

Says Wooldridge: 'The yellow gave our communications a much-needed consistency, while the slogan was a clear way of saying that we were no longer the newspaper for American expats, which we were sometimes still perceived as being.'

The next big push came in 1999, when the *IHT* ran a print campaign using the slogan 'Think!' – although the word was spelt backwards, turning it into: 'kn*IHT*!' The ads were run in the paper itself, in its partner newspapers, and in business and trade publications.

Wooldridge explains: 'We wanted to establish the initials *IHT*, because over the years we've been referred to as the *Herald Tribune*, the *Trib*, the *Herald*... a whole mixture of things, depending which country you happen to be in. Again, it was about having a consistent identity. Apart from that, we had the feeling that the average age of our readers was creeping up – a common problem among long-established brands – and we wanted to attract some new, younger readers.'

The campaign received positive feedback, but there was a feeling that the *IHT* still might seem a little old-fashioned to younger readers. It was lightly and subtly redesigned – 'tweaked' might be a more appropriate word – in 2002. *The New York Times* later recognized the need for further innovation. Certainly, the paper was one of the last in the world to have resisted colour photography.

The *IHT* has little time for brand extensions of the CD and t-shirt variety, but it does believe in touting the quality of its content. To this end it has a department called *IHT* Worldwide Events, which runs a busy annual conference programme. The *IHT* Oil & Money Conference was established over 20 years ago, for example, and to add a little glamour to the mix, the paper also holds an annual fashion conference in Paris. (The *IHT* has some of the best fashion coverage of all the international dailies, thanks to the contribution of Suzy Menkes, one of the world's most famous writers on the subject.)

'There is no question that when it comes to the perception of the brand, and the quality of its analysis, these conferences are hugely helpful,' Wooldridge states.

Another useful branding exercise is *IHT World*, a TV news analysis shown on the in-flight channels of 25 leading airlines, as well as on a number of pan-regional networks, including Euronews in Europe and Star in Asia.

For any brand targeting media-saturated frequent flyers, the Internet is a vital tool – and the *IHT* has made good use of its Web site. The newspaper says IHT.com attracts well over a million visitors a month and generates 25 per cent of new subscriptions. The site successfully takes advantage of the paper's leisure content – which tends to get overwhelmed in the print product – with archived fashion features by Suzy Menkes and restaurant reviews by Patricia Wells. Its 'At Home Abroad' section offers a useful guide to resources for expatriates. And the newspaper's stronger links with *The New York Times* – which has one of the most popular and comprehensive Web sites in the world – can only make the *IHT* online offering stronger.

THE *IHT* TODAY AND TOMORROW

In many ways, the takeover by *The New York Times* could not have come at a better time for the *IHT*. By the summer of 2003, the Paris-based paper had begun to look as if it was stuck in a rut. Its lengthy evolution from the English-language newspaper in Paris to 'The World's Daily Newspaper' had robbed it of some of its charm, making it seem corporate and worthy. The paper employed hardly any in-house writers – most of the content was sourced from *The Washington Post*, *The New York Times* or wire services. This meant that for all its modernization, the way the paper was produced had barely evolved from James Gordon Bennett's time. The redesign had not been radical enough, and the newspaper looked anaemic. Pagination was down – sometimes to as few as 14 pages, making it absurdly poor value for money, with a cover price of €1.85 in France and as much as €2.50 elsewhere.

Wooldridge says that the paper aims for between 22 and 24 pages, as its typically time-poor reader requires a precise appraisal of events. He also adds that the high price is strategic, positioning the paper as a premium product. 'Our readers are prepared to pay for the kind of journalism we do, and they feel an incredible amount of loyalty towards us,' he states. 'It is important to point out that we are a demand-driven newspaper. Many newspapers go in for bulk sales – sometimes described as "dumping" – where they provide thousands of papers to airports and hotels dirt cheap, or even free of charge, to push up circulation figures. We would prefer to cut back on our circulation than to do that. We supply airlines and hotels, but they have to pay.' (His words echo an advertisement that ran in the Paris *Herald* back in the 1920s: 'An Important Fact – the *New York Herald* is sold on its own merit and is not given away or distributed in hotels as a common handbill.')

None of this changes the fact that the *IHT* needs a boost. Wooldridge admits that the paper has had problems, mostly caused by its schizophrenic ownership. 'While journalistically it was great being owned by two of the biggest and best newspaper brands in the world, in a day-to-day business sense it was very limiting. The change of ownership has been the most liberating and wonderful event imaginable. The possibilities now open to us, which were unfortunately denied to us in the past, are limitless. We now have a single committed owner who really believes in what we are trying to do.'

In fact, *The New York Times* sees the Paris-based paper as the key to its own internationalization strategy. In 2003 it carried out extensive research to determine whether it should drop the *IHT* brand name altogether, perhaps turning the newspaper into *The New York Times International*. A resounding 'no!' came back from advertisers and readers.

Wooldridge says: '*The New York Times* is an incredibly powerful brand, but it was clear from the research that we have a great brand in our own right. It would be a shame to throw away that heritage, and the feeling of goodwill towards us.'

Besides, the end of 2003 might not have been an ideal time to rebrand the paper. Anti-American feeling was still rife in Europe after the latest excesses of the Bush administration and – in marketing terms, at least – the *International Herald Tribune* felt like less of a US product than *The New York Times*. Indeed, the *IHT* ran a series of features that were highly critical of Bush's foreign policy. ('Our readers don't want a party line, they want objectivity,' Wooldridge notes.)

The upshot of all this is that, as I write, the *IHT* is about to get some long-overdue attention lavished on it. Wooldridge promises more journalists, higher pagination, improved features and analysis, and a lot of additional marketing. 'We don't believe in all-singing, all-dancing re-launches, but there will be a gradual and noticeable improvement,' he says. 'And we'll actually be able to talk about it.'

Meanwhile, in a prepared statement about the improvements, editor Walter Wells states: 'We plan to increase content by about 10 per cent each day, paying greater attention to such areas as the media and technology. And with more of the insightful journalism that has always distinguished this paper, we will make a constant examination of the consequences that decisions and policies have on businesses and on individual lives. Our goal is to make the *IHT* not just the most loved newspaper in the world – which it has long been – but also an indispensable business tool.'

It is fair to say that the *IHT* serves a very real need. With its broad mixture of lifestyle, science and health features alongside the expected news and business coverage, it recognizes that its successful, hardworking readers are real people, not just moneymaking machines. The newspaper's figures show that 79 per cent of them are interested in literature, and 64 per cent in art and the theatre. More than 80 per cent are keen on sports. A daily newspaper addressing these subjects from an international perspective is pretty hard to find.

'We think this is our time,' says Wooldridge. 'Globalization continues, English has established itself as the international language of business, and the need for clear, concise, but comprehensive information has never been greater among people doing business around the world. I have no doubt whatsoever that we are entering a period of considerable success.'

The brand in brief

Media brand: International Herald Tribune

Founded: 1887

Owner: The New York Times Company

Circulation: 240,000 (Source: ABC)

Key marketing strategies: Innovative partnerships with domestic newspaper brands, print advertising, direct marketing

Brand extensions: Conferences and events, branded TV channel

Web site: IHT.com

8

The New York Times

'Our core purpose is to enhance society by creating, collecting and distributing high-quality news, information and entertainment'

One of the high points in the branding history of *The New York Times* was undoubtedly 31 December 1904, when the paper threw a New Year's Eve party to celebrate the event that put it on the map – literally. The newspaper had successfully lobbied to change the name of Longacre Square to Times Square in honour of its new headquarters.

In its day the attenuated Times Tower was one of the tallest skyscrapers in the city, although the newspaper was forced to leave for more spacious accommodation less than 10 years later. Today the wedge-shaped structure is little more than a giant advertising site, although a connection to the paper remains in the form of an electronic news ticker running around its base. *The Times* itself occupies a broader, squatter, but no less grandiose establishment at 229 West 43rd Street, a couple of minutes' walk from its old home.

The marketing low point came almost 100 years later, when *The New York Times* discovered that one of its star reporters had been begging, stealing, borrowing and inventing material for a whole series of articles. Horrified that its unspoken contract with its readers had been broken, the paper printed a front-page admission of guilt, and devoted two lengthy articles to detailing the errors and putting the facts straight. Media and PR experts were divided as to whether *The Times* had saved its skin by coming clean, or laid itself open to ridicule.

When the smoke had cleared, the paper said the matter had barely made a dent in its million-plus daily circulation. Now the incident is already fading into a hazy memory. Along with its London namesake, *The New York Times* is one of the most famous newspapers in the world, and it would take a great deal to dissipate the aura of respectability that surrounds the brand.

ALL THE NEWS THAT'S FIT TO PRINT

The New York Times probably has the strongest unbroken link with its past of any major newspaper. The current chairman of the company and publisher of the paper, Arthur Sulzberger Jr, is the great grandson of Adoph S Ochs, the newspaper proprietor and entrepreneur who bought the title in 1896 and was largely responsible for turning it into the media monolith that it is today.

This sense of continuity is ensured by a famous trust, drawn up in 1997 and based on an original trust established by Ochs, which was automatically terminated following the death of his daughter Iphigene Ochs Sulzberger in 1990. The trust states that the Ochs/Sulzberger family cannot give up their controlling share in the paper unless they unanimously agree that this would better serve the objectives of maintaining 'the editorial independence and integrity of *The New York Times* and to continue it as an independent newspaper, entirely fearless, free of ulterior influence and unselfishly devoted to public welfare' (The New York Times Company Web site, nytco.com).

The paper has always had a certain crusading, independent spirit. In 1851, Henry Jarvis Raymond and George Jones started a four-page paper called *The New-York Daily Times* in a dingy candlelit loft in downtown Manhattan. It changed its name to *The New-York Times* in 1857 (dropping the hyphen in 1896). Raymond and Jones planned to run a newspaper that covered the news objectively and accurately – no easy task in the corrupt, crime-ridden city portrayed fairly accurately in the film *Gangs of New York*.

The biggest crook of them all was 'Boss' William Marcy Tweed, whose Tammany Hall organization represented the Democratic Party in New York. Having arranged for one of his stooges to be elected mayor, Tweed virtually took control of the city, growing rich from backhanders and overpriced public works contracts. But in 1871 *The New York Times* published an exposé of Tweed and his cronies, a landmark piece of investigative journalism that effectively ended Tweed's political career. Criminal charges were brought against him and he died in jail in 1878. It was later estimated that he had stolen US$200 million from the city coffers. (For a full account of this exhilarating period, see Luc Sante's (1991) book *Low Life – Lures and Snares of Old New York.*)

Although *The New York Times* achieved an enviable reputation for dogged reporting, its emphasis on serious journalism put it at a disadvantage in the city's competitive and backbiting newspaper market – where its rivals included the *Sun*, the *World* and the *Journal*. Towards the end of the century, the paper was losing thousands of dollars a week, and its owners were forced to put it up for sale. It attracted the attention of one Adolph S Ochs, who already owned a successful news organization in the southern United States. In 1896 he bought *The Times* with the intention of turning it into the most respected newspaper in the city.

Born on 12 March 1858 in Cincinatti, Ohio, Adolph Simon Ochs was the son of Jewish immigrants. He had started out as a newspaper delivery boy in Knoxville, Tennessee. The young Ochs must have got newsprint under his skin, because he later became a printer's apprentice at the *Knoxville Chronicle*, and a compositor at the *Louisville Courier-Journal*. At the age of only 20, he borrowed US$250 to buy a controlling stake in the struggling *Chattanooga Times*, which he developed into one of the leading newspapers in the South. This grew into the Southern Associated Press.

Ochs had to borrow rather more money – this time US$75,000 – to gain control of the struggling *New York Times*. His plan was to tighten the paper's focus on quality, shunning all gossip and sensationalism. To get this message across to readers, he emblazoned the front page with the slogan 'All the News That's Fit to Print'. He also refused advertisements that he considered in poor taste. This might have been financial suicide, had he not attracted additional readers by slashing the paper's price from three cents to one.

Under Ochs, *The New York Times* flourished. He hired additional staff and invested in bureaux and correspondents. Aided by editor Carr Van Anda, whom he had poached from the *New York Sun*, he provided increasingly comprehensive national and international news coverage. Features like the book review section and *The New York Times* magazine were introduced. Photography appeared on the front page for the first time in 1910, and in 1918 the newspaper won its first Pulitzer Prize, for its coverage of the First World War.

Throughout the 1920s and early 1930s, Ochs built the paper into a force to be reckoned with. He died in 1935, having firmly established the principles to which the paper still adheres.

Janet Robinson, the current president and general manager of *The New York Times* (and senior vice-president of newspaper operations for The New York Times Company), says: 'Mr Ochs's philosophy still holds true today. The core purpose of *The New York Times* is to enhance society by creating, collecting and distributing high-quality news, information and entertainment... Content of the highest quality and integrity is the basis for our reputation and the means by which we fulfil customers' expectations and the public's trust in us.'

THE FAMILY FIRM

After the death of Adolph S Ochs, his son-in-law Arthur Hays Sulzberger became publisher of *The New York Times*. Sulzberger steered the paper through the Great Depression and the Second World War, of which it provided outstanding coverage. In 1945, *Times* reporter William L Laurence was the only journalist aboard the B-29 that dropped the atomic bomb on Nagasaki.

The New York Times celebrated its 100th anniversary in 1951. As the 1950s progressed, the paper began to offer greater in-depth analysis of the news, and to expand its coverage of subjects like fashion and the arts. Sulzberger retired in 1961, safe in the knowledge that the newspaper had achieved unprecedented levels of circulation.

Sulzberger's son-in-law Orvil E Dryfoos took the reigns for what proved to be a brief tenure, as he died in 1963. And so Sulzberger's son – and the grandson of Adolph S Ochs – Arthur Ochs Sulzberger found himself in the hot seat. Over the next 29 years, he was to oversee the paper's evolution into the modern *New York Times*. Notable innovations included making the paper more reader friendly by dividing it into four sections, and running opinion pieces by non-staff writers on the editorial page, creating the famous Op-Ed section.

One incident that added to the paper's notoriety (and reaffirmed its crusading image) was the publication in 1971 of the Pentagon Papers.

These leaked White House documents showed that the government had been economical with the truth about the country's involvement in Vietnam, and put a positive spin on a conflict that was turning into a disaster. The Nixon administration tried to block *The Times* from publishing further extracts. The matter ended up before the Supreme Court – which ruled in favour of the newspaper. Publication of the Pentagon Papers continued, and the American public discovered what was really going on in Vietnam.

Meanwhile, in 1967, after decades of sole ownership by the Ochs/Sulzberger family, *The Times* had begun selling shares to the public in order to fund acquisitions and expansion. This led to the creation of The New York Times Company, which along with the *Times* now owns the *International Herald Tribune*, *The Boston Globe*, several regional newspapers, sports magazines, digital media, and a string of local TV and radio stations.

In 1980 *The New York Times* took a decision that was to have a bearing on its future strategy. It began publishing a national edition, with satellite transmission to a printing site in Chicago. Over the next 10 years, *The Times* would place increasing emphasis on repositioning itself as a national newspaper. It launched an expanded three-section edition for readers in California in 1988, taking this nationwide in 1990. In 1997, it ran its first national brand image campaign, using the slogan: 'Expect the World.' Today, thanks to its 11 print sites nationwide, *The New York Times* is available to readers across the USA. (Its rivals say that the largest percentage of its circulation remains in the New York metropolitan area, however.)

Adolph S Ochs's daughter Iphigene died in 1990, having been regarded by many as the discreet driving force behind the newspaper. More than a century after Ochs acquired it, *The New York Times* is still a family firm. Arthur Sulzberger Jr took over as publisher in 1992 at the age of only 40, and was named chairman in 1997. His father Arthur Ochs Sulzberger was named chairman emeritus and remains on the board.

AN IMAGE UNDER PRESSURE

If anything, the Jayson Blair saga proves that solid brands can resist even the most damaging blows. But the events of summer 2003 were undoubtedly embarrassing for *The New York Times*, and the fallout may not have dispersed.

The simple facts were these: in May 2003 *The New York Times* revealed that one of its reporters, 27-year-old Jayson Blair, had left the paper after being accused of fabricating and plagiarizing stories. He had been caught lifting material for an article about a dead soldier's family from another newspaper, and an internal investigation had discovered that this was not the first time.

As British newspapers pointed out, the practice of recycling material from rival newspapers is common and even acceptable in the United Kingdom ('*The New York Times*' month of humiliation', *The Guardian*, 5 June 2003). But *The Times* had built its reputation on the authenticity and accuracy of its source material, and the fact that Blair had cribbed quotes and descriptive material from other papers was seen as a serious threat to its credibility. In order to protect its image, *The Times* took the remarkable step of publishing what amounted to a 14,000-word apology to its readers.

Although some observers questioned the wisdom of drawing attention to the problem in this way, *The Times* was generally praised for its honesty and the matter should have ended there. But the Blair affair seemed to reveal other rifts and suspicions in *The Times* offices. Soon, another senior journalist resigned after admitting that he had relied heavily on material from an intern for a feature he had written.

The paper wanted to get back on track, but anyone who was in New York that summer could tell that emotions were running high behind the imposing façade of 229 West 43rd Street. There were rumours of meetings at which harsh words were exchanged between journalists and senior executives. Only after the appointment of a new editor, Bill Keller, did the dust begin to settle.

Commenting on the affair in hindsight, the editor of a major British newspaper says: 'The entire *New York Times* editorial staff came under enormous pressure after September 11, with a lot of internal changes. I believe this caused cracks in the system which allowed undesirable practices to flourish.'

Janet Robinson, president and general manager of *The New York Times*, describes the paper's response to the problem. 'Our approach was to be open and forthcoming about what had happened, why, and what we were going to do to improve both our journalistic and managerial practices.'

She adds that a committee of journalists from both inside and outside *The Times* examined in detail the events surrounding the Jayson Blair case. They wrote a lengthy report that included recommendations of steps that could be taken to improve journalistic practices, training, staffing, communication, and performance management. The report was made accessible to the public by posting it on the company's Web site.

Robinson continues: 'As a result of the report and its recommendations, *The Times* in October 2003 named its first "public editor", who serves as a reader representative within the paper and helps maintain our high standards of accuracy and fairness.'

She believes that the saga had little impact on the paper's image. 'Our advertisers were extremely supportive. There were no postponements or cancellations of advertising as a result of the matter. While some readers cancelled their subscriptions, the number was relatively small.'

THE SPIRIT OF *THE NEW YORK TIMES*

New York Times readers are not average Americans. They are well educated and well off – three times as likely to have a post-graduate degree, according to the paper, and a household income of more than US$150,000 (or an individual income of more than US$75,000).

And they have a very specific idea about what the paper stands for. Along with 13,000 other brands, perceptions of *The Times* are measured by a syndicated tracking study called the Brand Asset Valuator, run by the advertising agency Young & Rubicam. This generates responses like 'reliable, trustworthy, intelligent, high quality, socially responsible and authentic'.

According to Janet Robinson, the paper's proprietary research reveals more specific characteristics. The paper's readers regard it as 'the most thorough and complete US newspaper', stating that it provides 'first rate coverage of the biggest story of the day… more detail on all topics than other papers… fields of coverage that are not found in other papers… and unexpected articles that surprise them'.

In the analysis that she prepared for this book, Robinson argues that 'in today's competitive media marketplace, simply providing a high quality product is not enough. Quality is a minimum requirement for entry.'

She goes on to say that a leading media brand must be seen not as good – but as the very best. 'A successful media brand... is looked to as "the word" on topics that are relevant to its audience.'

She observes that being perceived as the best in its field has enabled *The Times* to attract loyal readers who 'are very valuable advertising targets... Maintaining our position of credibility, authority and trust is [therefore] critical.'

The New York Times has expressed this positioning through a variety of marketing initiatives. The 'Expect the World' campaign of 1997 was reinforced in 2002 by a new slogan challenging readers to 'Look Deeper'. Print ads featured familiar objects shot in extreme close-up in order to attract and confuse the eye. They included the back of a playing card, military camouflage, and the curving exterior of New York's Guggenheim Museum – all rendered unrecognizable. The finishing touch was a visual trick that made it look as if the page was turning to reveal the solution.

One of the paper's most imaginative campaigns came just after 11 September 2001. In order to express its solidarity with the American people, *The Times* obtained permission to alter subtly a series of paintings by the artist Norman Rockwell – famed for capturing scenes of US daily life in the 1930 and 1940s. The paintings were changed to reflect responses to the Twin Towers attacks. The slogan read: 'Make sense of our times.'

The first ad used a 1943 Rockwell painting called *Freedom From Fear*, which shows a mother and father tucking their two kids into bed. The man holds a folded newspaper. Originally the paper's headlines reflected the Second World War, but the advertisement substituted these with the front page of *The New York Times* from 12 September. The second ad used a 1927 painting called *Outward Bound*, depicting an elderly man and a small boy staring out across the ocean. In the altered version, they are gazing at the denuded skyline of Manhattan. Both ads were run only in *The New York Times* itself.

Alyce Myers, the paper's vice-president for marketing services, comments: 'The ads were a wonderful way of demonstrating our sense of partnership with our readers, without taking advantage of the situation.'

Myers and her team are skilled in what might be called 'opportunistic' marketing. For instance, they once managed to convince the producers of the popular US quiz show *Jeopardy* to include *The New York Times* as a question category.

The paper has always been good at using its own iconic status for branding purposes. Poster ads for Father's Day, for instance, showed the paper folded into the shape of a tie. Other graphic treatments included *The New York Times* used as a dress or a beach towel.

Taking a different tack, the newspaper has achieved valuable media coverage with its sponsored Arts and Leisure Weekend. This began in 2001 and has become an annual event, normally taking place in January. Through promotions and partnerships, the newspaper offers its readers free or half-price entry to exhibitions, plays, films and concerts. Myers says: 'The event has become international in scale. We now have partnerships with museums not only across the United States, but in Paris, London and other major capitals.'

Following on from this success, the paper plans to launch *The New York Times* Food and Wine Festival in 2005.

While such initiatives are clearly aimed at the newspaper's core 40-plus, upmarket readership, *The Times* has also devoted marketing dollars to reaching niche groups. It is highly active in schools and colleges, promoting the paper as a learning tool for students. And it has launched a number of multicultural campaigns. Since 1999 it has run radio, print and TV ads aimed at New York's Hispanic, Indian, Korean and Russian communities.

Like other major newspapers, *The New York Times* is taking an increasingly sophisticated approach to direct marketing, using database management techniques to determine which approaches are best suited to specific target groups.

FIRST WE'LL TAKE MANHATTAN...

For the time being, the print version of *The New York Times* is not widely distributed outside the USA – yet international awareness of the brand is high. This is partly due to the global reach of American culture, and more recently to the Internet. But the company also promotes its brand through other newspapers.

The first glimmer of *The New York Times* News Service came in 1899, when an entrepreneurial salesman of phonograph records approached founder Adolph Ochs with the idea of selling *Times* news items to other newspapers. Ochs agreed, but the project failed to take off. However, the idea was resurrected in 1917 as *The New York Times* War Wire, which provided news of the First World War hours or even days ahead of rival services. *The New York Times* has been selling syndicated material ever since. Throughout the 1960s, the wire was expanded to Canada, Europe, the Far East, and Latin America. Today, branded *New York Times* news is carried by more than 600 newspapers worldwide, with a total circulation of more than 85 million.

But the newspaper's international ambitions do not end there. Having promoted itself as a national product, it now wants to take *The New York Times* brand global. In April 2002 it launched a series of weekly English-language supplements in overseas papers, beginning with *Le Monde* in France and subsequently extending to the four Grupo Reforma newspapers in Mexico, the Dominican Republic's *Listin Diario*, India's *Asian Age*, El Salvador's *Diario de Hoy*, and Denmark's *Politiken*.

The company's decision to take full ownership of the *International Herald Tribune* – in which it previously had a 50 per cent stake alongside *The Washington Post* – also forms part of its international strategy. From 2003, the IHT was clearly branded 'Published by *The New York Times*' (see Chapter 7). It is obvious that the Times would dearly love to rebrand the *IHT* entirely, perhaps as *The New York Times International*, but research showed that *IHT* readers were resistant to the idea.

As well as crossing national borders, The New York Times Company wants to traverse media frontiers. Janet Robinson comments: 'Our vision for *The New York Times* over the next 10 years is to transform ourselves from a product-oriented organization into one that focuses on our core competency of providing quality journalism through a variety of channels. This goal was established in 2001 and we are well on our way to reaching it.'

The newspaper's Web site, nytimes.com, has 12 million unique users. It continues to explore digital delivery systems, and users can already access an exact digital replica of the print product via the Web. Subscribers can also receive news on their mobile phones.

March 2003 saw the debut of the Discovery Times Channel, a joint venture TV channel from The New York Times Company and Discovery Communications. *The Times* also owns NY-TV, a production company supplying non-fiction television programming. Future plans include a branded radio programme on Bloomberg Radio in the USA.

The New York Times also gains valuable exposure among younger readers through its spin-off magazine *Upfront*. Published every two weeks in association with youth publisher Scholastic, it is aimed at teenagers and includes features of particular interest to the target group, culled mainly from the pages of the main paper.

The Times also produces a weekly large-type version for people with poor vision.

STRENGTH FROM INSIDE

The New York Times is no doubt hoping that the frustrations and uncertainties of summer 2003 are behind it. As far as this outsider can determine, things appear to have settled down at the newspaper.

This is just as well, as Janet Robinson backs the theory that superior brands grow from within. She says senior management at the paper have adopted a code known internally as 'The Rules of the Road'. 'These are standards of behaviour that all managers and employees are held responsible for in annual performance reviews. In other words, they are taken very seriously at *The New York Times*,' says Robinson.

The rules cover attitudes to the newspaper and to working conditions in general. They include: 'treat each other with honesty, respect and civility'; 'embrace diversity'; 'take risks and innovate, recognizing that failure occasionally occurs'; 'information is power – share it'; 'maintain perspective and a sense of humour'; and 'our journalistic work is sacrosanct'.

Robinson says that by institutionalising a culture of respect, *The Times* has achieved a very low turnover of staff. 'For journalists, the newspaper has always been a destination. Now, in part because the company practises these rules, the business side [staff] turnover matches that of the news side.'

Fortune magazine includes *The Times* in its annual list of the 100 best companies to work for in the USA. The company may have taken a knock or two, but it seems that people are still proud to work for *The New York Times*.

The brand in brief

Media brand: The New York Times

Founded: 1851

Owner: The New York Times Company

Circulation: 1.1 million weekdays; 1.7 million Sunday (Source: ABC)

Key marketing strategies: TV, print and radio advertising, promotions, sponsorship, cross-media branding, syndicated content

Brand extensions: TV, radio, books, events

Web site: nytimes.com

9

El País

'Everything we do must be excellent – otherwise our readers feel insulted'

I am sitting in Air Europe flight UX 1028 from Paris to Madrid, staring at the seat in front of me. A rectangle of cloth draped over the headrest says '*El País*'. I reckon this bodes well: even before I've reached Spain, the country's most famous newspaper is marketing itself to me.

I later discover that *El País* has a sponsorship deal with Air Europe's business class – when the stewards bring lunch, a subscription form is sitting on the little plastic tray. 'It is all part of our strategy of targeting business travellers,' explains the paper's marketing director Miguel Pereira later that day. 'They are a crucial target market for any up-market media product.'

The *El País* headquarters is a series of squat, blocky buildings in a dusty post-industrial area on the fringes of Madrid, far from the clamour of Puerta del Sol and the Gran Via. Despite the recession, the management continues to invest heavily in the newspaper, and Pereira proudly takes me on a tour of its new printing press.

With its metallic gnashing jaws, the press reminds me of a mechanical monster lurking in a glass-and-steel cavern. Its tentacles are the conveyor belts and 'feeders' that whisk the newly printed newspapers on their long journey to the loading bay – with pauses on the way for the automatic insertion of supplements, binding, and wrapping – where they land with a thump at a series of hatches in the wall. Vans are already backed up outside, doors open to receive the newspapers that only a few moments ago were rolls of blank paper.

'You should have been here on 11 September, when we prepared a special edition in record time,' says Pereira. 'The atmosphere was electric. Newspapers always function best in times of crisis.'

Pereira is one of the most enthusiastic marketing people I have met on my six-month tour of the world's great media brands. He lives and breathes his product as fully as any of the journalists who work on it – maybe even more so. 'I have been a reader of *El País* since I was a kid,' he confesses. 'I was incredibly excited when I got the job two years ago, but even then I did not realize how important the brand is. It turned out that nearly everyone feels the same way as me. Our readers have a huge emotional tie to the product. That's why everything we do in marketing must be excellent – otherwise they feel insulted.'

A POLITICAL BIRTH

In common with *Corriere della Sera* in Italy – but on a much more recent timescale – *El País* was a product of political and cultural upheaval.

The paper was launched on 4 May 1976. The dictator Franco had died less than a year earlier, and the country was in a fragile transitory phase after 40 years of repression. Adolfo Suaréz, the man Franco's successor King Juan Carlos had appointed prime minister, surprised everyone by embarking on a series of radical political reforms. Opposition parties resurfaced, and the first democratic elections since 1936 were held in June 1977. Suaréz's centrist party won that time, but during the next elections in November 1982 – after a failed coup by Francoist die-hards – the socialists took power in a landslide victory.

Against this turbulent background, the left-oriented *El País* fed a hunger for democracy and modernity. Its vigorous defence of civil liberties and its support for political and social change soon made it a symbol of contemporary Spain. Its early editorials defined it as independent, pro-democratic, and pro-Europe. From day one it became the country's best-selling newspaper – a position it has never relinquished. Its conservative rival *ABC* was over 70 years old, but remained staunchly associated with the monarchy and 'the old guard'.

Although *El País* is based in Madrid, it also has newsrooms in Barcelona – where its Catalonia edition is written and printed – Bilbao, Valencia and Seville. It has local editions in major cities throughout the country, as well as printing plants in Germany, Belgium, Mexico and Argentina, which enable it to reach Spanish-speakers all over Europe and Latin America. An international edition of the newspaper is distributed in the Americas. In addition, its branded Spanish-language news service provides stories for other media, particularly in Latin America. This gives *El País* valuable additional exposure, along with the English-language supplements that have appeared with the Spanish, Portuguese and Moroccan editions of the *International Herald Tribune* since October 2001. Periera says: 'Thanks to this, as well as our international edition and our distribution in the Americas, we are probably the best known Spanish-language newspaper in the world.'

On its home territory, *El País* seems to have a variety of different identities. During the week it is terse and sombre, while taking on a more relaxed and leisurely style at weekends. It has also broadened its readership through a number of supplements, notably the youth-oriented entertainment product *Tentaciones*, which appears on Fridays. The Saturday edition of the paper includes the cultural review *Barbelia*, and the travel supplement *El Viajero*. A glossy Sunday magazine, *El País Semanal*, is also highly regarded.

In its battle to retain younger readers, *El País* faces competition from the newer, punchier *El Mundo*, which launched in 1989 and gained a number of followers with its hard-hitting investigative reporting. But Pereira says the title is now regarded as somewhat sensationalist, as well as being a vehicle for its high-profile founder, the ebullient Pedro J. Ramirez. *El País* may suffer from being too closely identified with the socialist party, but it has an unbeatable reputation for serious journalism.

'We are known for being reputable, credible and objective,' Pereira states. 'When you read something in *El País*, you know it's true. It's the most trusted newspaper in Spain. We cannot deny our political roots – but it does us no harm to have been closely associated with the rise of a democratic society after 40 years of dictatorship.'

The paper's readers tend to be from the middle to upmarket demographic – educated, engaged with Europe, and with strong, left-oriented opinions on issues like the environment and immigration. But despite their apparent loyalty, *El País* recognises the importance of a vigorous marketing strategy.

CUTTING OUT THE CLUTTER

Miguel Pereira was trained in the United States, where the marketing of the media is a fine art, and any print product worth its salt has stacks of demographic data on its readers. When he arrived at *El País*, he realized that he was working in a very different environment.

'One of the problems with Spain is that it is a low subscription market – only 2 per cent of our sales come from subscriptions, compared to something like 8 per cent in other European markets. Because of that, there is little direct interaction with our readers. We know they feel a certain loyalty towards *El País*, but do we know exactly why? We are now trying to gather more information about them through direct marketing, generating a database from promotions and competitions. In Spain, where there is rarely one-to-one communication between the media and their audiences, a letter from *El País* can be a powerful tool.'

But while the drive to collect demographic data continues, there is a more pressing emphasis on maintaining newsstand sales. And that means giveaways.

Pereira sighs, as if almost unwilling to admit that *El País* would stoop to such obvious tactics. 'The Spanish newspaper market is swamped with promotions, collectibles and competitions,' he explains. 'Within that context we want to do two things – number one, to ensure that people buy us for the most important reason, which is our content. Quality of content is vital – everything else comes behind that. Number two – we want to be smart about the way we do promotions. If we are forced to play in that arena, we want to do it in a way that adds value to the brand. So instead of giving away all sorts of rubbish to attract extra sales, we try to offer the readers high-quality products with some sort of intellectual value.'

Recent promotions have included a series of books called *Classics of the 20th Century*, followed by classic Spanish movies on DVD. A series of reissued rock CDs has also proved popular. Pereira says the key to all these products is their unaccustomed subtlety. 'Nothing is over-designed or plastered with logos. We try to think how we can customize things for our readers in a more intelligent way. For instance, when you play the DVD, the main interactive menu has a small *El País* logo. We didn't just go out and buy a stack of cheap DVDs from China and slap our logo on their covers. We may be doing promotions, but we are retaining our core brand values of sobriety and trustworthiness.'

Having managed to dispense with what he clearly regards as a necessary evil, Pereira turns his attention to the innovation he believes is the newspaper's branding masterstroke: editorial marketing.

HOW TO SELL A NEWS STORY

'If our content is our biggest selling point, it makes sense that we should use that as a marketing tool,' explains Pereira. 'But how exactly do we "sell" the news? News is not static – it happens moment by moment.'

The way *El País* got around this problem is highly innovative, and maybe even unprecedented. In order to explain it in more detail, Pereira hands over to Arancha Ferreiro Galguera, the newspaper's first director of editorial marketing.

Galguera has the excited but faintly harassed look of somebody used to working under extreme pressure. This is probably because for the last few months, she has been a combination of marketing person and TV producer.

The toughest part of Galguera's day begins in the evening, when she sits in on the newspaper's 6 pm editorial meeting. By that time, the reporters have decided which news stories they will be writing up for the following day's edition. (Breaking news like 11 September is of course an unknown quantity, but all journalists have lists of diary items and hot topics they know they will be chasing.)

Galguera recounts: 'I make a detailed note of six news items that are going to be important for the following day's paper. We don't want to sell catastrophes – just solid social and cultural stories. We then shoot a one-minute TV spot in a special studio here at *El País*, using a former TV presenter whose face is known, but who does not have any political associations. We also record a 30-second radio ad. By around 10.30 pm these are edited and ready, and we send the tapes to all the major TV and radio stations.'

The radio ads begin airing at midnight and Galguera – who has been working since 10 that morning – usually hears the first burst on her car radio as she drives home. They continue throughout the night. The TV spots are shown between 7.30 and 9.30 am the next day. 'It's perfect timing, as many Spaniards like to turn on the TV while they are getting ready for work. And our research shows that the largest quantity of newspapers is sold before 10 in the morning.'

Compared to a standard consumer goods campaign, the *El País* promotion is relatively cheap, because it occupies slots away from prime time. The one-minute ads are bought as 'microspots', making them cheaper than normal commercials.

'None of our competitors are running campaigns anywhere near as innovative as this,' says Galguera. 'It is quite advanced, even by international standards. I have noticed that *El País* is a newspaper that really cares about marketing. At many companies, the marketing function is viewed as a "cost", but here the management realizes that shrewd marketing can sell a lot of papers.'

Miguel Pereira is extremely proud of the campaign, especially in the light of the effort it took to get it on air. 'It's highly complex, and many different elements needed to be put in place. For a start, something like this depends on unusually strong cooperation between the marketing and editorial teams. Then there are the shooting and production problems. And it also requires delicate negotiations with the TV stations, because they need to devote resources to receiving the spot at every day at 1 am, approving it, and getting it on air at 7.30 in the morning.'

This last part of the equation was not helped by the political nature of television in Spain.

'Media is very politicized here, and of course not all the TV stations are aligned with us. This campaign is a risky proposition for them, because for some extra advertising cash they are basically screening a news-based item that has not been properly approved – or at least, only approved at the dead of night. For all they know, we could have slipped in a sensitive piece about Silvio Berlusconi [the right-wing Italian prime minister, who has a stake in Spanish TV station Telecinco].'

Indeed, it took Pereira and his team over a year to get permission to screen the spots on the state-run channel, Television Espaniola, because *El País* is often critical of the current liberal government. The ads finally began running in October 2003.

'The point is that after all this struggle, we found ourselves in a position where we could give people a small but vital nudge just before they left their homes, which is the vital moment for newsstand sales. And even if people decide not to buy a copy, it is a great branding initiative – because day in and day out, we are pushing the quality of our content.'

PROGRESS MEANS SURVIVAL

El País celebrated its 25th anniversary in 2001 with a meeting at which its chief executive officer Pedro Garcia Guillén emphasized that the paper should look forward rather than backwards.

Says Pereira: 'After our 25th anniversary there was a great sense of achievement at the newspaper. But as our CEO pointed out – and I agree with him – we should not dwell on the past. In fact, he changed the senior management of the newspaper to reflect this strategy, getting rid of some of the old guard and hiring younger staff, including myself. This sent a message to the industry that we are a modern, dynamic, expanding company.'

Another example of this is the new printing press, a multi-million euro investment that gives the advertising sales department more flexibility when allocating ad pages, among other advantages. (The old press limited their ability to sell full colour and half page ads at the last minute.)

In fact, *El País* has no choice but to move forward, as the newspaper industry in Spain is so fragile that apathy would be fatal. Readership is low compared to other markets, with about 100 daily newspaper readers per 1,000 consumers, as opposed to three times that in northern European markets. 'And on top of that, those are declining numbers, falling at the rate of more or less 1 per cent a year. Our readership has remained stable due to our aggressive marketing, but the overall tendency of the market is decline, which is very worrying for us.'

Like all print titles, *El País* is anxious about the media consumption habits of young audiences, who increasingly prefer to get their news from the Web or via SMS. 'Attracting new, young readers is one of our biggest challenges,' Pereira admits. 'A newspaper doesn't have much allure for them – it's just that boring, old-fashioned thing that their parents read. It's not cool, it's not hip.'

In order to counter this trend, *El País* has launched an initiative in Spanish schools. Called *El País de los Estudiantes* (a play on words that translates as 'A Nation of Students'), it is a competition to design a student newspaper. In its third year at the time of writing, the event attracts over 34,000 students aged from 13 to 17.

'The competition appeals to students because it uses the Internet as a communications tool. The idea is that they create a student newspaper and post it online, each taking on the role of reporter, art director, editor, and so forth. We emphasize that the finished product has to be a traditional, ready-to-print newspaper, not a Web site.'

El País spends 'a fortune', according to Pereira, sending communication materials to teachers and guiding them through the competition process. They receive daily copies of the newspaper, tutorials from journalists, and 'press releases' advising them of stories they might want to use in their papers. *El País* staff judge the final results.

'It is a key part of our drive to do everything we possibly can to attract younger readers – the readers of the future.'

THE SEARCH FOR IDENTITY

Miguel Pereira believes that he is one of a new breed of media marketing executives – at least in Europe. 'Before I moved into newspapers, I was involved in fashion. And I still consider myself to be a marketing person rather than a newspaper person. So when I am devising strategies, I don't look at what other newspapers are doing – but what other industries are doing. I think that's the big difference in attitude between [Europe] and the United States.'

Newspapers should be considered fast-moving consumer goods like any other, Pereira opines. 'The more frequently you are purchased, the more you have to interact with your customer. Therefore, it's important that you present them with a clear brand identity, with attributes and added values that they can understand. Newspapers are not like refrigerators or cars, where it's one hit and then you can forget about it for a while. In fact they are more like breakfast cereals or fashion. As soon as you lose your grip on the customer's imagination, your sales start to fall.'

At the time I meet Pereira, he is wrestling with the idea of devising a new slogan, or 'brand claim', for the newspaper. 'Our original claim was "Abeirto a todos", which means "Open to everyone". But now we would like to come up with something that better expresses our drive and modernity. It seems a small thing, but it can really make a difference when you are trying to tell readers exactly what you can offer them on a daily basis.'

As with other established media brands, *El País* has the advantage of heritage – although not as much as some of the other names in this book. Pereira points out: 'When we launched more than 25 years ago, we came out of nowhere and took the lead. We are the proof that history is not everything. But I have to admit that when you have an extremely well-known logo, reinforcing your brand is an easier task.'

The brand in brief

Media brand: El País

Founded: 1976

Owner: Grupo Prisa

Circulation: 435,298 weekdays; 725,710 Sunday (Source: OJD)

Key marketing strategies: Marketing editorial content through TV and radio ads, promotions and competitions, building relationships with schools

Brand extensions: Branded books, DVDs and CDs

Web site: Elpais.es

10

Die Zeit

'We decided to treat the newspaper like a luxury brand'

They used to call it 'Auntie Zeit'. A heavy publication in both senses of the word, the prestigious German weekly was leaden in its seriousness, and looked as severe as an uptight relative. But over the past 10 years it has gradually been revamped, with more pictures creeping in, and then colour, and then a lifestyle section. Now the newspaper is considered so handsome that it regularly wins plaudits from the US-based Society for News Design. And yet it still manages to retain an intellectual air that makes it the paper of choice for Germany's thinkers and academics.

The paper's senior editorial team says a lot about its positioning in the market. *Die Zeit* has a trio of managing editors. The first of these is Josef Joffe, who does not hide his conservative views and who can pick up the phone and get straight through to US national security advisor Condoleezza Rice, according to colleagues. Joffe works closely with fellow editor Michael Naumann, a left-winger who served as minister of culture under Gerhard Schroeder from 1998 until 2000. They are joined by none other than Helmut Schmidt, the former West German chancellor, who was recently described as 'the wisest man in Germany'. Together, they maintain the paper's diverse range of political opinions, and its overall independence.

The paper is still located in its original home, a building called the Pressehaus in Hamburg. From its windows you can see the offices of *Der Spiegel*, the weekly news magazine. But if you had looked out of the window in 1946, when *Die Zeit* was born, you would have seen a very different picture.

OUT OF THE RUINS

The Allied bombing of Germany decimated Hamburg. What had been a thriving commercial port was smashed to rubble. As much as 50 per cent of the city's residential areas, 40 per cent of its industrial districts and 80 per cent of the harbour were laid to waste. More than 50,000 residents died in air raids, and 70,000 men lost their lives fighting. A further 70,000 people were killed in a nearby concentration camp. The landmark church of St Nikolai was reduced to a blackened tower, like the stump of a decayed tooth.

After the city's surrender, in April 1945, it was occupied by British troops. One of the occupying force's main tasks was to rebuild democracy – with a particular emphasis on creating a free press. Newsprint was strictly rationed, so the British offered printing 'licences' to two democratically minded entrepreneurs: Gerd Bucerius and Axel Springer. Legend has it that Springer – who became one of the titans of the German media – flipped a coin with Bucerius to decide who would run Hamburg's daily paper, and who would take charge of its weekly. Springer got the daily, and Bucerius launched *Die Zeit*. (The reality is a little more prosaic, as Springer initially launched a regional title called *Nordwestdeutsche Hefte*, with the daily *Hamburger Abendblatt* only following in 1948.)

There is little to indicate that Bucerius knew much about running a newspaper. Born in Westphalia in 1906, he had studied law in Freiburg, Berlin and Hamburg, and then worked as a judge in Keil during the 1930s. An opponent of National Socialism, he was married to a Jewish woman, Gretel Goldschmidt, whom he had arranged to be spirited to safety in England. He had also defended Jewish clients at considerable risk to himself. Nevertheless, he survived the war years and emerged with an untarnished reputation as a courageous free thinker.

One of *Die Zeit*'s founding journalists was another remarkable figure, Marion Countess Doenhoff, who became editor and who worked at the newspaper for the rest of her life. By the time she died at the age of 92 in March 2002, she was regarded as the doyenne of German journalism. A member of the East Prussian aristocracy, Countess Doenhoff was forced to abandon her family's estate to the invading Russian forces in the winter of 1944. Her homeland remained cut off behind the Iron Curtain for decades. Deeply involved in the Resistance against the Nazis, Doenhoff was part of a network that masterminded an attempt to assassinate Hitler. Many of her close friends were executed when the plot was uncovered, and Doenhoff herself was interrogated. Her writings on the subject of the German Resistance helped soothe deep-rooted feelings of shame after the war, and meant that *Die Zeit* contributed to the country's psychological recovery.

Despite the input of such impressive personalities, and the fact that it played a leading part in Germany's post-war intellectual development, *Die Zeit* was barely profitable. It limped along for years, sustained only by its owner's shares in more successful projects – such as the news magazine *Stern*, launched in 1948, and the publishing house Gruner + Jahr, set up with John Jahr and Richard Gruner in 1960. Bucerius later sold his stake in G+J to another German media giant, Bertelsmann, in a deal that enabled him to regain control of *Die Zeit*. It remained under his charge until his death in 1995, when it was transferred – in accordance with his wishes – to the Holtzbrinck publishing group, a long-term investor. Holtzbrinck continued the modernization process that has re-established *Die Zeit*'s status as the country's best-selling quality newspaper.

DRIVEN BY DESIRE

From a print-heavy, dauntingly earnest newspaper, *Die Zeit* has evolved into a product with a positioning close to that of the UK's *Economist* – piercingly intelligent, but in step with contemporary life.

In an article written for the Society for News Design's journal, *Die Zeit* editor-at-large Theo Sommer recalls: 'Ten years ago [the newspaper's] circulation had reached an unprecedented and unrivalled 500,000, but the emerging Fun Generation rather snickered at its staid appearance. The paper's black and white matter-of-fact style, long the hallmark of its seriousness and the bedrock of its success, suddenly came across as stolid and stodgy, humdrum and heavy.' ('Old Auntie Zeit Is Back', *Design Journal*, Fall 2003.)

Careful retuning has changed this perception. After years of decline, sales are creeping back to peak levels. And while the paper's content is as serious as ever, its packaging has undoubtedly become more attractive. *Die Zeit*'s marketing director, Stefanie Hauer, says: 'We have come a very long way in terms of approachability, without sacrificing any quality. There is a better mixture of long and short articles, of words and pictures. It would be wrong to assume that we have become superficial, however. The writing is so literary that I occasionally have to read a sentence twice.'

Needless to say, *Die Zeit*'s readers are an upmarket, brainy crowd. 'Our research shows that more than 60 per cent of them have university qualifications. Many of them are from the worlds of academia, the arts, science and politics. These are people who surround themselves with books, and are happy to read. To them, *Die Zeit* is a pleasure – they lock themselves away on a Saturday morning and wallow in it.'

This realization led to a major branding initiative using the slogan '*Genießen sie Die Zeit*' (literally, 'Enjoy the time'). Hauer explains: 'We decided to treat the newspaper like a luxury brand. This is a weekly publication, so it can't promise an instant fix of news. We offer commentary and analysis. We don't tell you it's raining, we tell you what annual rainfall levels mean for our society. To get the most out of the newspaper you need to spend time with it, to lose yourself in it for a while. In other words, this publication is not a "must have" product, but a "want to have" product.'

In the high-speed, information-overload world of modern media, where everything is about getting facts fast (think of Reuters' slogan 'Know. Now.') this is a bold strategy.

'Every revolution has its counter-revolution,' shrugs Hauer. 'We can't compete with the Internet, so why pretend that we can? Besides, our readers are not fast food consumers. They are classical music consumers.'

The first print and cinema ads featured readers enjoying the newspaper in the same way that they might savour a cup of coffee, a glass of wine, or a piece of chocolate. And the cinema ads were not shown in thousand-seated multiplexes, but in small art-house theatres where they were more likely to reach their target audience. The next stage of the campaign used images from one of the paper's most popular articles, which features personalities describing their recurring dreams, next to sumptuous black and white photographs of them feigning sleep.

'As a tie-in promotion we asked readers to send us examples of their dreams. It may seem a rather populist approach, but because we are considered such an austere title we can get away with it. It's almost a way of showing that we don't take ourselves too seriously.'

The campaign successfully differentiated *Die Zeit* from its competitors. More importantly, it waved away suggestions of stuffiness by suggesting that those who invested their time in the newspaper would reap the rewards. Or as Hauer puts it: 'We are a luxury for the mind.'

SEDUCING SUBSCRIBERS

Of course, like every other newspaper, *Die Zeit* has to get involved in down-to-earth matters like direct marketing. Newsstand sales for weekly newspapers tend to fluctuate, so they rely on subscriptions to keep their circulation figures stable. *Die Zeit* has around 263,000 subscribers out of its total sales of 450,000. It is using a combination of standard and creative marketing techniques to raise this figure.

Hauer says: 'The classic tools are ads and cards in the newspaper offering trial subscriptions. We also offer newcomers a range of promotional giveaways if they convince friends to subscribe. When it comes to gifts, *Die Zeit* readers are the same as everyone else. They like electrical items like stereos or TV sets, or something big. A rather plain office chair has been a favourite for some years now.'

Die Zeit also inserts flyers into other magazines aimed at its target audience. Among the most successful publications are *Der Spiegel* and *National Geographic* – but also niche special-interest journals like *The Parliament* and *Psychology Today*. 'By far the most successful magazine is the TV guide for the cultural channel Arte. So again, we can see that our target audience is well educated and loves to read. These flyers will never win a beauty contest, but they are extremely efficient.'

The newspaper also does direct mail and telemarketing using its own database of addresses. 'These can be former subscribers that we are trying to get back, or names we've gleaned from competitions. We do several big reader contests per year.'

These tools are familiar to the marketing departments of almost every newspaper around the world. But *Die Zeit* also adds something extra to the mix. 'Our figures showed that only about 40 per cent of readers continued with their subscriptions after the trial period. So what was it that made the others uncomfortable with the newspaper? We thought we knew, so we designed a welcome package including a letter and another flyer. On the flyer, you meet five real readers of *Die Zeit*, who tell you why they love it and how they read it. They point out what it means to them, talk about their favourite sections, and make the paper seem less intimidating. For instance, a bank manager says: "Of course I can't read all the articles – no one can. But even if I have time for only three or four, it's worth it.'"

Die Zeit makes sure its subscribers feel appreciated. In every issue, the newspaper runs a full-page section detailing a range of offers available exclusively to subscribers – from theatre tickets to backstage passes at concerts or dinners with film directors. Hauer says: 'Organizing all this costs quite a lot of money, but we felt that subscribers in general had become more demanding and wanted a reward for their loyalty. This is a very good argument for making them stay – and a good reason for other readers to subscribe.'

For an old-fashioned kind of newspaper, *Die Zeit* has also made efficient use of the Internet. The Web site Zeit-online is now regarded as one of Germany's most useful sources of news analysis, attracting 1.5 million visitors a month, according to Hauer. In a single year it drove 8,000 new subscriptions. An online competition attracted more than 80,000 entrants. And readers regularly receive e-mail newsletters and special offers using the latest Flash technology.

PROMOTIONS OF DISTINCTION

And now the fun part: as well as designing methods to seduce and cosset subscribers, 'Old Auntie Zeit' has embraced modern branding techniques in every form. As managing editor Josef Joffe says: 'All of us must compete for attention, no matter how profound our message and how weighty our authors.'

His view is backed by editor-at-large Theo Sommer, who confirms: 'We have at long last abandoned the classical view of the founding generation that shipping the paper to the newsstands is all it takes in terms of marketing. Running after the readers, we used to think, is a rather ungainly strategy. But today we run numerous projects which are all designed to strengthen the relationship between the paper and its readers.'

For instance, the most groundbreaking aspect of *Die Zeit*'s new technology strategy is its use of downloadable audio files. Every week, journalists and professional speakers turn 15 *Die Zeit* articles into MP3 files that can be downloaded from its Web site. In this way, people who spend most of their day behind the wheel of a car can listen to *Die Zeit*'s main features, in full, while travelling back and forth to work or to meetings.

'It was a success from the start,' says Hauer. 'We also run one of the articles every Friday at 6.30 am on a station called Classic Radio. That's when a lot of Germans are just getting ready for work, so it is an efficient commercial for the newspaper.'

With its eye on the next generation of readers, *Die Zeit* is distributed to schools and colleges. It organizes a quiz for young readers every year, and sponsors debating tournaments at universities. But the newspaper's determination to invest in new activities deriving from its brand values extends even further, as Hauer explains.

'One of our major projects is Zeit Events – *Die Zeit* live, so to speak. We invite people to a reading by Günter Grass or a debate between our editors and opposition leader Angela Merkel. You don't reach as many people as with mass media, but it is a very intensive form of communication.'

Even more forward thinking in broadsheet newspaper terms is the Zeit Shop, which sells a range of lifestyle products, both general and branded. 'We make sure the products on sale are of a very high quality, to match our position in the market,' stresses Hauer. 'You might find a *Die Zeit* watch in the store, but the branding would be so subtle as to be hardly noticeable.'

Other articles on sale include calendars, limited edition photographs, fountain pens, books, CDs (from jazz classics to *Die Zeit* articles), wine, and even a designer hi-fi. These can be bought from the shop itself, or ordered online.

Perhaps more impressive still is Zeit Reisen, the newspaper's travel service, for which it produces a glossy brochure. It's a far cry from a traditional tour operator. 'We're not just taking you on a trip to Paris to see the Eiffel Tower – I mean, so what?' says Hauer. 'Instead, you can go to the Himalayas with Reinhold Messmer, a famous mountaineer, or join Germany's most famous chef Wolfram Siebek for a cookery course in the South of France or in Tuscany.'

The trips don't come cheap, either. Fancy a 'safari' in Finland with a team of huskies? It's yours for €1,930 per person. Or if you'd prefer a voyage to the Antarctic 'in the footsteps of Shackleton', you need only find €6,730. Nevertheless, the tours are popular and once again emphasize the newspaper's positioning as a luxury brand.

READERS UNDER SCRUTINY

So why have I heard of *Die Zeit*? When I was casting around for a German newspaper to include in this book, why was it the first brand that popped into my mind? Hauer says: 'Our overseas readership is actually increasing, which is surprising given the amount of information that is available over the Internet. At the moment we have about 13,000 subscribers abroad, and the bulk of those are in the German-speaking markets of Austria and Switzerland. The rest are obviously expatriates. I think we are a popular choice for the latter because – although we are seen as quite expensive – the dense nature of the paper means that it offers good value for money.'

The newspaper also distributes several thousand issues through airlines, and has an obvious appeal for business travellers.

Hauer says the next challenge facing *Die Zeit* – and many other media brands – is to determine how the different strands of its marketing work alongside one another. 'Our goal is to create a database marketing tool that can document all the contacts our readers have with the brand. We want to build a contact history that tells us when the same subscriber buys something in our shop, or takes part in a reader contest, or subscribes to an e-mail newsletter.'

Despite all *Die Zeit*'s marketing initiatives, Hauer stresses that editorial content remains largely untouched by commercial concerns. 'There is a gulf between the marketing department and editorial. That is how our journalists prefer it, and I respect that. We have little or no influence on content.'

The newspaper will continue evolving and modernizing at its own pace, but it remains true to the philosophy expounded by its greatest editor, Marion Countess Doenhoff: 'We make the newspaper we like.'

The brand in brief

Media brand: Die Zeit

Founded: 1946

Owner: Verlagsgruppe Georg Von Holtzbrinck

Circulation: 456,000 (Source: IVW)

Key marketing strategies: Print, cinema and online advertising, direct marketing

Brand extensions: Sponsored debates, shop, CDs and books, upmarket travel service, MP3 audio files via Web site, radio show

Web site: Zeit.de

11

Corriere della Sera

'We built this brand over 125 years – with the wrong promotion we could destroy it in six months'

News stories become history almost before the ink is dry, so it's inevitable that the history of a newspaper should reflect that of its country. And nowhere is this more apparent than in Italy.

Corriere della Sera, the country's most famous newspaper, was founded in 1876 – just 15 years after Italy's birth. For hundreds of years, the country had been a mosaic of kingdoms and city-states, fought over by Spain, France and Austria. But by the mid-19th century, the pressure to create a united Italy had swelled into a movement called the *Risorgimento* (revival), which found its most heroic and effective leader in Giuseppe Garibaldi, a tough sailor turned freedom fighter. After Garibaldi and his guerrillas kicked the Austrians decisively out of their Lombardy stronghold, Vittorio Emanuele II became the first king of a united Italy.

Alessandro Cannavò, a senior journalist at *Corriere della Sera*, recites this tale with the relish of a schoolboy recalling a particularly satisfying playground scrap. Responsible for features and special supplements at the paper, Cannavò is considered an expert on its history, having spent months putting together a special issue for its 125th anniversary in 2001. Infectiously enthusiastic, he breezes into the meeting room clutching a scooter helmet, his grin is broad and welcoming, and his comments about Italy, politics and the press are laced with undisguised irony.

'You can't separate *Corriere della Sera* from Italian history, or indeed from politics,' he points out. 'Until 1861, Italy was an idea rather than a nation. This newspaper was the concrete expression of an entirely new political situation.'

But Italy was not complete until 1870, with the conquest of Rome – which had remained the dominion of the Pope under the protection of France. Despite Garibaldi's battle cry of *'Roma o morte!'* ('Rome or death!'), Italian troops were unable to take the city until the French pulled out, following the defeat of Napoleon III in the Franco-Prussian war. Once Rome was under Italian control, though, there was no question that it would become the capital of the new country. After all, had it not once been the hub of a great empire?

And yet Rome's position has always been more symbolic than deserving. Milan – capital of the northern region of Lombardy – is the country's financial powerhouse. Business, fashion, the media, the great cafés and restaurants of the elite: these are the elements that fuel the city *Corriere della Sera* calls home.

'It has always been that way, even in the 19th century,' says Cannavò. 'Milan was the centre of intellectual and business life, the capital of the bourgeoisie. This had a cultural impact, too: it's no coincidence that La Scala, Italy's most famous opera house, is here in Milan. When it launched, *Corriere della Sera* was a reflection of this intellectual, cultural and financial wealth.'

The paper's founder, Eugenio Torelli Viollier – a Neopolitan, ironically, and a shrewd businessman – saw that while Rome was the political capital, the rich Milanese had a taste for inside information, because it gave them an edge in business. However, this focus also meant that, for decades, *Corriere della Sera* was regarded as the local newspaper of Milan – a criticism that is still aimed at it today.

EDITOR AND BRAND-BUILDER

In fact the paper owes its national status to its longest-serving editor, Luigi Albertini, who held the post from 1900 to 1925. Today's newspaper editors have to accept that they are part of a huge team, often with surprisingly little influence over matters like distribution, promotion and advertising revenue. But there seems little doubt that Albertini actually ran *Corriere della Sera*. It was during this period that the paper moved to its current headquarters in Via Solferino, a location that subsequently became a brand name in itself – like Fleet Street in London and Times Square in New York.

'Albertini made the paper what it is today. You might say he created the brand,' says Cannavò. 'A great admirer of *The Times* in London, he even had the paper's boardroom built to look like the one at *The Times* – very opulent and English, with lots of polished oak. He believed a newspaper should be serious and weighty, as well as a forum for debate.'

When the First World War broke out, Albertini decided the paper would overtly support *interventisme* – the idea that Italy should not stand aside, but take part in the fighting. Like many others, Albertini was worried about the ambitions of Austria, Italy's old foe, and felt his country should move to defend itself.

'It was a controversial decision, because until that moment the paper had seen itself as being above politics,' explains Cannavò. 'When it was founded, the idea was that it should be detached and independent, rather than in opposition or pandering to a particular political viewpoint. It was felt that if the newspaper gave both sides of the story, its readers were intelligent enough to make up their own minds. But Albertini decided that on this crucial matter, the paper should express an opinion – while giving readers all the opposing views, too, of course.'

Eventually, politics ended Albertini's reign at *Corriere della Sera*, when he came up against that well-known former journalist, Benito Mussolini. After the First World War, the growing gulf between Italy's rich and poor caused many workers to turn towards Socialism, and there was a rash of strikes. Mussolini had previously edited the socialist newspaper *Avanti*, but had become dispirited by what he saw as the inertia of the far left and instead embraced the far right. Playing on a widespread fear of Socialism, he promised to silence the dissenters and turn Italy into a more dynamic, modern country. In 1922, his Black Shirts marched on Rome and demanded that the government hand over power to the Fascists.

'Naturally, when he came to power, Mussolini also wanted a pro-government national newspaper,' says Cannavò. Albertini resigned. So began *Corriere della Sera*'s long dark period as a government mouthpiece (although Cannavò points out that many of the journalists left to fight with the Partisans against the Fascists).

With the return to liberty and democracy at the end of the Second World War, the newspaper regained its old form. Once again taking a stance on a vital issue, *Corriere della Sera* supported those who wanted to abolish the monarchy. Italians felt that the king had betrayed the country by letting it fall into the hands of the Fascists. And so in 1946, Italy became a republic.

HISTORY VERSUS YOUTH

During the post-war era, *Corriere della Sera* re-established itself as a trusted news source, a crucible of intellectual debate – and a breeding ground for superlative writing.

'I believe it is the newspaper's journalists who have created its international reputation and outlook,' says Cannavò. 'Thanks to them, this is not just a Milanese paper, and not even an Italian paper; it is global in spirit.'

Reporters like Luigi Barzini, who covered the first Peking–Paris rally in 1907, embody the spirit of *Corriere della Sera* for Cannavò. Perhaps one of the world's first embedded journalists, Barzini accompanied one Prince Scipione Borghese and his chauffeur in a souped-up Itala car for the entire 7,100 miles of the race. Responding to a challenge laid down by French newspaper *Le Matin*, the trio completed the journey from the Chinese capital to Paris in two months, with Barzini sending hair-raising reports to *Corriere della Sera* via telegraph. He later wrote a book about his exploits.

With similar reverence, Cannavò mentions Indro Montanelli, 'the prince of Italian journalism', who died in 2001 at the age of 92. Imprisoned by the Fascists during the Second World War for an article condemning Mussolini, he survived to cover the Hungarian uprising of 1956 for *Corriere della Sera*, and became an outspoken critic of Russia during the Cold War. He was a civil rights champion and a campaigner for press freedom, as well as pioneering 'a dry, clear and gripping style that continues to influence Italian journalists today'. He eventually left the paper in the 1970s to set up a rival title, *Il Giornale*.

Another famous contributor is Oriana Fallaci, who specializes in profiling influential political figures, and was the first woman to interview the Ayatollah Khomeini. More recently, her book about 11 September, *The Rage and the Pride*, sold more than 1 million copies in

Italy, where the highest sales figure a bestseller can normally hope to achieve is 500,000.

Cannavò says: 'Just about every famous Italian writer you can name has appeared in our pages, from Gabriele D'Annunzio to Italo Calvino. Our dedication to quality has remained consistent since the paper's birth.'

Asked to describe his newspaper's brand qualities, Cannavò mentions two key words: 'Trustworthiness and heritage.' As we have already discussed, any serious newspaper must aim to win and keep its readers' trust. But heritage can be a disadvantage.

Twenty-eight years ago, exactly 100 years after the launch of *Corriere della Sera*, a newspaper called *Repubblica* came on the scene. Crisp, colourful and tabloid, compared to the unwieldy broadsheet of *Corriere della Sera*, it positioned itself as a younger alternative to the elderly icon of Italian journalism – a marketing stance it maintains to this day. It is also outspokenly left wing, having no truck with *Corriere della Sera*'s balanced centre-right approach. It now has a circulation of 651,000, compared to just over 714,000 for its older rival.

And yet, by continuing to innovate while referring to its past, *Corriere della Sera* has remained the pre-eminent brand name in Italian newspapers. Thoroughly engaged with the modern notion of a single Europe, it includes the European flag on its masthead. Cannavò says: 'We believe Italy should play a prominent role in Europe. After all, the country was one of the six original founders of the European Community in 1957.'

Despite its protestations to the contrary, it seems that *Corriere della Sera* cannot help becoming mired in politics. And the trap is even harder to escape during a period when Silvio Berlusconi, the right-wing Prime Minister, also owns a rival media group.

Shortly before I arrived in Milan, I heard that the newspaper's then managing editor, Ferrucio de Bortoli, had resigned, amidst speculation that Berlusconi's government was putting pressure on him to report events in their favour. Stefano Folli has replaced him, but Cannavò says there is no question that this represents acquiescence. 'If anything, since then we have come down even harder against Berlusconi,' he says.

In business terms, however, these are relatively minor problems compared to the real challenge facing *Corriere della Sera* – declining newspaper sales.

A NEWSPAPER OF TWO SOULS

To bring this issue more sharply into focus, Cannavò cedes his place at the meeting room table to Alessandro Bompieri, the newspaper's commercial director. Bompieri is a quieter and more restrained figure, with a trim goatee beard and glinting spectacles that lend him a faintly intellectual air. He also has some cunning marketing strategies.

'After hearing about our history, you may rightly come to the conclusion that we are a newspaper with two souls,' he says. 'Our first soul is a Milanese one. Here we are regarded as the local newspaper, and we really don't have any competition. We also have a much wider range of readers, demographically speaking. In the regions, we tend to be regarded as the newspaper of the elite – doctors, lawyers, business-people and so forth.'

The problem is that almost 50 per cent of the newspaper's 400,000 circulation is in Lombardy alone, and 25 per cent of this is in Milan itself. This is still enough to make it the best-selling news-paper in the country, but in other regions it drops to second place after rival *Repubblica*.

'It is clear we need to build sales in the regions, but an additional complication is that newspaper sales have been falling in Italy since the 1990s. With 115 newspapers sold per 1,000 inhabitants, Italy has one of the lowest newspaper readership figures in Western Europe. The emergence of the Web, cable television, rising prices, longer working hours, economic recession and the appearance of free newspapers handed out on the metro have all eaten into our sales.'

To address these matters, *Corriere della Sera* has devised two strate-gies. 'Which is quite appropriate for a newspaper with two souls,' Bompieri smiles.

The first strategy is the least controversial, and covers the regions. Bompieri says: 'Our research showed that in the regions, there were many potential readers who liked the idea of *Corriere della Sera*, because having it under your arm is like wearing a badge saying, "I am a member of the elite." But they felt held hostage by their local news-papers, because they needed to be informed about news in their region. What gives us the edge in Milan, of course, is that we are seen as local already. So we decided to embark on a strategy of localization.'

Since 1997, the newspaper has been rolling out a series of local supplements – three so far – contained within the main paper. The layout, graphics and sequence of sections mirror those of the national newspaper, and the content is designed to deliver the insight and weight of the main title, but in a localized form.

'The aim was to convince the elite to choose us over their local papers, and to lure younger readers.'

So far, the results have been extremely gratifying. The first supplement, *Corriere del Mezzogiorno*, was launched in 1997, and since then sales in the region have increased by 47 per cent. The most recent, the Venice edition, launched at the beginning of 2003 and by June that year sales had already risen 15 per cent.

'Of course, this is an extremely long-term project and we can't expect our sales to shoot up over night,' observes Bompieri. 'But we are constantly increasing our circulation in a market where, overall, sales of newspapers are shrinking.'

In addition, the newspaper has targeted Italian-speaking readers abroad, forming partnerships with newspapers in Argentina, Venezuela, Brazil and Australia – all of which have significant Italian communities – to distribute *Corriere della Sera* in supplement form.

MARKETING MAKES THE NEWS

The second strategy is less obvious and – to a journalist, at least – perhaps a little alarming. Bompieri explains: 'In this market, maintaining your existing readers becomes even more important than recruiting new ones. Therefore, it is vital that you understand what your readers like about your newspaper, what they want from it, and what they might like to change. Good research is key.'

Bompieri and his team spent months looking for the perfect research tool, but found nothing to support their specific needs. In the end, they decided to create a new model themselves.

'We have a panel of readers who represent our target readership. For seven days each month we conduct 200 interviews, every day, asking them what they think of the paper's contents. Each article is graded out of 10 in terms of its quality and relevance to them. Then, with further questions in focus groups, we try to determine why some articles work for them, and others don't.'

The following day, the marketing department take the results to the editorial team, which can use them as a reference for tweaking the newspaper's contents. Bompieri says: 'Because of the heritage and style of the newspaper, we can't make revolutionary changes. But there should be a day-by-day evolution. The real aim of this instrument is to make the newspaper as much as possible in line with the needs of the readers.'

This is not to say that the research has changed the paper's political positioning, he stresses. 'At this time it is probably easier to create a newspaper like *Repubblica*, which is on the left and prides itself on attacking the right-wing government. But we have no intention of giving up our independent position. Instead, we decided to give to the editor elements that would help him improve the quality of the newspaper, and present our position in the best possible way.'

Although many journalists would bristle at the idea that the marketing department should advise them on how to write, the research does seem to be having a positive effect. Articles are even more fully researched than before, and the newspaper has adjusted the delicate balance between information and entertainment. The result is a younger, clearer, punchier product.

Says Bompieri: 'When we began the research four years ago, the average score for all of our articles was 7.2 out of 10 in terms of quality and relevance. This has risen to 7.6.'

EXTENDING AN ICON

While such initiatives are resourceful and effective, Italian newspapers rarely adopt more traditional marketing methods like TV and poster advertising. Few papers even have a formal marketing function. Italians still consider newspapers as elements of their culture, rather than products to be consumed, so promoting them alongside soft drinks and detergents would seem bizarre, and even demeaning. Still, brand-building is a necessary part of the marketing mix, and *Corriere della Sera* has found a way to do this while playing on its cultural heritage.

Bompieri says: 'We have the usual competitions and promotions within the newspaper, designed to sustain circulation, but from a marketing point of view our tactical activities are more interesting. The idea is to build the brand while extending our business.'

Brand extensions, in other words. Bompieri says the paper has launched a series of products in areas 'where being branded *Corriere della Sera* is a competitive advantage'. He adds: 'As other marketers have discovered, there is no point in diluting your brand by attaching it to products outside your target market. So we are careful that our products are of an extremely high quality, and aimed at an upmarket audience.'

The first of these was a series of books called 'The Great Novels', with authors ranging from Alberto Moravia to Ernest Hemingway. These are published in hardback, with attractively understated jackets, and a cover price of no higher than €4.90. A second series, 'The Great Italian Novels', quickly followed. At the time of writing, the initiative had been so successful that the newspaper had decided to publish a series of 30 art books, of the hefty coffee table type that normally cost more than €25, but in this case would retail at only €5.90.

'The crucial thing here is that while the books are very reasonably priced, we do not sacrifice quality. We use the finest design, paper and reproduction,' says Bompieri. 'This brand's reputation was built over 125 years, and you can destroy it in six months with the wrong kind of promotion.'

In the same vein, *Corriere della Sera* has produced a series of videotapes, this time under the banner of 'The Classic Films'. The movies retail at just €3.50, but their packaging is of a similarly superior quality. 'We choose products directed to a target audience for which *Corriere della Sera* is a sort of trademark. This gives us a competitive advantage. If we were to brand products aimed at the wrong audience, it would bring nothing to the brand and it would not help sell the product.'

Interestingly, the *Corriere della Sera* branding on all the products is so subtle as to be almost non-existent. The name of the newspaper is printed in miniscule Roman lettering, and on the spine is a simple heraldic device featuring an intertwined C and S.

'That's because here we are using the *Corriere della Sera* name as a guarantee of quality, rather than plastering it all over the product in huge letters in an obvious bid to promote the newspaper. We don't even use the regular *Corriere della Sera* masthead or typeface. The "CS" device is our trademark for sponsoring cultural activities, like classical music concerts for example. It was a very old logo that we resurrected three years ago to brand products and events that were in the spirit of *Corriere della Sera*, but did not concern the newspaper itself. We will be building on this with future products.'

For Bompieri, the strategy has one overarching advantage. 'We are building on our brand not by spending money, but by making money.' He grins. 'In a way, this is very dangerous, because our bosses are getting a bit too used to the idea of making a profit out of marketing.'

The brand in brief

Media brand: Corriere della Sera

Founded: 1876

Owner: Rizzoli Corriere della Sera

Circulation: 714,000 (Source: Accertamenti Diffusioni Stampa)

Key marketing strategies: Localization, international distribution, market research leading to editorial evolution

Brand extensions: Branded classic novels, videotapes and art tomes

Web site: Corriere.it

12

Libération

'All great newspapers are born out of periods of extreme social change'

It is appropriate that the headquarters of *Libération* are located a Molotov Cocktail's throw away from the place de la République in Paris – with its watchful statue of Marianne, symbol of the French revolution, whose plinth bears the words *'Liberté, égalité, fraternité'*. Even though the newspaper grew out of a very different period of French history, it places great emphasis on its stance as a supporter of individual rights.

In a narrow street just around the corner, *Libération*'s smart black-fronted building looks more like it belongs to an advertising agency than a newspaper. A couple of middle-aged yet rebellious leather-jacketed types stand outside, smoking – they look very much like my idea of *Libération* reporters, not to mention its readers.

I'm early, so I wait at a tiny smoke-filled café across the street, drinking a bitter espresso and reading a copy of that day's *Libération* from the free pile on the counter. I am vaguely aware that some of the intense, black-clad men in the café could also be on the newspaper's staff. I look through the paper critically, because it has had a bit of a facelift to mark its 30th anniversary, and I need something insightful to say about its brand positioning to its managing director, Serge July.

I needn't have worried. When I am ushered into July's office, with its huge polished black desk, he is chatting on his mobile phone with somebody called 'Maurice'. They are talking about advertising, and I realize that the person on the other end is Maurice Levy, chairman of Publicis – the biggest advertising agency in France.

'Of course I believe advertising has an important role to play in selling newspapers,' says July in answer to my query, after he has hung up. 'But the problem is that our own advertising income is down at the moment, in common with everyone else's, so we don't have an enormous budget to play with.'

Instead, *Libération* has made rather clever use of public relations, with its 30th anniversary and the redesign snatching several column inches in rival newspapers. Even the right-oriented daily *Le Figaro* printed a half-page interview with July in its media section. All this has revived interest in a paper that had begun to look as if it was flagging, with circulation down 4 per cent at the time of writing. In fact, while the other French media bite their nails and wait for the recession to end, *Libération* has come out fighting.

IRON IN THE SOUL

The paper has always seen itself as something of a firebrand. It launched in 1973, but it grew out of the 'events' of 1968 – when radical students and workers took to the streets in a movement that began as a political protest, but swelled into a revolt that exposed deep divisions within French society. This was the time of the barricades, but also of a new youth culture and a re-examination of traditional values. It was the period that gave the world, among other things, French New Wave cinema.

There cannot be many tabloid-format newspapers that were created by great philosophers. But the driving force behind *Libération* was none other than Jean-Paul Sartre, the writer and thinker who developed the theory of existentialism. Sartre was into other 'isms' as well, notably Communism, and he had long wanted a platform for his political views. He had also flirted with journalism throughout his career, founding the review *Les Temps Modernes* with his lover Simone de Beauvoir in 1945, and writing for *Le Figaro* and the now-defunct *Combat* throughout the late 1940s. As the 1960s roared to their energized, chaotic close, Sartre saw that a new generation was beginning to seize and act on the values that he had been trying to disseminate for 20 years.

He founded the press agency Libération in 1970, resurrecting the name of a long-dead Resistance newsletter. The project evolved into the newspaper of the same name. In a bitterly ironic turn of events, only a few days after *Libération* launched on 22 May 1973, Sartre suffered a debilitating stroke. Barely able to write, he was forced to relinquish his position as managing director of the paper. But events had begun to snowball, and by the end of the 1970s *Libération* was selling over 30,000 copies a day.

Serge July explains: 'The French newspaper scene as we know it today was largely created after the war. Of course there were plenty of newspapers before 1944, but the majority of them had collaborated with the Nazis, so they were forced to close. A new generation of journalists and managers came on to the scene, and created newspapers from scratch. Then there was a long period of calm until the 1960s and early 1970s, when many students and activists began launching papers. But only one survived – *Libération.*'

The obvious question is – why? For July, it is almost a matter of chance. 'All great newspapers are born out of periods of extreme social change,' he says. 'In France, there was one period like this after the liberation, and then another at the end of the 1960s, with 1968 as its defining moment. Everything was changing in terms of music, culture, fashion, morality, and yet the post-war newspapers were not really covering these things. They left it to the magazines, which only did part of the job. *Libération* came along and did it better and more professionally than anyone else. And of course the readers were already there – and had been for quite some time before we existed.'

July says the brand positioning of the newspaper was forged at that moment, and has not changed since. 'I always use the formula: "The newspaper for a changing society" – it's a little simplistic perhaps, but it expresses the idea that we are the newspaper for people who want to question things, overturn things, and change them for the better.'

Libération is regarded in France as the newspaper of the left, but July says its stance is more complex than that. Sartre's legacy, he claims, was not so much political as attitudinal. 'We represent the people, and are suspicious of institutions. If you look at our rivals, *Le Monde* and *Le Figaro*, they are much more part of the establishment. We are deeply suspicious of the establishment. Our reporting staff can be quite militant – but without links to any particular party. No matter who is in power, we see ourselves as the newspaper of opposition. Our relationships with left-wing governments have been as turbulent as those with the right. The key word is "liberty", freedom of thought – that's what we're about.'

Libération launched at the brink of a new era, hoisting the banner of the counter-culture just as that culture was about to become the dominant force in society. In a sense, *Libération* became part of the mainstream at the same point as its readers.

A FRENCH PROBLEM

Libération's circulation grew steadily until the 1980s, but it was clear that the newspaper was never going to equal the sales figures of its more establishment rivals – and certainly not those of the Anglo-Saxon press. This is because of a certain peculiarity in French reading habits. To put it simply, the French don't like national newspapers.

For one thing, the strength of the printing and distribution unions has made newspapers expensive – all the big three titles cost a euro or more. For another, the French have access to no fewer than five information-led radio stations, from the punchy, updated-every-fifteen-minutes France Info to the more discursive Europe 1. Not only that, but local newspapers are far more popular and influential than the national press, with the biggest local title, *Ouest France*, selling more than 764,000 copies a day (compared to the leading national, *Le Monde*, which sells 361,000). And if those two media don't satisfy the French thirst for knowledge, they can always get a global overview from one of the weekly news magazines, the main titles being *Le Nouvel Observateur*, *L'Express* and *Le Point*. All these information sources don't leave much room for national newspapers, which the French tend to purchase only once or twice a week – if at all.

Says Serge July: 'The English love their daily newspapers, but the French are far bigger consumers of magazines. That is why the news magazine concept worked so well here, while it barely exists in the United Kingdom. And of course, a national newspaper cannot compete with either the immediacy of radio or the relevance of the local press.'

In 1981, Serge July and the *Libération* team came up with a potential solution to this problem – the newspaper as magazine. They developed a formula in which the paper would focus on one *'événe-ment'*, or news event, a day, providing a deeper analysis of the subject rather than a slew of headlines and news briefs. The rest of the contents would be a mixture of commentary and features, looking 'behind the scenes' of world events, culture, and the arts. The paper would even have a photograph or an illustration on the front page, just like a magazine.

'We realized at the time that our competition was not so much the rest of the daily press as the news magazines. After all, like us they tended to address changes in society with more depth. They spent more time on analysis, rather than skimming over the day's events. We there-fore felt that our job was to convert weekly news magazine readers into daily readers of *Libération*.'

By adopting the codes of a magazine in a tabloid newspaper format, *Libération* succeeded in distinguishing itself from its competitors, and made potential readers feel more comfortable. The photography on its front cover became increasingly eye-catching, and the back-page profiles of leading figures in news, entertainment and literature became one of the best-loved features in French journalism.

RISE OF THE 'BOBOS'

Libération's shift from counter-culture pamphlet to cosmopolitan journal-of-record coincided with the evolution of its readership. The rebels of 1968 (loosely gathered under the term *soixante-huitards*) and their creative offspring, far from hurling bricks and assaulting policemen, were now working in advertising and the media, when they weren't designing clothes, cars or buildings. They mutated into the demographic the French media refer to as 'BOBOS' – bourgeois bohemians. Property owners with families, they have plenty of money while remaining engaged with issues like sustainable devel-opment and the environment. And these days, they are *Libération*'s key target market.

The only problem is that there are not enough of them, and they still do not buy *Libération* every day. Instead, July says: 'Our policy of exploring important subjects in great depth means that there are big circulation increases around major events, for instance the morning after 11 September, or during the presidential elections in 2002.'

This was the moment when, owing to a low turnout of voters in the first round of the elections, the incumbent president Jacques Chirac found himself up against National Front leader Jean-Marie Le Pen in the crucial second round. The truculently right-wing Le Pen is a *Libération* reader's worst nightmare – hence the paper's front cover, which was black apart from the single white word 'NON'. Many people carried the newspaper as a banner during the anti-Le Pen demonstrations that same day. The next day's paper read simply 'OUI', urging French citizens to vote for Chirac. And when Le Pen was finally vanquished, *Libération*'s front cover sighed 'OUF!' – the French version of 'Phew!' Three days and three newspaper covers in the history of a nation.

But while the covers won awards and circulation was briefly at an all-time high (the 'NON' cover sold 700,000 copies, according to July), *Libération* was not achieving the readership it wanted on a daily basis. With its 30th anniversary looming, the paper's management realized that it needed another revamp.

'The same formula had been in place more or less unchanged since 1981. Our task was to encourage new readers, without losing the existing ones. People who are loyal to brands tend to fear change, and we didn't want to frighten anyone by saying that we were going to drastically overhaul the newspaper. So rather than abandoning or drastically changing our look, we managed to embellish it and deepen it.'

The result is a sharper, less-cluttered *Libération*, with a clear index on the front page, and better-signposted sections within. The most significant change has been the introduction of two news analyses each day, rather than just one. July explains: 'It had occurred to us more than once over the years that we limited ourselves by focusing on just one major news event per day. Never was this more apparent than during the conflict in Iraq. Clearly, we needed to run the war as our lead story, but we were aware that there were equally important things happening elsewhere in the world. So when it came to the redesign, we seized the chance to add a second analysis.'

BRANDING ON A BUDGET

Serge July admits that these days, when it comes to marketing newspapers, it is necessary to think around the problem rather than addressing it head-on. 'As I explained earlier, the state of the economy means that we simply do not have the budget to run huge cross-media advertising campaigns.' (Until 2004 the press was banned from advertising on French television, as it was seen as a competing medium. But now newspapers are allowed promote their contents over the airwaves, very few of them can afford it.)

'Our objective is to make our readership more loyal, and more regular. We know from our most popular issues that we have a potential readership of more than 500,000. We are targeting them by encouraging subscriptions through advertising in our own pages, and by creating clearer and more sophisticated contents.'

But the hinge of the paper's 30th anniversary campaign was a glossy coffee-table book called *The Libération Almanac*, which told the last 30 years of French history via the newspaper's covers. Sold through the newspaper's Web site and in bookshops across France, the almanac was designed by Oliviero Toscani, the Italian advertising genius behind clothing brand Benetton's 'shock' campaigns. The book cost €30 and was divided into seven sections: individuals; the body; beliefs; the new France; the globe; the wounded earth; and *Libération*'s choice. These titles very much reflected the newspaper's editorial themes.

'We were able to use the almanac to promote the *Libération* brand in a subtle way. The book did not talk about the background of the newspaper or advertise it in any way – apart from using its pages to tell the story, alongside other relevant visuals. But the advertising campaign that we ran on radio, and in our own and other newspapers, clearly expressed the idea that *Libération* moves with society.'

To keep *Libération* moving, at the time of writing its management had expressed interest in finding an external partner who could bring much-needed investment to the newspaper. 'We would like to introduce more sections, and a magazine supplement, but of course all these things cost money,' admits July. 'Yet if we want to continue to evolve with society, we must keep our eye on the future.'

The brand in brief

Media brand: Libération

Founded: 1973

Owner: Libération SARL

Circulation: 156,077 (Source: OJD)

Key marketing strategies: Advertising within its own pages to encourage more regular purchasing; radio; press

Brand extensions: Books, most recently *The Libération Almanac*

Web site: Libération.fr

Birth of a media monolith: Ted Turner launches CNN – and changes the face of television news.

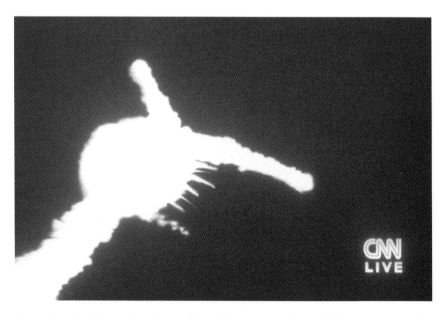

'The CNN effect': the channel built its reputation on live coverage of dramatic news stories – like the Challenger shuttle explosion in 1986.

The broadcaster was once again on the scene as the Berlin Wall came down, symbolizing the end of the Cold War.

Behind the scenes: the bustling CNN newsroom at the broadcaster's Atlanta headquarters.

Although Turner no longer owns CNN, he was the first news broadcaster to spot the potential of satellite technology.

Defining moment: in 1991, when CNN beamed live images of the Gulf War from Baghdad, terrestrial channels across the globe used the images complete with the CNN logo.

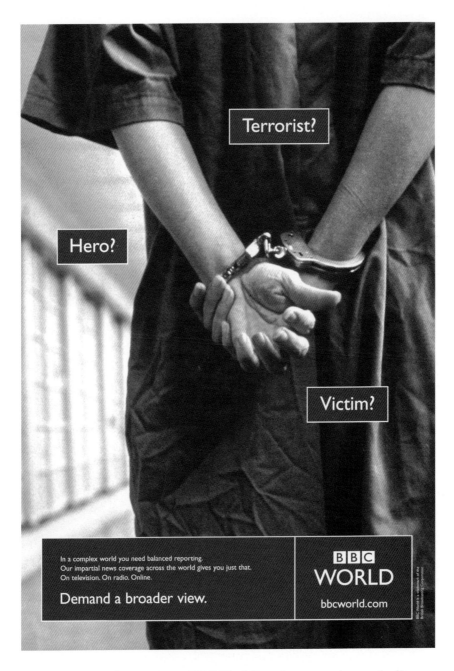

Asking the tough questions: BBC World's print campaign underlines its objective approach to news stories ...

Fitness?

Fashion?

Exploitation?

In a complex world you need balanced reporting.
Our impartial news coverage across the world gives you just that.
On television. On radio. Online.

Demand a broader view.

BBC
WORLD

bbcworld.com

BBC World is a trademark of the
British Broadcasting Corporation

Global community?

Commercial madness?

Criminal tool?

In a complex world you need balanced reporting.
Our impartial news coverage across the world gives you just that.
On television. On radio. Online.

Demand a broader view.

BBC
WORLD
bbcworld.com

With its 'What's important' TV advertising campaign, The Times *emphasized the need to look beyond accepted truths. Is the banana just a harmless fruit when it is used in sexist imagery?*

And is the bottle just a harmless object when it can cause alcoholism and death?

'Our advertising agency hated the logo.' MTV hired a small New York design company to come up with its 'graffiti' logo, which is now the Nike 'swoosh' of youth broadcasting.

THE WALL STREET JOURNAL.

VOL 1—NO. 1. NEW YORK, MONDAY, JULY 8, 1889. PRICE TWO CENTS.

The stock market trembles: the very first issue of The Wall Street Journal *on 8 July 1889. It was four pages long and cost two cents.*

FURNISHED BY

DOW, JONES & CO.

Financial News Agents,

No. 15 WALL STREET.

FOR CUSTOMERS' AFTERNOON LETTERS.

NEW YORK, Thursday, May 15, 1884.

MORNING GOSSIP.

Windsor thronged last night. It was known that the investigating committee was at work for the Metropolitan Bank, and everybody agreed that the market to-day would depend a good deal upon whether the bank would be able to resume or not.

If it was in a condition to be carried through by the Clearing House banks, other failures would be obviated and relief would be felt.

The announcement that the bank will resume is therefore assurance of a better feeling to day.

Everybody agreed that the action of the Clearing House saved the street and would prevent a money panic to-day.

The point was made that the loan certificates would act as an inflation measure. It would ena.le parties holding securities to borrow money on them, as the bank making the loan would be secured. Under these circumstances it was thought that the large operators could secure certificates to almost any extent. Some of the large houses made arrangements last night for the certification of all their checks before 10 o'clock this morning.

9 A. M.—The Metropolitan Bank is open. None of the officers are down, but the clerks say they are told that the bank will open between 10 o'clock and noon.

President Rolston of the Farmers' Loan & Trust Company, laid particular stress on the action of the Clearing House. He said that each bank left to itself and forced to stand a run could be broken ; but united by this action, none of them could be hurt. This action by the Clearing House had heretofore brought everything out all right.

Bank Presidents at the Windsor admitted calling loans and refusing to certify, private bankers did the same with the result of looking up money. This caused some of the failures. Customers would be helped to-day by certification and loans. Parties who could not respond to calls yesterday, would be allowed to renew loans to-day. Money would be eased by this action

Large shorts covered yesterday, and in a good many instances went long in order to steady the market. Conspicuous among the buyers were H. N. Smith, Mr. Johnes, Mr. Van Emburgh, Mr. Chapin, Soutter & Company, and H. L. Horton & Company. Mr. Smith was a large buyer of Western Union.

Mr. Gould bought and sold, apparently keeping his account about even.

The withdrawal of support in Western Union Monday, was on the discovery by Mr. Gould of inside selling.

The *Tribune* interview with Dr. Green is worth reading.

One result of the disturbance is expected to be conservatism in railroad management. The disposition of the companies will be to make themselves as strong as possible financially, and no risks will be run in paying unearned dividends or interest.

It was stated positively that the Metropolitan elevated difficulties were settled. Mr. Kneeland stated that a settlement had been nearly reached, the first time he has said anything of the kind. The terms of settlement were not obtainable. Rumour said that the Manhattan Company would issue some sort of bond for the purpose of retiring the Metropolitan stock. Another statement was that the arrangement would be similar to that made with New York Elevated

9 A.M.—Cashier McGourkey, of the Metropolitan Bank, says : " We shall resume at 12 o'clock.

Atchison, Topeka and Santa Fe dividend 1½ per cent. payable to-day. Pullman dividend 2 per cent. payable to-day." Canadian Pacific books open to-day.

Mr. O. M. Bogart says he can give no statement as yet. If the Metropolitan Bank resumes it will help him.

Notice has been posted on the doors of the Metropolitan Bank, signed by Mr. Scriba, Bank Examiner, that the bank will resume business at 12 o'clock to-day.

London quotations at 12:30 were equivalent to following here with exchange 4.90: Reading, 37¼ ; Central, 125½ ; St. Paul, 66¾ ; Illinois Central, 117¾ ; Erie 2nds, 101½.

Understated debut: the flimsy afternoon newsletter that grew into a mighty newspaper.

'Accuracy, reliability, promptness and independence.' The attributes demanded by Dow Jones customers remain unchanged.

Seeing red: The Economist's *justly famous UK poster campaign uses witty wordplay to make readers (and potential readers) feel as if they are in on a slightly superior joke.*

Newton

Giuliani

Steve Jobs

Tellement plus que l'économie | The Economist

The European version: to get its message across to those who speak English as a second language, The Economist *used a more visual approach, while retaining its wit.*

Newsrooms vary little across the world – they all have an air of controlled chaos. This is an everyday scene at El Pais *in Madrid.*

Like many 'heavyweight' newspapers, El Pais *uses its Sunday magazine to attract younger as well as female readers.*

In common with Corriere della Sera *in Italy,* El Pais *used a promotional series of branded books to emphasize its values of seriousness and quality.*

'We must do everything we can to attract the readers of the future.'
Here, El Pais is distributed to university students.

PART 3

THE MAGAZINES

13

Time

'*We are currently in what might be described as a golden era of news, and products like* Time *have taken on a new relevance*'

The corridors of the austere 48-floor Time-Life Building on Sixth Avenue in New York are eerily quiet on this Monday morning. There is a muted whir of air conditioning, the discreet sound of people tapping away at keyboards, and that's about it. I remark on this quietness to the woman who is escorting me to my interview. 'It's because everyone is working,' she tells me. *Time*, I get the impression, is a very serious place.

It is also a legend. *Time*'s mission statement is there for all to see in its main entrance hall: 'To serve the modern necessity of keeping people informed.' Instantly identifiable by its red-bordered cover, it was the first weekly international news magazine, created by Henry R Luce and Briton Hadden in 1923. It is also famous for nominating its Man of The Year (now Person of the Year) every December. The first was aviator Charles Lindbergh in 1928. But getting on to the cover of any issue of *Time* is a mark of prestige, a sign that you've made it. In its early days it was said that the publication had 'a disrespect for authority and a reverence for success'. In that respect, *Time* is plugged straight in to the American dream.

Time is owned by Time Inc., which publishes some 140 different magazines and is a division of Time Warner (currently trying to recover from its ill-fated merger with AOL). The magazine has a worldwide circulation of 5.5 million, 4 million of which is in the

United States. It has separate editions for the USA, Canada, Europe and Asia – plus a separate magazine called *Time for Kids*. Its Web site, Time.com, has around 3 million unique users a month.

All in all, not a bad achievement for a magazine set up by a couple of reporters from *The Baltimore News*.

MR LUCE AND MR HADDEN

Henry R Luce and Briton Hadden might have been thrown together by fate in order to leave their mark on American journalism. They were both born in 1898 – Hadden in Brooklyn, and Luce in Tengchow, China, where his parents were missionaries. Already, their different backgrounds seemed to provide the American salt and foreign spice that gave *Time* magazine its unique flavour.

Initially educated at a British boarding school on the Chinese coast, at 15 Luce was sent to the Hotchkiss School in Connecticut. Luce was a scholarship student and appears to have worked incredibly hard to support himself. He worked as a waiter after school, and edited copy at *The Hotchkiss Literary Monthly*. He was also assistant managing editor of the weekly school newspaper, whose editor was Briton Hadden.

The fussy and rather straight-laced Luce was very different to Hadden, a lively extrovert, but the balance worked. Luce wrote later: 'Despite the greatest differences in temperaments and even in interests, somehow we had to work together. We were an organization. At the centre of our lives – our jobs, our function – at that point everything we had belonged to each other.' (*'Time*'s Founders', Time.com.)

The pair continued to work together at Yale University, where Luce was editor of the *Yale Daily News*, with Hadden as chairman. In 1916 they signed up as reserve officers and were sent for military training in South Carolina. They were shocked by the diverse and unreliable news that came in about the First World War, and discussed the need for a new kind of publication that would dispense with propaganda and report straight facts.

It would be a few years before their idea bore fruit, because in 1920 they graduated and went their separate ways – Luce to study history at Oxford University, and Hadden to become a reporter at the *New York World*. When Luce returned to the USA, he took a job on the *Chicago Daily News*. But at the end of 1921, they found themselves working together again at *The Baltimore News*. Competing for scoops during the day, in the evening they drew up plans for the project that was to become *Time*. By 1922 they had raised US$86,000 from 74 investors, and despite being short of their US$100,000 goal, they decided to quit the *News* and get on with launching their magazine.

Time made its debut on 3 March 1923, with Hadden as editor and Luce as business manager. The magazine cost 15 cents.

A DIFFICULT DEBUT

Although there had been weekly magazines before, Hadden and Luce felt that they devoted too much time to analysis and not enough to a simple explanation of the news. As for newspapers, they had the opposite problem – too many bland news bites with no detail. *Time* would provide a summary of the week's most important events, explaining them in full, while cutting out any extraneous material.

Their prospectus for the magazine explained their goals in detail: 'People are uninformed because no publication has adapted itself to the time which busy men are able to spend on simply keeping informed... *Time* is interested – not in how much it includes between its covers – but in how much gets off its pages into the minds of its readers.'

Time would be different, the document went on to say, in that it would deal with 'every happening of importance' and present these 'as fact rather than comment'. It would also strive to be as up to date as possible.

But the real key to *Time*'s success was the way it was divided into easily navigable 'departments' – such as foreign news, the arts, business, people, and sports – enabling readers to extract quickly and easily the information they wanted.

The current president of the Time Group, Eileen Naughton, says the magazine's proposition has remained virtually unchanged since that day. 'The founding precept was that there was so much information available to people that there was no way of synthesizing it. So *Time* had a fairly logical and formulaic way of covering the week's events. As a concept, it was remarkably prescient.'

By all accounts the magazine's first few months were chaotic, with newsgathering techniques that amounted to little more than filleting articles from the week's papers and rewriting them. But soon the magazine had settled into a unique and groundbreaking style – mainly due to the insight and perseverance of Hadden.

Briton Hadden would only get to edit the magazine for six years, but during that time he introduced many of the elements that survive to this day. *Time*'s archive reports that Hadden wrote no stories of his own – restricting his contribution to eccentric missives run on the letters page to provoke reader response. Otherwise, he concentrated on ensuring that his reporters produced the magazine he had envisaged, telling them: 'Let all stories make sharp sense. Omit flowers. Remember you can't be too obvious.'

A lover of words, he carried a copy of Homer's *Iliad* in his pocket, and in its back cover he noted verbs and adjectives that he considered intriguing. Under Hadden, *Time* magazine popularized words like 'tycoon', 'pundit' and 'kudos'. Hadden's genius lay in his ability to take enormously complicated ideas that were completely foreign to him, and not only work on them until he understood them, but also put them on a page in a clear and readable form.

In the winter of 1928, Hadden fell ill with a streptococcus infection. He died at the age of 31 on 27 February 1929 – exactly six years to the day after the first issue of *Time* had gone to press.

THE MARCH OF TIME

Henry Luce took over as editor of *Time* and ensured that the magazine exceeded his friend's aspirations. The publication had already achieved a number of milestones – the introduction of a glossy cover in 1923, the red border in 1927, and its first colour cover the following year – and under Luce it continued to innovate.

In an early example of cross-media branding, *Time* launched the first *March of Time* radio programme in March 1931. The magazine's circulation department is thought to have dreamt up the idea for the show, which was broadcast on CBS. At first it focused on domestic news, but during the war it broadened to cover international events.

The show was such a success that *Time* decided to develop it into a newsreel for cinemas. It had plenty of competition, but *Time* had an efficient marketing department and the resources to shoot dramatic overseas footage. More than 500 cinemas signed up to receive *Time*'s newsreels, and the ponderous narration by Westbrook Van Voorhis became the conscience of the nation. (Orson Welles satirized it in the film *Citizen Kane*.) Unfortunately, the end of the war killed the radio version – which went off the air in 1945 – while TV negated the need for the cinema newsreels, which ended in 1951.

Meanwhile, the magazine demonstrated a chilling ability to single out those who would leave an indelible mark on history, naming Adolf Hitler its Man of the Year in 1938, and Joseph Stalin in 1939.

A Latin American edition launched in May 1941, and the following year the magazine's overall circulation hit 1 million. Colour was introduced as a regular feature inside the magazine as early as 1951, although *Time* would not become a full-colour publication until the 1970s. Luce had also been busy expanding the *Time* group, launching *Life* and *Fortune* in the 1930s, and *Sports Illustrated* in 1954.

When Henry Luce died in March 1967, at the age of 68, *Life* magazine described him as: 'A man who revolutionized modern journalism.'

By then, *Time* was already part of the American press landscape, but its international expansion continued in March 1973 with the launch of *Time Europe*. Over the years, the conservative tone it had displayed under Luce softened, and its coverage became more neutral and centrist. It began to develop its technology coverage, to such an extent that it named 'The Computer' Machine of the Year in 1982. The resulting flurry of controversy reinforced *Time*'s ability to make headlines in other media, thus maintaining its high profile. In 1993, the magazine made its content available online for the first time, launching a full Internet site and a daily news service the following year.

In 1996, Walter Isaacson became the 14th managing editor of *Time*, and thoroughly shook up the magazine, introducing more detailed reporting and livelier writing. In January 2001 Jim Kelly succeeded Isaacson in the editor's chair. His goal, he said, was to 'assume our readers are passionate and curious about the world, and to prove to them week after week that *Time* offers them something they can't find anywhere else'.

It's fair to say that *Time* has had plenty of imitators – titles like *L'Express* in France and *Der Spiegel* in Germany were directly inspired by it – but no other magazine can compete with the impact of its red-bordered brand power. Interbrand listed *Time* as number 66 in its ranking of the world's 100 most valuable brands in 2003.

It's interesting to note that *Life*, one of the most popular magazines of its day, ceased publication in 1971, a victim of increased competition, rising costs, and falling advertising revenue. For many years it existed only as a book-publishing venture, although Time Inc has recently tried to resurrect it through a series of 'collectible' special editions. In terms of impact, though, the brand remains a shadow of its former self.

Time, on the other hand, marches on.

AN AMERICAN ICON

'Coca-Cola has its red can, and *Time* magazine has its red border,' says Eileen Naughton, president of the Time Group. 'It pulls all our editions together and gives us a coherent brand identity. The red cover connotes accuracy, authority, and balanced journalism.'

As the custodian of one of the world's best-known brands, Naughton is a powerful and influential woman – but she is also welcoming and chatty, especially when it comes to talking about the magazine. For Naughton, *Time*'s great balancing act has been to stick to the resolutions made by Luce and Hadden, without getting mired in the past.

'I'm not sure that the general perception of *Time* is that it is provocative – but it really is,' she points out. 'If you read it every week, you're going to discover some pretty eye-opening material. And yet at the same time, it's a front row seat at history.'

Naughton says *Time* adheres to its original mission by taking the week's most important news items and exploring them in a depth that TV and newspapers don't have the time or space to attempt. Far from being out of date, she says that the formula developed by Luce and Hadden has become more relevant as information sources have proliferated.

'People get their information in different ways. It's a pleasure to sit down for 40 minutes or so with *Time*, and really ingest the information. You have a higher level of engagement with a magazine than you do with television or a newspaper, which you tend to consume in chunks, while multi-tasking. And there are a lot of people who enjoy that connection.'

Time has made a few concessions to modernity, however. The layout is certainly more flexible than it was before. 'Under the founders the formula was pretty rigid – the length of each weekly feature was always the same, it was always written in a neutral *Time* voice, it was created from a fairly narrow range of resources coming in to the New York office.'

Now, as Naughton puts it, *Time* is a 'mega news gathering operation', with 28 bureaux around the world. In Iraq, the magazine had three writers and two photographers 'embedded' with the troops. 'Technology has enabled us to become a more immediate and visually rich product, especially with the digital transfer of images almost directly from the photographer to the page. This allied with the editorial team's intuitive visual sense has given us an incredible equity in photojournalism over the past few years.'

Time's readers are more or less the people you might think: educated, literate, fairly affluent, aged between 35 and 45, with an even split between male and female. Some of them believe *Time* has become more commercial over the years. One of them commented: 'You get a little tired of cover stories about "the new yoga".'

Naughton says: 'The magazine was never designed to cover just politics. Obviously that's an important component, but it's not the mainstay. We cover the stuff of life, and that embraces an unlimited range of issues. I think our readership would become fatigued pretty quickly if we didn't try to surprise them once in a while.'

From a sales point of view, *Time* can afford to take risks with its covers, because 98 per cent of its circulation comes from subscriptions. Only about 200,000 magazines of the entire 4 million US circulation are bought at newsstands.

A CONVERSATION WITH READERS

Newsstands are important, however, from a marketing perspective. *Time*'s red border is highly visible on shelves, and many copies are distributed to kiosks at airports and stations. Because of this, there is no need to plug specific issues, and *Time* can use advertising to build its brand.

Time has been running regular branding campaigns for over a decade, but its tack has changed over the past couple of years. Naughton explains: 'We are currently in what might be described as a golden era of news, and products like *Time* have taken on a new relevance. After September 11 we found that a lot of lapsed subscribers took up their subscriptions once again. Our advertising is designed to encourage that trend.'

A print campaign called 'Join the conversation' used the *Time* red border to highlight news photographs. For instance, a red border around an Asian woman wearing a mask to ward off the SARS virus, with the accompanying question: 'What is more infectious – the organism, or the fear?' Or the crippled actor Christopher Reeve, accompanied by the question: 'At what point does hope overcome science?'

The fact that *Time* is part of the Time Warner group gives it considerable benefits when it comes to print advertising. Naughton confirms: 'We have access to other consumer magazines which will run our campaigns at very favourable rates. We were able to run our print campaign in *Fortune*, *People*, *Parenting*, and *Sports Illustrated*, among others. This gives us very broad exposure. And because the campaigns are visually compelling, we get a lot of pick-up. If these magazines need an extra page of advertising, they'll often run a *Time* ad.'

CNN is also part of the Time Warner group – another helpful connection. The news channel frequently covers controversial stories broken by *Time*, and the magazine's journalists regularly appear in front of the cameras as guest commentators. Naughton says: 'Our public relations team works very actively with CNN and other news outlets to promote our journalists as experts in their field, and to generate coverage for the articles within the magazine.'

The famous Person of the Year cover always generates masses of media coverage, even though it began as a mistake. 'In fact the founders had pretty much missed the Charles Lindbergh [first solo Atlantic flight] story, so putting him on the cover was an admission that they hadn't written enough about him. The Man of the Year quickly became an institution – we changed it to Person of the Year in 1999 to make it a bit more politically correct.'

The person chosen must be the figure who, for good or for ill, has had the biggest influence on history during the year. This can sometimes put *Time* in a sticky spot – having already devoted covers to Hitler and Stalin in the 1940s, it considered making Osama Bin Laden its Man of the Year in 2001.

'There was a lot of debate internally, which we then opened into a national, public debate,' says Naughton. 'Perhaps fortunately, there is a rule that the person must be still living, and at that stage it wasn't clear whether Bin Laden had been killed or not. So we made Rudy Giuliani [the former mayor of New York] Man of the Year instead.'

It was the popular choice – even something of a cop-out from a non-American point of view. Naughton defends the decision. 'Giuliani was incredibly important for this city and this country during that year. He became a symbol of our steadfastness. But the different reactions to our choice illustrate how powerful the Person of the Year concept has become in terms of provoking debate.'

Time has become adept at developing special issue concepts that generate external publicity – such as the Pictures of the Year issue in December, the Health edition in January, and the Coolest Inventions number in October. 'As well as being popular with readers, these are frankly very effective advertising vehicles,' Naughton points out.

SELECTIVE DISTRIBUTION

Magazines, even serious ones like *Time*, are never above creating advertising vehicles. In 2002, Naughton became concerned that *Time* was relying too much for advertising revenue on the technology, financial services and automotive categories – all of which were suffering during the recession. She felt that the magazine needed to look more closely at areas like fashion, retail and personal care.

She noted that the European edition had been covering fashion for some time, having followed the demands of its readers. It was also getting advertising from luxury brands. So the US edition adopted European thinking and produced a Style and Design supplement. 'It may seem out of our orbit, but fashion is a 40 billion dollar global industry,' Naughton insists. 'We held a gala party to launch the supplement, and many designers told us they were delighted *Time* was taking this subject seriously. It was not meant to be frivolous – once again, this is the stuff of life, and we should be covering it.'

Not so long ago, *Time*'s other problem from an advertising perspective was its huge circulation. What did advertisers do if they wanted to reach a certain target group of readers? *Time*'s subscriber database provided the solution. The magazine launched *Time Global Business*, a supplement distributed only to 1 million select subscribers, described as: 'high income top managers, scientists, engineers and technical specialists'.

Now, *Time* runs other targeted supplements. A report called *Inside Business* is aimed at a slightly wider, less elite range of 1.8 million readers. A family-oriented insert called *Connections* goes out to 1.5 million women, while *Generations* only goes out to readers aged 50 or over. This could become a trend within publishing – using specially tailored supplements to 'cherry pick' groups of readers within a subscriber base. 'We call it "selective edit",' says Naughton. 'As a reader, you don't necessarily realize that your *Time* magazine is any different to anybody else's. But you may be receiving *Generations*, while your son is getting the *Inside Business* insert.'

Despite the necessarily sophisticated and commercial nature of contemporary publishing, Naughton says the original spirit of the magazine remains intact. The essential serious-mindedness of the product survives.

'*Time* must have some of the most highly educated staff of any magazine, and they were all drawn here by what the magazine stands for. There is a lot of pride in what we do – we are selling a product that enriches people's knowledge. We are all strongly aware that *Time* is a leadership brand, and that our job is to preserve and extend it.'

The brand in brief

Media brand: Time

Founded: 1923

Owner: Time Warner

Circulation: 5.5 million (Source: ABC/Time Inc)

Key marketing strategies: Print advertising, public relations, tailored editorial content for specific target groups

Brand extensions: Books

Web site: Time.com

14

National Geographic

*'If archaeologists unearthed a copy in 100 years, they
would see exactly what our world is like right now'*

We used to fight over *National Geographic*. Nobody was quite sure
why we had a subscription to the magazine, or who had taken it out,
but it would arrive at the office every month in its understated yellow-
ish package, and whoever got in early enough would steal it. A few
days later, our boss – the editor of a now-defunct media magazine –
would wander about looking under press releases and foraging through
stacks of other, more turgid publications, before finally asking in a
studiedly casual tone: 'Has anybody seen *Nat Geo*?'

It can get to you like that, *National Geographic*. With its thick,
glossy pages, its faintly retro typeface, its chatty, informative prose and
its superlative photography, *Nat Geo* is a treat – as luxuriant as a slab of
chocolate. But because it is worthy and intelligent, it is also a guilt-free
pleasure. Nobody is going to sniff at you for reading *Nat Geo* on a
plane, the way they might if you were tucking into *Maxim* or one of the
fashion glossies. Perhaps that's why polls like the European Business
Readership Survey and Europe 2003, both conducted by Ipsos-RSL,
list *National Geographic* as one of the most popular publications
among elite business people, nestling incongruously alongside titles
like *The Economist* and the *Harvard Business Review*.

National Geographic is unique – neither travel magazine, nor
wildlife publication, nor archaeological review, it is a mixture of all
three and several other things besides. It is part of a 116-year-old

society founded by explorers, it has a circulation of 9 million via 24 local editions, and its brand name has been applied to books, documentaries, feature films, maps, spin-off magazines, an extraordinarily popular Web site, a 24-hour television channel, clothing, gifts and even holidays. The magazine's yellow-bordered cover is instantly recognizable, whether you happen to be looking at the English or the Romanian edition. *National Geographic* was once considered an American icon. Now it is an icon, full stop.

A MYSTERIOUS GATHERING

On the evening of 13 January 1888, a group of 33 extraordinary men made their way through the dank streets of Washington DC by foot, horseback, and horse-drawn carriage. Their destination was a place called The Cosmos Club, located on Lafayette Square opposite the White House. The men who had arranged to meet at the club that night were a disparate bunch: explorers, geographers, teachers, cartographers, lawyers, military officers and financiers. But they were united by a taste for adventure and an intense curiosity about the world around them.

They were, as one of them later pointed out, 'the first explorers of the Grand Canyon and the Yellowstone, those who had carried the American flag farthest north, who had measured the altitude of our famous mountains, traced the windings of our coasts and rivers, determined the distribution of flora and fauna, enlightened us in the customs of the aborigines, and marked out the path of storm and flood'.

The group gathered around a large mahogany table to sketch out plans for the organization that would become the National Geographic Society. A non-profit concern, its aim would be to 'increase the diffusion of geographical knowledge', and its qualifications for membership would be 'as broad and liberal... as is consistent with its own well-being and the dignity of the science it represents'. The National Geographic Society was officially incorporated two weeks later.

The society's first president was Gardiner Greene Hubbard, a lawyer, financier and philanthropist who had helped to found a school for the deaf. In his introductory address, Hubbard said that as he was 'neither a scientific man, nor... a geographer' his appointment would send a message that the society would not be confined to professional geographers. Instead, it would be open to all those who wanted to encourage research and spread knowledge 'so that we may all know more of the world upon which we live'.

Since then, the National Geographic Society has remained something of a family concern. Its second president was the inventor Alexander Graham Bell, Hubbard's son-in-law. Later, Bell's own son-in-law, Gilbert H Grosvenor, took the reigns. Gilbert M Grosvenor, today's chairman, is Gilbert H's grandson.

The first *National Geographic* magazine was published nine months after the founding of the society, and sent to just 200 people. A dry-as-dust scientific journal with a dull brown cover, it bore no resemblance to the vibrant, photography-packed magazine its readers know today. But its mission statement struck the right tone, explaining that 'as it is not intended to be simply the organ of the Society, its pages will be open to all persons interested in geography'.

NOT JUST BLACK AND WHITE

The magazine has come a long way since then. In February 1905, Gilbert H Grosvenor, who had taken over as editor a couple of years earlier, took the groundbreaking decision to run photographs in the magazine. He went the whole hog, too, filling 11 pages with photographs of Lhasa in Tibet. He half-expected to be fired, but many society members congratulated him. Not everyone was happy with the change, though, as the magazine's current editor-in-chief, Bill Allen, recounts.

'One of the members apparently said that it would never be considered "a magazine of substance" if it published photographs. It's pretty incredible when you consider that today, photography is one of our greatest strengths.'

Indeed, a year later, when Grosvenor published some early flash photography of nocturnal creatures, two society members resigned in disgust, saying the magazine was turning into 'a picture book'. Their opinion seems to have had little effect on Grosvenor, as he became president of the National Geographic Society in 1920, a post he held until 1954.

In the early years of his tenure, the society and the magazine sealed their reputations with a string of impressive achievements, from the first colour underwater photographs in 1926 to the first flight over the

South Pole in 1929. The first colour aerial photographs were published a year later. By the Second World War, the National Geographic Society had amassed such an important collection of photographs, maps and other cartographic data that it was able to throw open its doors to the US military.

Ironically, the magazine still had problems opening up to the possibilities of colour photography – the first colour photos began appearing on the magazine's cover in 1959, but the first all-colour issue didn't hit newsstands until 1962.

Nevertheless, *National Geographic* was regarded as an unmatched journal of scientific discovery, with some of the most impressive collaborators in the history of exploration. In 1952, for example, it published an article by the legendary undersea explorer Jacques-Yves Cousteau. Ten years later, astronaut John Glenn carried the National Geographic Society flag on the first US orbital space flight. And in 1963, Americans climbed Mount Everest in an exhibition sponsored by the society. This led to the first branded *National Geographic* television programme, *Americans On Everest*, which was screened on CBS. The society's flag finally made it to the moon with the Apollo 11 astronauts in 1969.

EXPLORING OPPORTUNITIES

By the 1970s, *National Geographic* had become a brand to be reckoned with. But the first hint that it was to grow into a vast international business did not come until 1984, with the launch of a spin-off travel magazine called *National Geographic Traveler*.

In the meantime, the core brand continued to focus on what it did best – funding groundbreaking exhibitions, and providing the perfect showcase for adventure and discovery. When undersea explorer Robert D Ballard began investigating the wreck of the *Titanic*, the results were reported to the National Geographic Society. The magazine also became increasingly experimental, from printing a hologram on the cover of its centennial issue in 1988, to devoting the whole issue to France in 1989 in celebration of the country's bicentennial.

In 1994 the society launched its first local-language edition, in Japan, marking the launch of the strategy that would take the brand to a whole new level of global recognition. The following year, National

Geographic Television (now NG Television & Film) became a separate, taxable subsidiary. It fell under a new for-profit arm called National Geographic Ventures, which would later move into satellite TV, film production, mapping technology, gifts and apparel. It signed a partnership with Rupert Murdoch's Fox Entertainment Group, which helped fund its expansion into the global TV market. The first president of National Geographic Ventures was John M Fahey Jr, who is now president and chief executive officer of the National Geographic Society and is widely credited with having led its modernization and international expansion.

Perhaps not surprisingly, the launch of National Geographic Ventures provoked accusations that the non-profit society had lost sight of its original aims – which were to promote knowledge. But editor-in-chief Bill Allen says: 'We became increasingly aware that we had to reach different people in different ways. My main concern is that people know about the wonderful job the society does, and the wonderful work our writers and explorers do. If we have to reach people through a magazine in their own language, television, the Web site, or whatever, that's what we will do. Our goal is education, and we want to make sure enough people come to us so we can continue doing what we do.'

The magazine's vice-president and worldwide publisher Sean Flanagan, who is responsible for its advertising sales strategy, backs this view. He says: 'Since it was founded the National Geographic Society has funded something like 7,000 expeditions and explorations. Clearly, we need to create revenue to support that. This is not about getting rich, this is about doing our job.'

The society's headquarters in Washington DC reflect this double role – containing both a museum and a hi-tech television studio.

The final years of the century were a time of incredible change for *National Geographic*, as the magazine suddenly woke to the possibilities of international distribution and new technology. Local language versions were launched in quick succession in Spain, Latin America, Israel, Greece, France, Germany and Poland. The Web site went online. In 1997, National Geographic Channels International was launched. The same year, the first 108 years of the magazine were published on CD-ROM. And another spin-off title, *National Geographic Adventure*, was launched to make use of the abundance of material provided by the explorers and writers associated with the society.

National Geographic entered the 21st century with a burst of energy, launching no fewer than six local-language magazines in 2000 (in Korea, Denmark, Sweden, Norway, the Netherlands and Brazil). The following year, it made its debut in China, Finland, Turkey, Thailand and Portugal. The magazine's local editions are published simultaneously around the world, containing about 15 per cent of original tailored content alongside translated articles from the parent magazine. Also that year, the National Geographic Channel launched on cable and satellite in its home market in the United States.

Local language editions have continued to appear – most recently, at the time of writing, in Romania and Russia – as have other spin-off projects, such as the magazines *National Geographic Explorer* and *National Geographic Kids*. In July 2002, another significant branding development appeared in the form of the first feature film produced by *National Geographic*. *K-19: The Widowmaker* starred Harrison Ford and told of a Cold War Russian submarine disaster, based on a true story. Both entertaining and educational, it clearly delineated the style of films the organization wants to produce in the future.

Despite all the spin-offs and marketing activities, *National Geographic* has never stopped funding exploration. Its Committee for Research and Exploration has an annual budget of more than US$4 million. It founded its Expeditions Council in 1998 to encourage exploration of parts of the world that remain largely unknown – particularly beneath the sea. Projects have included expeditions to the Black Sea to search for ancient shipwrecks and evidence of a cataclysmic flood. In April 2000, the society assembled a team of 'explorers in residence' to 'redefine exploration for the new millennium'. In the last few years alone, expeditions supported by *National Geographic* have uncovered the fossil remains of giant crocodile, found Inca mummies in Peru, and climbed Everest in an anniversary expedition marking 50 years since Edmund Hillary conquered the summit. The society has also set up the National Geographic Conservation Trust, a grant-making body to support conservation activities around the world.

In addition, the society still places a great deal of emphasis on education. As well as producing branded magazines, books and maps aimed at kids, it has worked hard to get the neglected subject of geography back on to the curriculum. As part of its centennial celebration in

1988, it put up US$200 million to create the National Geographic Society Education Foundation. A national competition is held in the USA every year, with 5 million students from 15,000 schools competing for college scholarships totalling US$50,000. The national winners go through to an international competition held every two years. In 2003, the *National Geographic* World Competition involved students from 18 countries.

But whether for charity or revenue, there is no doubt that *National Geographic* has become expert at leveraging its brand. In March 2002, in a disquieting but compelling mixture of marketing and reportage, the magazine announced that it had located Sharbat Gula, the Afghan girl who had gazed levelly from the cover of the June 1985 issue in what became an iconic image. The magazine ran an advertising poster contrasting the original photo with a picture of the adult Sharbat, whose clear-eyed innocence had been shattered by struggle and war.

THE MAGAZINE TODAY

Bill Allen has been editor-in-chief of *National Geographic* since 1995, and he has a very clear idea of what the brand stands for. 'Our key attribute is accuracy, but not in the conventional sense of the term. I believe our job is to present a vivid, unbiased and completely true picture of the world around us. I like to think of the magazine as a kind of time capsule. If you buried a copy of *National Geographic*, archaeologists should be able to unearth it in a hundred years, and get a completely accurate picture of what our world looks like right now.'

It's a pretty big ambition, but the magazine does everything in its power to ensure that this vision is realized. Writers can spend as long as two years researching stories – which often involve trekking to the ends of the earth – and each fact is painstakingly checked and double-checked. 'We're not interested in the tip of the iceberg,' says Allen. 'We're interested in every last droplet of moisture that makes up the iceberg. We have to get things right because our readers trust us as a brand, not as individual reporters. You won't hear someone say, "Did you read what Bill Allen wrote about such and such," but, "Did you read what *National Geographic* wrote?"'

He adds that while those who write in the magazine are often explorers, they are first and foremost journalists. 'The magazine has to be entertaining as well as informative, so we try to keep the writing crisp and lively. The photography is part of that, too. When you look at the style of the magazine in the 1940s and 1950s, it's almost laughably dry. These days we have dramatic introductions, and plenty of break-out quotes and boxes that bring the reader into the article. Some of these subjects are pretty complicated, so we have to make them as accessible as possible.'

National Geographic receives thousands of suggestions for articles from freelance journalists and photographers. Allen admits that being a 'name' helps to get a piece commissioned, but the magazine has also given relative unknowns their first big break. 'Clearly we're looking for the best of the best, but if you've been a careful reader of the magazine and you know what to say and how to say it, there's no reason why you shouldn't be given a chance. We have discovered many superb writers and photographers that way.'

While the magazine's boyish enthusiasm for insects, wild carnivores and archaeological digs gives it an escapist twist, Allen is keen to reflect topical issues. 'We didn't ignore the conflict in the Gulf, for instance. In fact, we sent award-winning reporter Alexandra Boulat to Baghdad to go behind the headlines, and find out how this situation was affecting everyday citizens. It's one of the best things we've done. We also spent several years researching a story on modern slavery.'

The lengthy and occasionally perilous nature of *National Geographic* assignments can also be used to justify its cross-branding initiatives – for instance, a film crew may tag along with a writer so a story about Afghanistan can also be a documentary for National Geographic Television and Film. The magazine itself includes a section called 'Beyond the printed page', which promotes the Web site, the National Geographic Channel, and the organization's television and film productions. Says Allen: 'Our people risk their lives to bring back this information. I don't see why we shouldn't want to diffuse as widely as possible, using our various media. That was our original mission statement, after all.'

Allen believes that all human beings are instinctively curious about the world, hence the magazine's ability to bridge demographic and cultural divisions. (In fact the average *Nat Geo* reader in the United

States is aged between 38 and 50, typically high-earning and well educated.) 'Anybody should be able to open *National Geographic* and find at least one subject that passionately interests them, and at least one that they want to learn more about.'

Ironically, this mass appeal does not prevent the brand from being perceived in different ways in its various markets. 'In Poland, for example, we are considered a youth brand. The launch party for our national edition over there was very trendy – there was a rock band and everything. It was great.'

With his instinctive grasp of the magazine's identity, Allen is more involved in marketing than most editors. He is also aware of the publication's need to remain contemporary and relevant – especially in its home market, where it is occasionally viewed as a little earnest.

'I like to push the boundaries a little. One of the most popular magazines in America is *Sports Illustrated* – particularly its swimsuit issue, which features gorgeous models wearing the garments concerned, and always sells millions of copies. Well, last year we produced the *National Geographic* swimsuit issue, as a way of showing that we didn't take ourselves too seriously. We explored the social history of the swimsuit in an extremely well-researched and interesting piece.'

The idea caught the attention of the US media, and Allen did more than 45 TV interviews in the space of a week. 'It was a fantastic branding exercise. Can you imagine how many advertising dollars that kind of exposure would have cost us? The only sad part is that it was for something light, and not our reports on Afghanistan or the trade in human beings. But hopefully it brought more people to the magazine.'

Allen says the magazine uses these kinds of 'alternative' marketing devices quite often. 'Television advertising is extraordinarily expensive. Fortunately, we can promote the magazine across our own media. We also rely heavily on direct mail to encourage new and renewed subscriptions.'

The direct marketing strategy is seductive because it urges readers to become 'members' of the National Geographic Society, instantly making them feel part of an undeniably impressive organization. Overseas editions are run under licence, and have separate marketing budgets. 'We wouldn't presume here in Washington to know how to market a magazine in, say, Russia,' Allen points out. 'But we give advice and many of the foreign titles use similar methods to ourselves.'

Magazine vice-president and worldwide publisher Sean Flanagan also has some firm views on the brand identity. 'If I had to choose key words, I'd use "discovery, research, and education". But our two main advantages from a marketing point of view are our extraordinary history, and our high level of reader involvement. People are passionate about the magazine, and they read it from cover to cover. Those who have taken out their first subscription renew 70 per cent of the time, which is an extraordinarily high figure. And then of course you have the fact that our brand touches something like 250 million lives through its various media, and has no real competition.'

Certainly, while there are many other travel and adventure magazines, there is nothing quite like *Nat Geo*. As Flanagan says: 'Trends come and go – but tradition remains.'

There is no doubt that the brand will continue to expand, exploring new niches and broadening its global reach. Already, more than 40 per cent of readers live outside its domestic market (less than 10 years ago, 80 per cent of its readership was in the USA). One in four read it in a language other than English. A Spanish-language edition of *National Geographic Traveler*, called *Viajes*, is the top-selling travel magazine in Spain. Following that success, a history magazine called *Historia National Geographic* was launched there in November 2003. At the time of writing, a *National Geographic* branded children's magazine was scheduled for launch in China, Korea, Germany, Bulgaria, Croatia, Romania, Russia, Slovenia and Latin America. And the National Geographic Channel, from its launch in the United Kingdom, Australia and Poland in 1997, is now available on every inhabited continent.

The National Geographic Society's mission statement on its Web site clearly states its goal. 'After more than a century the National Geographic Society today is propelled by new concerns: the alarming lack of geographic knowledge among our nation's young people and the pressing need to protect the planet's natural resources. As our mission grows in urgency and scope, the Society continues to develop new and exciting vehicles for broadening our reach and enhancing our legendary ability to bring the world to our millions of members.'

The brand in brief

Media brand: National Geographic

Founded: 1888

Owner: National Geographic Society

Circulation: 9 million via 24 editions (Source: *National Geographic*)

Key marketing strategies: Cross-media promotion, worldwide distribution, direct marketing, press and poster advertising

Brand extensions: Spin-off magazines; 24-hour cable TV network; branded movies and TV documentaries; books and maps; videos and DVDs, digital photo library; branded clothing, luggage and gifts; travel programme

Web site: Nationalgeographic.com

15

Playboy

'We'd never want to be in a position where people didn't rip us off, because that would mean the brand had lost its cachet'

At the beginning of 2004 *Playboy* turned 50. It's the ideal age for a playboy – mature but not over the hill, roguish but not a dirty old man. One imagines a lounge lizard with a martini in one hand and a wink for the ladies, a blend of David Niven and Austin Powers.

Naturally I was hoping to interview the creator of *Playboy*, Hugh M Hefner – 'Hef', a marketing genius if ever there was one – but the lines to the Playboy Mansion were permanently engaged. Truth be told, Hef's daughter, Christie Hefner, runs Playboy Enterprises, and it was through her that I learned of the empire's plans for its next half century.

Playboy has been more than just a magazine for many years now. It was launched in December 1953, and within a decade the TV show, the clubs and the branded retail products were already in existence. And it had something else, too – a genuine identity, a panache that went beyond the products themselves.

Christie Hefner comments: '*Playboy* is the only magazine title to have ever become a true global brand. By that I mean it's not just a recognizable name, but also an attitude, a lifestyle, a symbol that people identify with. Whether it's on running shoes in China, sunglasses in Brazil or t-shirts in France, it stands for sexy, fun, adventurousness. People who wear the *Playboy* logo are self-confident, open-minded and romantic.'

Playboy's founder certainly seems to have possessed some of those qualities.

HEFNER, MARILYN, AND THAT RABBIT

He's been called Hef since he was a teenager, and somehow the nick-name has the right ring to it – a fun-loving, hearty sort of name, some-body you might want to slap on the back. Good old Hef. No wonder he became the life and soul of the party.

Hugh Hefner was born in Chicago on 9 April 1926, the eldest son of conservative Protestant parents. He showed creative promise early on, founding the school newspaper and drawing cartoons for various army papers during military service. After being discharged in 1946 he took art classes ('anatomy, of course', dryly notes the official biog from the *Playboy* press office). He became an art student at the University of Illinois, where he edited a satirical campus magazine called *Shaft*, introducing the Coed of the Month feature. In 1949 he married class-mate Mildred Williams.

Hef initially wanted to be a cartoonist, but it soon became clear that this was not going to be the route to success. He got a job as an adver-tising copywriter, first at a department store, and then at a Chicago-based men's magazine called *Esquire*. When the magazine relocated to New York, Hef demanded a pay rise. His request was turned down, so he decided to stay behind and launch a publication of his own. His idea for a Chicago city magazine failed to spark the interest of investors, however. So Hef supported his family by working as the newsstand promotion director of a publishing company, and then as circulation manager of *Children's Activities* magazine. All these jobs provided the experience that enabled him to market *Playboy* successfully later on.

Hef never let go of his dream. By now, he had developed the concept of a risqué but sophisticated magazine for men, which he felt certain would find an audience in a tie-loosening post-war America. In 1953, he managed to convince a printer and a distributor to help him get the first issue of his publication on to the shelves. He borrowed US$600 from the bank, using his own furniture as collateral, and raised further funds from friends and family, ending up with a total of US$8,000.

Hefner cobbled together the first issue of *Playboy* on his kitchen table. He was originally going to call it *Stag Party*, but a rival magazine named *Stag* heard about his plans and threatened legal action. One of his friends suggested *Playboy*, so Hef went with that instead. The debut issue was an odd beast, containing nude pictures of Marilyn Monroe (purchased from the local printer of a calendar), a Sherlock Holmes short story, and a feature on desk design for the modern office. It was 44 pages long and cost 50 cents.

'Hef never envisioned the magazine becoming the phenomenal success it has,' says Christie Hefner today. 'The first issue didn't even have a date on its cover, in the hope that newsstands would keep it on sale longer than one month in order to fund the second issue.'

In fact, the first issue sold a respectable 51,000 copies – enough to cover Hef's costs and make a second edition worth while. After that, circulation grew rapidly, and in 1955 Hefner launched the first *Playboy* branded product: cufflinks bearing the rabbit head logo.

Although a cartoon rabbit had appeared in the original magazine, the famous symbol did not surface until the second issue. Arthur Paul, the magazine's art director, designed what must by now be one of the most ripped-off logos on the planet. At first glance it's impossible to tell whether the glittery t-shirts on sale at Spanish beach resorts are genuine Playboy Enterprises products, or cheap attempts to cash in.

Christie Hefner says: 'We work hard to fight piracy, both litigating aggressively and working with governments and trademark holders around the world. But, in truth, we'd never want to be in a position where people didn't rip us off, because that would mean the brand had lost its cachet.'

For the moment, that seems unlikely. More than 1,500 *Playboy*-branded products are sold in around 125 countries and territories, with global retail sales of approximately US$350 million in 2003. If anything, the logo is better known than the magazine that spawned it.

PLAYBOY VERSUS THE PURITANS

By the end of the 1950s *Playboy* was selling a million copies a month. Hefner had already moved into television, starting a syndicated show called *Playboy's Penthouse* in 1959. He had also scored a big success with the Playboy Jazz Festival at the Chicago Stadium – marking the start of a long tradition of supporting popular culture that *Playboy*'s detractors tend to overlook, or of which they are unaware.

Playboy was not only about bare flesh. In its heyday, the magazine published short stories by Arthur C Clarke, Ian Fleming, Alberto Moravia, Isaac Bashevis Singer and William Styron, among many others. Addressing a group of curvaceous Playmates assembled for a 1979 reunion, Hefner said: 'Without you, I'd be the publisher of a literary magazine.'

Indeed, Hef had a cultural agenda as well as a financial one. His editorials in the 1960s championed personal liberty and freedom of expression, and kicked against the American heritage of Puritan repression. Later he set up the Playboy Foundation, which would support charities fighting for civil liberties, combating censorship, and promoting sexual education. Over the years, the Foundation has donated US$16 million to various non-profit groups. After his conservative upbringing, Hef may have realized more than most that many Americans were still pioneers at heart: God-fearin' folk with guns. With the help of *Playboy*, the Swinging Sixties were about to blow all that away – at least for a little while.

The first Playboy Club opened in Chicago in 1960, as if raising the curtain on the decade. Membership was an annual US$25 and drinks, cigarettes and food all cost US$1.50. Soon there were 15 clubs and 500,000 members (or 'key holders' as they were called). Apparently, Hef was unsure about the 'Bunny Girl' outfits until he saw the prototype costume, complete with white furry tail. After that, the bunnies became as much a part of the era as The Beatles.

The Playboy clubs closed in the 1980s, when the brand was in the doldrums, but there are rumours that they might reopen. Christie Hefner is equivocal. 'I closed the clubs after they had had an incredible run – over 20 years – because it's a low-margin business, and one in which nightclub concepts tend to come and go. We are interested in re-entering the business, but only where the club is joined with a casino, so that it's a multifaceted entertainment centre with a much higher profit margin, return on investment and lifespan.'

But all that was all in the future, because in the late 1960s and early 1970s, *Playboy* was on a roll. A second syndicated TV series, *Playboy After Dark*, launched in 1969 – and unlike its predecessor, it was in colour. In 1971 Playboy Enterprises went public, with listings on the New York and Pacific stock exchanges. At that point the magazine was selling 7 million copies a month, there were 23 Playboy clubs, resorts and casinos (with more than 900,000 members), and the company's assets included book publishing, merchandising, a model agency, a record label and a TV and film production company. The following year, *Playboy* magazine launched its first overseas edition, in Germany. (There are now 18 editions worldwide.)

There were still a few golden years ahead. In the 1970s Hefner relocated to the second Playboy Mansion, in Hollywood, his spiritual home. Hef has always felt an affinity for the movie business. *Playboy* money was behind films like Roman Polanski's *Macbeth* and Monty Python's first full-length feature, *And Now For Something Completely Different*. And in 1980 Hefner helped to fund the restoration of the Hollywood sign, then in serious disrepair. Little did he know it, but his own empire was about to fall into a similar state.

DOWN – BUT NOT OUT

The 1980s were a depressingly conservative period in the United States. Making money was more important than having fun, drugs were only there to make you work harder, and a sexual partner was just another status symbol. Repression and hypocrisy returned in their new guise of political correctness.

Playboy entered a period of depression, and Hefner himself suffered a stroke in 1985. He stoically referred to it as 'a stroke of luck', because it forced him to slow down and consider his options. In 1989, having long been divorced from Mildred – Christie Hefner's mother – he married the magazine's Playmate of the Year, Kimberly Conrad.

Meanwhile, Christie Hefner had taken over the running of Playboy Enterprises, and she quickly set about trying to put it right. She recruited a new management team, restructured operations, and eliminated unprofitable businesses. Showing an instinct for consumer trends that was to serve her well over the next few years, she started a pay TV service and launched a line of videotapes. In 1986 she closed the remaining Playboy clubs, their allure now sadly faded.

While Hef remained editor-in-chief of *Playboy* magazine and the spiritual leader of the company, Christie was now firmly established as chairman and chief executive. She says: 'My vision for the company... was that its future was to be electronic and global. While the magazine remains the soul of the enterprise, the definer of the Playboy brand and the creator of our unique content... the majority of our profits [now] come from television – and our fastest growing profit centre is Playboy.com.'

Throughout the late 1980s and early 1990s, Christie Hefner remodelled the company along these lines. In 1993 the brand's biggest licensee, Chaifa Investment, opened the first Playboy retail products store in China, eventually setting up more than 300 Playboy retail outlets in China and Hong Kong. Playboy Enterprises began to sell branded television programmes overseas, and expanded its cable TV operations. Today, it operates 22 international networks and its various audiovisual products, including videos and DVDs, are distributed in more than 200 countries worldwide. Playboy Enterprises also bought the steamy Spice adult cable channel in 1998, but is careful to differentiate it from *Playboy*'s soft-focus, rather kitsch positioning.

Just as she had spotted the Playboy brand's relevance to the home video and cable TV market (sex always drives nascent media), Christie Hefner quickly realized the potential of the Internet. *Playboy* became the first national magazine on the Web in 1994, with the launch of Playboy.com. Later it launched Playboy Cyber Club, a paid subscription site. These days it also runs PlayboyNet Español, a Spanish-language version, and sites aimed at audiences in Germany, Taiwan, Brazil and the Netherlands. And that's not all: PlayboyStore.com sells *Playboy*-branded products, and Playboy Auctions is a virtual auction house for admission to Playboy events. In addition, the online network includes gambling sites that can be found at www.playboy.com/gaming.

Christie Hefner does not understate the role the Web has played in injecting life back into the brand. 'Playboy.com was one of the elements in our marketing strategy of strengthening the connection to the brand among 18- to 29-year-olds, as they were early adopters online. And indeed, the majority of visitors to Playboy.com are not readers of the magazine – or any magazine, for that matter.'

A NEW GENERATION

The 1990s saw the rise in the United Kingdom of 'the lad mag'. The concept is generally acknowledged to have been ignited by a title called *Loaded*, launched by IPC in 1994. With its blend of sex, fashion, sport, interviews with male icons and heavily ironic 'un-PC' humour, *Loaded* was a joyous backlash against the uptight yuppies of the previous decade. In fact it was a budget version of the *Playboy* formula, with lager and soap starlets in place of champagne and Playmates.

Loaded soon spawned imitators, such as *FHM* and *Maxim*. The jokes got bawdier, the girls got raunchier, and circulations soared. Pretty soon the formula crossed the Atlantic. Established US men's magazines like *GQ* and *Details* cringed under the assault of this new tribe of publications, which were altogether scruffier, sexier, and less reverential than themselves. Here at last were men's magazines that seemed to be aimed at heterosexuals.

The phenomenon did not go unnoticed at *Playboy*, which was after all an older and (by then) less fashionable version of the same thing – the granddad of lad mags, if you like. Inevitably, in 2002 Hugh Hefner appointed James Kaminsky, former editorial director of *Maxim*, as the first new editorial director of *Playboy* for 30 years. (He replaced *Playboy* stalwart Arthur Kretchmer, who had decided to bow out.)

Kaminsky's brief was to revive flagging interest in the publication among 18- to 34-year-olds – the audience that had defected to magazines like *Maxim*. At the same time, it would have been unwise to tamper with the classic formula too much. What emerged was a compromise between the *Playboy* of old and the men's magazines of today. There's still plenty of skin, but a redesign has given the publication a more contemporary twist. Good writing, a part of the *Playboy* mix that seemed to have been abandoned over the years, has been reintroduced. There are more general features, accompanied by sharper photography. And finally, an eight-page men's fashion spread.

Is *Playboy* still pornography? Was it ever? Perhaps – but only in the sense that glossy magazines about cooking and travel and interiors are a kind of pornography: images to fantasize over. The more pertinent problem for *Playboy* is that the taboos it broke are now part of the mainstream. Bare flesh is the currency of advertising and video games, and sex is plentiful on the Web. The magazine's counter attack seems to have been to go into reverse.

'In many ways, *Playboy* today is a direct descendent of the magazine 50 years ago,' underlines Christie Hefner. 'It's a unique blend of celebrities, pop culture, lifestyle, fashion, cars, electronics, food and wine, big ideas and great writing, both fiction and non-fiction.'

She says that in its early years *Playboy* was a 'wish list', an escapist fantasy portraying a lifestyle that was beyond the reach of most of its readers. 'Today it's more of a guidebook, helping young men get the most out of life, to seek the special but the attainable... The magazine is undergoing an evolution to connect with the next generation of readers, the ones who've grown up on video games, the Internet and ESPN. Hence we're using more photography, more side-bars, more entry points and less jump pages to ensure that readers stay with us, even for the serious journalism.'

It remains to be seen whether younger readers will respond to the title's retro appeal, but for the moment its sales are holding steady. In the United States, the magazine's total paid circulation is 3.15 million – a long way off its 1970s peak, but still higher than that of *Esquire*, *GQ* and *Rolling Stone* combined, and ahead of *Maxim*. In addition, the company says that an estimated 5 million adults read the various international editions (in Brazil, Bulgaria, Croatia, Czech Republic, France, Germany, Greece, Hungary, Italy, Japan, Mexico, Netherlands, Poland, Romania, Russia, Slovenia, Spain and Taiwan).

Hefner says: 'On average, the overseas editions have 75 per cent local content. That localization – the politicians, celebrities, writers and sports teams that are familiar to each country – is why the magazine is so successful internationally. The positioning is very consistent from country to country, however. What is different is that outside the US, especially in countries that have had a history of repression, *Playboy* resonates powerfully as a symbol of freedom, both personal and political.'

As for herself, Hefner does not have any problem being a woman at the helm of a distinctly male-oriented business. 'It hasn't influenced my views of *Playboy*'s opportunities. And it has probably helped me attract talented women into management.'

Indeed, the company's chief finance officer and head of corporate communications are both women. Similarly, Hefner does not feel that there is any snobbery towards the brand. 'I've found that the business people we deal with admire both the brand and the company – and that includes institutional investors, our media partners around the world, the press and distributors.'

PLAYBOY AT 50

Playboy entered its 50th year in reasonable shape, with revenues hovering around US$300 million. After a long period in the red, it was due to go back into profit. The magazine's influence on contemporary culture may have waned, but this hardly seems to matter, as the modern *Playboy* is a multi-strand corporation embracing publishing, entertainment, licensing and online.

Christie Hefner says: 'The key brand extensions are first of all our two electronic media businesses, Playboy TV and Playboy Online. Then there is our consumer products business, which includes entertainment products such as video games, slot machines and music, as well as fashion items like lingerie, jewellery and casual clothing. Our next brand extension will be our Playboy concept stores. The first one, which opened in 2002 in Tokyo, has been extremely successful and we are developing plans to open others with local partners in major markets.'

The stores will sell fashionable clothing and accessories – once again dovetailing with Hefner's strategy of making the brand relevant to younger consumers.

Having said all that, the magazine was still very much to the fore during the 50th anniversary celebrations, which provided an ideal marketing opportunity. The list of events and spin-offs seemed endless – starting with a bumper special issue of the magazine, naturally emblazoned with a golden rabbit's head. In a nod to the past, it featured articles by Norman Mailer and Hunter S Thompson. The rather more youthful-looking anniversary Web site allowed visitors to vote for the sexiest centrefold of all time, and chronicled the search for the 50th anniversary Playmate (proving that the rabbit had not changed his… er… spots too much).

Meanwhile, Playboy Licensing released a 'designer collection' of limited edition clothing and accessories. The designers involved ranged from Versace and Vivienne Westwood to Dunhill and Burton Snowboards (a snowboard with a Playboy bunny on it – how cool is that?). The entertainment arm produced an anniversary TV documentary, soon to become a globally distributed DVD and video. Commemorative stamps and coins were issued. A photographic retrospective, *Playboy 50 Years: The Photographs*, hit the bookstores.

There was more. Fans of the brand could attend The Playboy Club Tour, a four-month-long 'consumer experience' resurrecting the spirit of the clubs and calling at 50 cities in the USA. Hosted by a group of Playmates in bunny costumes, the tour nights were held at swish nightclubs, allowing those who had shelled out for a ticket to mingle with models and local VIPs 'among photographic images of *Playboy* covers and other sensual imagery'. Then there was the gala launch of the anniversary issue in New York, the VIP anniversary weekend in Las Vegas, and no fewer than two anniversary parties at the Playboy Mansion – one of them, of course, on New Year's Eve.

And where does Hef, now in his seventies, fit in to all this? As the last of the anniversary champagne runs out and the final firework fizzles and dies, can he still recognize the brand that he launched on his kitchen table 50 years ago? Is he even involved with the business any more? Christie Hefner says: 'Hef is the creative guru and marketing genius for the company, while I concentrate on strategy, management and operations. I see myself as the steward of the brand, and the person responsible for creating shareholder value.'

HEF'S VISION

There is no doubt that Hugh Hefner created one of the greatest media brands of all time. In 1959, only six years after *Playboy* was launched, a reader was able to send a letter to the magazine's offices simply by drawing the iconic rabbit head on an envelope.

As a magazine, *Playboy* pushed boundaries, tore off the plain brown wrapper, and told men to stop being ashamed of their sexuality. In an age before antiseptic coat hangers became the standard perception of female beauty, it worshipped glamorous women. Since Marilyn Monroe's 1953 appearance, the magazine has featured the likes of Sophia Loren, Kim Novak, Jane Fonda, Natassja Kinski, Cindy Crawford, Drew Barrymore, Sharon Stone, Kim Basinger, Farrah Fawcett and Madonna. Say what you like about that lot, but they aren't cut-price starlets.

In addition, *Playboy* set the standard for men's magazines to come, providing a showcase for some of the most talented authors, artists and photographers – from Woody Allen to Andy Warhol via Vladimir Nabokov. The *Playboy Interview* became a brand in its own right. Alex Haley conducted the first one, with legendary jazz trumpeter Miles Davis. Other interviewees have included The Beatles, Muhammad Ali, Bob Dylan, Frank Sinatra, Dr Martin Luther King, Bill Gates, Fidel Castro and Jimmy Carter.

Not only that, but Hefner was one of the first publishers to realize that a magazine could have a life beyond the printed page. As soon as he produced those first bunny cufflinks, he moved into territory that had previously been occupied only by entertainment factories like Hollywood and Disney. It's difficult to think of another magazine brand – even *Vogue* – that has so successfully evoked a specific lifestyle and then exported it into new areas.

Like it or not, *Playboy* is part of America's cultural heritage. And as I mentioned earlier, Hef himself has never been a slouch on the culture front. The Playboy Jazz Festival remains an annual event, and Hefner recently embarked on a project to restore and screen jazz-themed films.

Still heavily committed to the film industry, which he sees as the greatest expression of the American Dream, he has a personal library of some 4,000 films, and regularly holds screenings at the Playboy Mansion. The Playboy Foundation has instituted an annual Freedom of Expression Award at the Sundance Film Festival. And while you wouldn't imagine Hefner to be a fan of the caustic British screenwriter Dennis Potter, he recently underwrote a Potter retrospective at the Los Angeles Museum of Contemporary Art. He sponsored a US TV series called *American Cinema*, and collects and restores rare early films (the 1920s British crooner Al Bowlly is a particular favourite).

Hefner has already been the subject of numerous magazine articles, books, and TV documentaries, but I hear that Hollywood is soon going to pay him the ultimate accolade – a big-budget feature film based on his own life.

The brand in brief

Media brand: Playboy

Founded: 1953

Owner: Playboy Enterprises Inc

Circulation: 3.15 million (Source: ABC)

Key marketing strategies: Cross-media branding, diversification

Brand extensions: Cable TV networks, film and television production, videos, DVDs, books, online, branded fashion and accessories

Web site: Playboy.com (plus spin-off gaming sites)

16

Paris Match

*'We are regarded as a French institution – like Renault
or Chanel'*

One of the best anecdotes about *Paris Match* concerns, almost
inevitably, Grace Kelly and Prince Rainier III of Monaco. The story
goes that in 1954, when Kelly was in the South of France shooting *To
Catch A Thief*, a *Paris Match* reporter was sent to Monaco to interview
Prince Rainier. The prince was an elegant but rather imposing figure,
and to spice up the story a bit, the reporter decided to engineer a
meeting between the beautiful young actress and the future ruler of the
principality. The rest, as they say, is history.

It's difficult to determine whether this story is true – most reports have
Kelly meeting the prince at the Cannes Film Festival, an encounter that
was undoubtedly covered by the magazine. But the point is that the tale
contains many of the elements that make *Paris Match* so compelling:
glamour, sophistication, a dash of intrigue and a gigantic scoop.

Paris Match is one of the few non-English language magazines to
have gained worldwide recognition. The title has an international
edition, and almost 84,000 of its 700,000 readers live outside France.
This may be because it projects a certain idea of Parisian chic, or
because it shows the world through a French prism, or simply because
its photo-heavy format makes it accessible to Francophiles who speak
French as a second language.

One thing is certain – *Paris Match* is a brand. Its white and red logo
is instantly recognizable, and the mere mention of the name conjures

up images of café terraces and glasses of Ricard. More importantly, *Paris Match* has built its reputation on some of the most stunning photography and important news features in the history of French journalism.

MATCH IGNITES

It began in 1928 as a sports magazine called, simply, *Match*. Its creator was the legendary French journalist Léon Bailby, who was also the proprietor of the now long-defunct newspapers *L'Intransigeant* (the most popular French evening paper of the 1920s) and *Le Jour*. He sold the title in 1938 to Jean Prouvost, a French industrialist who had made his fortune in the textile trade before becoming a media baron. Owner of the newspaper *Paris-Soir*, which ironically put Bailby's *L'Intransigeant* out of business, Prouvost later started another famous French magazine, *Marie-Claire*.

The war broke out before Prouvost had time to develop his vision for *Match*, and circulation was suspended under the Occupation. The magazine was re-launched as a weekly newsmagazine on 25 March 1949 under the title *Paris Match*, with Winston Churchill on the cover. Its logo and basic offering have remained more or less unchanged since then. That same year, a journalist named Roger Thérond became editor at the age of only 26. Over the next 50 years he was to have an indelible impact on the magazine.

With its odd but alluring blend of celebrities, culture, fashion and hard news, *Paris Match* quickly found an audience. The French have always preferred magazines to national newspapers, which are considered poor value for money and have much smaller circulations than their British counterparts (in recent years, fewer than 400,000 a day). *Paris Match* provided all the crucial news and gossip in one colourful weekly dose.

Throughout the 1950s and 1960s, *Paris Match* documented French and international events through a combination of eye-catching visuals and gripping reportage. But in the early 1970s the title hit a rough patch, faced with increasing competition and an ageing readership. Its saviour was Daniel Filipacchi, the founder of Filipacchi Media (now Hachette Filipacchi). The dynamic Filipacchi had been a photographer for *Paris Match* and *Marie-Claire*, while at the same time organizing jazz concerts and running a record label. He published a jazz magazine with his friend and business partner Frank Ténot, and in the 1960s the pair made a fortune from a publication called *Salut Les Copains*, covering French pop music. (They also had a radio show of the same name – a nice bit of cross-media promotion.)

In 1976 Filipacchi bought the struggling *Paris Match* from Prouvost and began to turn it around. He reinstalled his friend Roger Thérond as editor of the title. Thérond had left the magazine eight years earlier to work for the rival weekly *L'Express*, but Filipacchi seemed to realize that his fellow photography enthusiast had a unique insight into the true 'personality' of *Paris Match*.

Nicknamed *L'Oeil* (The Eye) due to his instinctive grasp of what separated a great photograph from a merely good one, Thérond later built one of the world's greatest photography collections. He retooled *Paris Match* around the theme of photography, reducing text and giving more room to images. This inspired the magazine's famous slogan: *'Le poids des mots, le choc des photos'* ('The weight of words, the power of images') – a phrase that many French people still repeat as soon as you mention the magazine. He established the tradition of starting each article with a double-page photograph, a banner headline, and only a few lines of opening text.

Slowly, *Paris Match* attracted new readers and regained its place as one of the country's leading newsweeklies. Thérond was not afraid to balance shocking photos of war and strife with glamorous pictures of celebrities and royalty. In a recent film about *Paris Match* – issued on DVD exclusively to the magazine's advertisers – there is an old recording of Thérond saying: 'The magazine does not intend to depict life as marvellous, but to depict life as it is.'

When Thérond left the magazine in 1999 (he died two years later at the age of 76), his identification with the title was so complete that its future seemed dangerously uncertain. Alain Genestar, a highly capable journalist who had previously run the Sunday newspaper *Le Journal du Dimanche*, succeeded him as editorial director. A new era had begun.

FANNING THE FLAME

The most important aspect of the *Paris Match* editorial floor is known as *'le mur'* – the wall. And that's exactly what it is: a wall covered with a metre-high strip of corkboard, on which the page layouts of *Paris*

Match are tacked one by one as the magazine counts down to press day every Tuesday.

This is a fairly common system in newsrooms around the world, but it is doubly important at *Paris Match* due to a peculiar idiosyncrasy – which is that the magazine does not have a structure. Actually, that's a slight exaggeration. In fact it has two sections, known as the *cahier froid* and the *cahier chaud*. The 'cold' section covers culture and lifestyle, and is written well ahead of press day. It is the only section of the magazine to contain advertising. The 'cold' pages are on the outside edges of the magazine, wrapping like the earth's crust around the molten inner core of the magazine, the 'hot' news pages. These can be changed right up until the last moment, with the result that they are completely unencumbered by advertising. The *cahier chaud* is between 62 and 70 pages long, sometimes even 80 pages on a good news week.

Olivier Royant, second-in-command at the magazine, conducts my tour of the wall. I have arrived on press day, and the editorial team are trying to decide whether to replace a spread of the actress Lucy Liu with some photos of floods in Marseille – a story that only broke last night. (In the end, they decide to go with the actress, as that week's issue lacks the essential element of glamour.)

The success or otherwise of the *cahier chaud* as a piece of reading matter depends on its rhythm, which again is decided on press day. The double page spreads are shuffled around until Genestar and Royant are happy with the way the section 'flows'. Genestar himself has said that the reader should experience the magazine like a conversation, switching from the serious to the amusing and back again. 'The notion of rupture creates the architecture of the magazine,' he comments. 'I don't believe in being contained. Each issue is driven by what we desire. We take hours to decide, swapping this layout here or that photograph there. And then, suddenly, *c'est bon!*'

Royant calls the *cahier chaud* 'a triumph for journalism'. He adds: 'I find it hard to imagine any other magazine in the world that could get away with banishing advertising from its central pages. It is another one of those things that makes *Paris Match* an extremely special publication.'

Later I discuss this aspect of the magazine with Edmond Tran, the head of advertising sales at *Paris Match*. Far from being frustrated by the situation, he seems to revel in the challenge.

'While it competes for advertising with the other French newsweeklies, and although it has elements in common with international titles like *Stern* and *Newsweek*, *Paris Match* is completely unique,' he states. 'Apart from its highly visual nature, it distinguishes itself by covering news with a capital 'N', no matter what that might be. Hence you have everything from the war in Iraq to the marriage of an actress, with no attempt at hierarchy or any suggestion that one thing is more important than the other. That is for our readers to decide. The flowing, free-form quality of the *cahier chaud* reflects that.'

Both Royant and Tran point out that because *Paris Match* has very few permanent subscribers, immediacy is an important marketing factor. Edmond Tran says: 'Of the 630,000 copies sold in France, something like 65 per cent are sold at newsstands. That means each issue of the magazine must be highly compelling, because if our readers decide we are not interesting one week, then they might not buy us the next – and then our sales for the entire month are down.'

For the same reason, every week's cover tends to feature a personality. 'Personalities sell the magazine – after more than 50 years of experience, we know that,' says Tran. 'Magazines with high numbers of subscribers can occasionally risk covers devoted to general features about fashion or cars. But we depend on a strong visual hook to sell the magazine, so each cover must be a person our readers can identify with.'

From an editorial point of view, Royant finds this aspect of the magazine highly contradictory. 'In a way, the cover lies about what the magazine is. You'd think that it was a "people" magazine, when in fact it contains a great deal of hard news. Fortunately, our readers understand that we give them a formula that embraces every aspect of life.'

The cover image is also the magazine's most important marketing tool, with posters blanketing news kiosks just before each issue comes out. *Paris Match* does not have what the French refer to as *maronniers* – the annual editions about wine or holidays that guarantee extra sales. But it does know that certain faces sell well. Stick French crooner Johnny Hallyday on the cover, and you can shift plenty of copies.

'With our large readership, we can get interviews with people who may not talk to anyone else,' Tran explains. 'And of course it helps that we are regarded as a French institution, like Renault or Chanel. When [French president Jacques] Chirac finds his popularity slipping in the polls, it doesn't hurt if he appears in *Paris Match* holding his baby grandson. That's the kind of influence you can exert with a circulation of 700,000 and an estimated weekly readership of over one million. We are a means of communicating with the French people.'

(A French friend of mine observes that in the *Tintin* comic books, jumped-up opera diva Bianca Castafiore refuses to talk to the press, except to a certain magazine called 'Paris Flash'.)

But *Paris Match* courts controversy, too, making its relationship with celebrities and politicians precarious. For instance, the magazine was the first to publish photos of former French president François Mitterrand with his 'secret' daughter, Mazarine. Royant says: 'Lots of people knew of this girl's existence, but nobody wanted to talk about it. We got a photograph of Mitterand emerging from a restaurant with his arm over her shoulder, a very affectionate gesture, so we decided to run with it and bring the whole thing out into the open.'

Royant admits that the magazine uses paparazzi photographs, a fact that had a negative effect on its circulation following Princess Diana's death in a Paris car crash in 1997 – apparently after a high-speed chase by paparazzi. But readers soon tired of being judgemental and came back for more. Royant says: 'We deal in revelation and provocation – that's the nature of this publication and we can't fight it, otherwise we'll kill it. Naturally, as the leading newsmagazine, we sometimes face accusations of irresponsibility from those who are not leaders. And it's true that there are privacy laws in this country, which leaves us open to legal action. We get sued all the time. But we'll carry on bringing our readers the news.'

Another contributor to the *Paris Match* film is the crusading lawyer Robert Badinter, who in a landmark 1977 court battle managed to save the murderer of a child from the guillotine, commuting the sentence to life imprisonment. When Badinter was made justice minister in 1981, his first act was to abolish the death penalty. In the film, Badinter describes how the support for his work generated by *Paris Match* strengthened and inspired him.

'*Match* played an important role... during the great battle against the death penalty. It was always present and its coverage was very committed. At the time it was forbidden to take photographs in court, but a *Match* photographer took some with a concealed camera, and today the archives of *Paris Match* are the only place where I can find images that capture the intensity of the trial and of the period.'

Olivier Royant stresses that although *Paris Match* is prepared to go to considerable lengths to give its readers the inside story, there are certain lines it won't cross. 'We will always maintain our dignity. We're never vulgar or in poor taste, and we're not out to destroy anyone.'

He says the magazine's aim is to reveal 'the backstage lives' of politicians and celebrities. 'We show you the side you don't see on television or in newspapers, when these people are in the spotlight. For instance, in a recent issue we gained exclusive access to [US defence secretary] Donald Rumsfeld's office. We followed him at work as he went about his daily business. It showed what he's like as a human being, not as a public figure.'

Using the Rumsfeld piece as an example, Royant points out that *Paris Match* publishes far more 'quality' journalism than celebrity tittle-tattle. 'We have more than a hundred top-class correspondents, and access to some of the best photography on the planet. Photographers love us because we are the only magazine that still uses uncluttered double page spreads, showing their work to its best advantage. *Paris Match* is by no means a downmarket product.'

In fact, it is difficult to determine what market the magazine is aimed at. Everyone from wealthy executives to the concierge of my apartment building seems to read *Match*. Royant laughs at this observation. 'I know – it's totally irrational. You read studies and attend magazine publishing workshops, and everybody says, "You have to go niche, you have to go niche"… and meanwhile we're the exact opposite to niche. And yet it seems to work. I'm sure it's something to do with our heritage. If someone launched *Paris Match* tomorrow, they might not be able to get it off the ground.'

TELEVISION IN PRINT

While the recession has meant that the magazine's circulation figure has remained flat, it is still the second most popular weekly in France, after the television and culture title *Télérama*. Edmond Tran also insists that advertising revenue is buoyant.

'In terms of attracting advertisers, *Paris Match* can sometimes be a difficult sell from a marketing point of view,' he says. 'We don't have a niche market, and our readership is evenly split across genders – in fact it's about 58 per cent female. We report on everything, and we appeal to everyone, which is both a strength and a weakness.'

This did not stop jewellery brand Bulgari launching a recent French advertising campaign through *Paris Match*. And here, Tran launches into an anecdote. 'One of the items in the campaign was a diamond necklace worth several thousand euros, worn by the model Gisele Bundchen. I was later told that a woman walked into a jewellery store in Monaco with a copy of *Paris Match* under her arm, opened it to the advertisement concerned, and said: "I want this."'

Apart from its lack of focus, *Paris Match* faces a branding challenge familiar to all well-established titles. 'We're an institution, and we've been around for ever – but we don't want to appear old,' says Tran. 'It's another reason why we have to keep quality as high as possible. There is no room for apathy.'

It's fair to say that *Paris Match*'s marketing is far from groundbreaking – consisting of little more than the poster campaigns mentioned above, supported by a peppering of radio spots. But there are signs that the magazine's owners are waking up to the brand's potential. In December 2001, Hachette Filipacchi's parent group Lagardère launched Match TV, a satellite channel. Although French cross-media ownership rules prevented the company from using either the *Paris Match* name or logo, it made no secret of the fact that the channel would cover people and events in the same spirit as its sister brand. Its schedule includes a programme called *Match Magazine*, presented by Alain Genestar. At the end of 2003, the show also began broadcasting on terrestrial TV.

'The magazine format translates perfectly to the screen, because with its wide range of subjects, the publication itself is rather like a television channel,' points out Tran.

In addition, the magazine's Web site, which had remained largely unchanged since 1997, was dramatically redesigned in September 2002. Users can scrutinize the latest news and pictures, find out what's coming up in the next issue, and access an archive. *Paris Match* also seems to have begun exploring more sponsorship opportunities, for instance supporting a Botticelli exhibition at the Musée du Luxembourg.

Olivier Royant says the magazine's ability to break news stories can be a marketing plus. On the week of my visit, *Paris Match* published a photograph of Jacques Chirac apparently wearing a hearing aid – not a big deal, one would have thought, but it generated reams of coverage in the French press. 'When the rest of the media get hold of *Paris Match* and it has a hot story, it makes headlines, which creates a buzz around the magazine,' he says. 'News organizations have an enviable ability to generate marketing with very little expense, by utilizing their core skills.'

The experience of the 1970s shows that *Paris Match* cannot afford to be complacent, but despite its somewhat casual approach to marketing, its continued high profile seems assured, both at home and abroad. Says Tran: 'We can never be sure exactly who our overseas readers are, but it is obvious that they are people who want to get a French perspective on topical events. And in our home market, of course, we are simply France's window on the world.'

The brand in brief

Media brand: Paris Match

Founded: 1949

Owner: Hachette Filipacchi (Lagardère)

Circulation: 718,271 (Source: OJD)

Key marketing strategies: Posters, radio, sponsorship

Brand extensions: Match TV

Web site: parismatch.com

17

The Economist

'Quality, wit, and depth of analysis appeal to readers all over the world'

The most famous British business magazine occupies a stark glass-and-stone tower, plonked down in an uncompromising slab of court-yard just off St James's Street in London. Futurist architects the Smithsons created the building in the early 1960s – which is exactly the sort of detail that *Economist* readers would appreciate. On the day of my visit, the rigid structure contrasts sharply with a series of ovoid Chinese sculptures resembling giant blobs of mercury on display outside. It's tempting to assume this juxtaposition is deliberate, because it nicely reflects the contents of *The Economist*, whose intel-lectual veneer masks a sly sense of humour.

The reception area continues the theme, with plenty of polished marble and designer leather seating, and a briskly efficient receptionist whose mouth does not even twitch when I make a facetious remark about being early. And yet here is more art – this time photographs of various personalities wearing the same leather jacket (I recognize Jeffrey Bernard and John Hurt). I later discover that two of them – Pip Piper and Peter Dunbar – are former *Economist* art directors. The temporary exhibition is by the photographer Shakespeare Lane, who rescued the leather jacket from a Chelsea skip in 1973. Once again, it is an unexpectedly quirky touch.

But the permanent centrepiece of the reception area is the bust of a stern-looking gentleman, whose real-life gaze must have been difficult to meet if his likeness is anything to go by. This is James Wilson, the man who started it all.

THE HAT-MAKER'S LEGACY

Wilson, the fourth son of no fewer than 15 children, was born in the Scottish border town of Hawick, Roxburghshire in 1805. Although apprenticed as a teenager to a hat-maker, he was precociously interested in economics and spent much of his spare time swotting up on the subject. In 1824 he moved to London and, with the help of his brother and the financial assistance of his father, set up the hat-making business Wilson, Erwin and Wilson.

Despite his grounding in economics and his shrewd business sense, Wilson made one serious error of judgement during his long career. In the late 1830s he speculated heavily in indigo and lost a fortune (the bottom fell out of the indigo market when German factories produced a synthetic version of the natural dye, previously sourced from a subtropical shrub). But rather than being crushed by the experience, he emerged from it toughened and resolute.

Committed to the idea of free trade, Wilson became involved in the battle to abolish the Corn Laws. The laws were complex and various, but their cornerstone was a duty on imported corn, which had been introduced to protect large landowners. Its opponents, mainly manufacturers and merchants, felt it was effectively a subsidy that supported agriculture while hampering industrialization and the development of overseas trade. Sir Robert Peel, the Conservative Prime Minister, repealed the laws in 1846.

Meanwhile, in 1843, Wilson founded *The Economist: The Political, Commercial, Agricultural and Free Trade Journal*. Its purpose, he said, was to stimulate 'every man who has a stake in the country... to investigate and learn for himself about public affairs'. While not an immediate success, the journal quietly established itself and Wilson eventually felt confident enough to withdraw from its day-to-day running to enter politics – although he remained nominal editor until 1857.

Wilson became MP for Westbury in Wiltshire in 1847, but in the 1850s his career took an unexpected turn, when he became first a secretary at the board of control (also known as the India Board), then Financial Secretary to the Treasury, and finally Financial Member of the Council of India. This job took him to Calcutta, where he died on 11 August 1860 of dysentery exacerbated by overwork. To the very end, according to *The Economist*'s own biography of its founder, he was a man of 'sound judgement, clarity of thought and exposition, extraordinary grasp of detail and common sense'.

It has all the ingredients of a Dickens novel: a hat-maker who rises to become a leading businessman, a magazine editor and a politician. More importantly, the story also explains the spirit of *The Economist*, whose advertising often suggests that with knowledge and tenacity, even the humblest worker can rise to great heights. As one memorable poster puts it: 'It's not what you read at university that counts.'

ACCESSIBLE ELITISM

Posters, of course, are the key to *The Economist*'s marketing strategy in its domestic market. The witty captions in white-out-of-red are now as much a part of the London landscape as red buses and post boxes. In a meeting room at The Economist Tower (inevitably, the chairs are upholstered in red leather) brand marketing manager Jacqui Kean explains how this deceptively simple advertising campaign became a legend. With her are Toby Green and Annabelle Watson, respectively account director and account planner at AMV.BBDO, the agency that created the campaign in 1986 and, remarkably, keeps it fresh and relevant today.

First, though, Kean offers a few more insights into the brand's positioning. '*The Economist* is an institution, and if you look at the branding and the product itself, they are very much aligned. All the attributes that are present in the newspaper itself are carried through to the marketing: intellectual rigour, independence, irreverence, and an international outlook.'

A short sketch of *The Economist* would describe it as a weekly international news publication, covering business, politics, finance, science, technology, culture and the arts. Although it is 50 per cent owned by The Financial Times Ltd, and is therefore an associate of Pearson plc, an independent board of trustees must approve the appointment of *The Economist*'s editor, and the constitution of the company is designed to ensure its independence.

You may have noticed that Kean refers to *The Economist* as 'a newspaper', one of the quirks of the brand's positioning. Although in terms of format this is clearly a magazine, it is referred to as a newspaper because, according to Kean, 'it's concerned with news and works very much to a newspaper deadline, with much of the editorial being updated just before going to press each Thursday'. Whether this makes any difference to the readers is a moot point, but it is another example of *The Economist*'s endearing eccentricity.

Yet another is the fact that none of its journalists get bylines – a fact that surprises most career reporters, an egotistical bunch who expect their names to appear with their articles, preferably accompanied by a photograph of themselves. But the journalists at *The Economist* are an anonymous lot, their identities subsumed entirely by the brand. The reader meets them only when they die, and are granted terse, pithy obituaries. My request for an interview with Bill Emmott, the current editor-in-chief, is greeted with a revealing lack of enthusiasm.

Kean explains: 'One of the tenets of *The Economist* is that the editorial line prevails over any private views the journalists might have. The opinions expressed are those of the magazine. The Monday editorial meetings may be like a debating society, with ideas being bandied around and vociferous disagreements – but at the end of the day the editor gets the casting vote about what is going to run and the correct approach to covering it.'

Politically, it would be easy to pigeonhole *The Economist* as a right-wing, conservative publication. (In 2003 it firmly supported the war in Iraq, for example.) But a closer examination reveals that it is anti-monarchy and in favour of legalizing soft drugs. Says Kean: 'The magazine is pro-free market, pro-globalization, and anti-statist. It is liberal on many social issues. The important thing is that it is consistent and that all its views are expertly argued, even if you don't happen to agree with them.'

While this makes *The Economist* sound like a rather inaccessible publication, it is actually a surprisingly palatable read, with its flowing sentence construction and ironic undertone. Perhaps the most fascinating aspect of its marketing efforts is that even as it strives to convince readers that it is witty and approachable, it endeavours to retain its clubby elitism. Kean and her colleagues are by no means fazed when I describe it as 'the perfect primer for sounding clever at dinner parties'.

AMV.BBDO's Annabelle Watson says: 'In fact, that was effectively the insight that started the whole white-out-of-red campaign. In focus groups, people said they liked being spotted on the tube reading *The Economist*. It has a certain cachet, and makes a statement about you. A lot of our ads dramatize the *Economist* reader as being more intelligent than his peers.'

In a rare TV advertisement for *The Economist*, screened in 1995, a young man is seen on a plane just before takeoff. An imposing yet familiar figure ambles up the aisle and settles into the seat beside him. It is Henry Kissinger – hardly the least intelligent person on the planet. As the young man looks discreetly pained, the caption reads: 'Ready for a nice chat?'

SEEING RED

But *The Economist* is best known for its poster advertising, and the saga of one of the most successful campaigns in history is as quirky as the magazine itself. For a start, it is a campaign that, tactically speaking, should not work at all. As Watson points out: 'It was a bold move, using a mass medium to advertise a niche product. But over the years we have discovered that broadcasting a brand's status makes those who have bought into it feel good about themselves – and those who have not want to be a part of it.'

The aim of the advertising now seems relatively simple: to make existing *Economist* readers feel that they are part of a club, and to inform prospective readers that this club is easy to enter. Regardless of their age, wealth, or position, they require just one thing – intelligence.

And yet it took the advertising wizards a surprisingly long time to hit the right note. *The Economist* began working with AMV.BBDO – then called Abbott Mead Vickers – back in 1984. At that point the publication had a UK circulation of around 70,000, and it was felt that this was unlikely to increase. Instead, advertising was needed to keep *The Economist* 'front of mind' with business readers for those vital readership surveys. (The results of these surveys are important for luring advertisers to a magazine.)

As Alfredo Marcantonio, the former vice-chairman of AMV.BBDO, describes in his excellent book *Well-Written and Red* (2002), *The Economist*'s then worldwide advertising director (and now publisher), David Hanger, had been impressed by AMV's work for Sainsbury's. Indeed, the agency's co-founder David Abbott is now widely regarded as one of the best copywriters in advertising history. Abbott's proposition was spot on – he wanted to create an 'aura' around the magazine, suggesting that it was something 'you would be proud to be seen reading on a tube, a train or on an aircraft' while also emphasizing that this elite status could be obtained simply by popping to the newsagents.

Ironically, something about the way his pitch was received gave Abbott the idea that *The Economist* had not been impressed. Distracted by other business, he decided that he did not want to work on the account, after all. But the magazine had other ideas, and found itself in the position – highly unusual for an advertising client – of having to persuade Abbott to take the job. Fortunately, he acquiesced.

Early ads included one with the line: 'Of course *The Economist* isn't elitist. Nearly every company chairman I know seems to read it.' But while the sardonic tone is familiar, the bland black-and-white layout was still many leagues away from the execution that entered advertising history.

That's not to say the early work was bad. One groundbreaking ad emerged from the difficult relationship between AMV's copywriters and *The Economist*'s editor, who insisted on checking (and sometimes changing, or even refusing) every ad. After the agency's diplomatic protests, the editor relented and handed over a copy of *The Economist*'s 'style sheet', a list of journalistic 'do's and don'ts' produced by Johnny Grimond, one of *The Economist*'s senior editors. David Abbott was enthralled by the document, which seemed to capture the magazine's intellectual rigour. He printed a large extract as an advertisement under the line: 'How to write for *The Economist*'. According to Marcantonio's book, the ad caused a major stir, with people ringing up and asking for extra copies to pin on their office walls. They also wanted to refer to the rest of the document, hence the publication of *The Economist Style Guide* in book form.

But while AMV's ads occasionally struck gold, the client felt that they lacked coherence – none of them were instantly recognizable as an *Economist* ad. As Jacqui Kean recounts, rather than irritating David Abbott – whose work for *The Economist* had garnered a number of awards at this point – this criticism provoked the inspiration behind the campaign we know today.

'The story is that David Abbott had the magazine on his desk and that as he stared at the masthead, he realized that if it were blown up, it would be more or less the size of a 48-sheet poster. So why not just take the red and white masthead itself, and turn it into an advertisement? It would be very different, and inextricably linked with the product.'

Marcantonio's book confirms that this was indeed the case. Abbott felt that a simpler execution would be a good way of avoiding all the tedious copy approvals and run-ins with *The Economist*'s journalists. He tells Marcantonio: 'I also thought that it was a good idea that the advertising should feature only words, because that's what I thought was the ethos of *The Economist*.'

Among the batch of ideas that Abbott produced was the ad that became the first in a long-running series: '"I never read *The Economist*". Management trainee. Aged 42.' (Trivia fans may be interested to note that from the very start the slogan was not in exactly the same typeface as the masthead, but an adapted version called Bauer Classic.) The client loved the ad. David Hanger recalls that his reaction when he saw it in situ was, 'We've got it!'

The ad was groundbreaking for a number of reasons. For a start it deployed bright colour, which was unusual for an all-print ad at the time. Additionally, products aimed at a business audience tended to avoid outdoor campaigns because of 'wastage'. In other words, while many potential *Economist* readers would see the ad, there was a danger that it would be lost on 90 per cent of passers-by. In fact this was not the case, as it had the effect of making *The Economist* accessible to a wider audience, generating a feeling of warmth about the brand, and attracting the attention of advertisers who might not have considered the magazine otherwise.

Lastly, the ad broke the mould of traditional media brand advertising by saying absolutely nothing about the issue's contents. Or as AMV.BBDO's Annabelle Watson puts it: '*The Economist* ads talk about what the magazine is, rather than what's inside. Even now, most media brands prefer to run ads describing special issues, competitions or particular articles. Some newspapers are currently trying to get away from that, and turning towards brand-building campaigns, but *The Economist* was the first to do it with any real conviction. The aim was long-term rather than short-term circulation increases.'

'Management Trainee' became the most talked-about ad of the year, and the trade magazine *Campaign* voted it the year's best media poster at its annual awards ceremony.

ONE STEP AHEAD

Although in purely visual terms the campaign seems to have changed very little since that first execution, it has been forced to adapt to survive. Every year in around May and October there are two 'bursts' of posters, roughly seven or eight at a time. This strategy keeps brand awareness extremely high, as it never gets a chance to die down to zero after each spike of advertising, but it also means there is a constant demand for fresh themes and ideas. To aid this process, each phase has had a mission statement, or key proposition, designed to inspire copywriters. And these are always in step with the times.

Jacqui Kean says: 'At the outset the proposition for the campaign was "Gives you the edge in business". The resulting ads reflected the Margaret Thatcher years, when there was an accent in British society on success and status. In today's climate some of the executions seem far too strong – particularly the one that said, "If you're already a reader, get your chauffeur to hoot as you pass this poster." Although it was right for the time, we would not run it now.'

With many ads referring to boardroom battles and financial gain, *The Economist*'s marketing strategy was in danger of seeming out of step with the 'caring 90s', which had dawned with recession, remorse and re-evaluation, as if the country had emerged from a decade-long party. Gordon Gekko, the grasping anti-hero of quintessential 1980s movie *Wall Street*, was no longer the target audience.

'Interestingly, the notion of success has always been at the heart of the campaign, but definitions of success have changed,' points out Kean. 'The next phase of the campaign came in the era when John Major was in power, people were losing their jobs, and the media was accusing the Tory government of sleaze and corruption. So we adopted the rather ironic proposition of "Don't get found out".'

Standout ads from this faintly paranoid period include 'If your assistant reads *The Economist*, don't play too much golf'; 'On the edge of a conversation – one of the loneliest places on earth'; and 'In real life, the tortoise loses'.

When Tony Blair's New Labour swept to power in 1997, *The Economist*'s ads reflected a new feeling of optimism. This was the era of Cool Britannia and Britpop – a sensation that the spirit of the 1960s had returned and that British society might at last become both fun and inclusive. Says Kean: 'The proposition here was "surpass yourself". While we were still targeting a business audience, we also wanted to widen our appeal to attract younger readers. We wanted to be seen as an inspirational read.'

Appropriately, *The Economist*'s ads became increasingly playful – sometimes bordering on the surreal. A new generation of creatives had entered the agency, and they were keen to have a crack at the famous campaign. One ad showed nothing but a white keyhole, intimating that the magazine could provide tantalizing new insights. Another used a bright green background instead of the familiar red, explaining the substitution with the line '*The Economist* is full of surprises'. Perhaps one of the most daring posters in the series twisted a well-known piece of advertising lore. The ad read: 'A poster should contain no more than eight words, which is the maximum the average reader can take in at a single glance. This, however, is a poster for *Economist* readers.'

In society at large, any feeling of playfulness waned with the crash of the dotcom economy, and the rapid slide into recession. Faced with a new era of austerity, AMV.BBDO and *The Economist* were already rethinking their strategy in mid-2001. Then came 11 September, which *The Economist* itself described on its front page as 'The day the world changed'. By the time the aftershock had subsided, *The Economist* had defined its new strategy as 'Stay one step ahead'. Kean explains: 'The idea is that when things are politically and economically uncertain, *The Economist* gives you all the information you need to make sense of events and run your business and your life effectively.'

Despite David Abbot's retirement in 1999, this proposition has ensured that *The Economist*'s ads remain as fresh and relevant as ever. But the creatives needn't stick slavishly to the brief, as Toby Green explains.

'The campaign has been with us for so long that there is an almost intuitive understanding of the brand within the agency. Some of the creatives have worked on it from the very start. Although the propositions are important guidelines, to a certain extent the brand overrides them. Sometimes a line comes out and it just feels like a perfect *Economist* ad. The only important thing we need to remember is that the ads should reflect the zeitgeist. The propositions are a way of monitoring that.'

And there is no shortage of prospective ideas. Usually, a single creative team within an agency handles a client's brief, but *The Economist* campaign is left open for anyone at AMV.BBDO to submit lines. 'There is an incredible amount of competition,' says Green. 'Everyone wants to get a line printed. You even get people who aren't in the creative department submitting ideas. The guys who work in the studio mocking up the ads often have a go – a couple of years back two lines in the campaign came from somebody who worked there.'

The campaign has also utilized unexpected media and unusual locations, from the roof of a red London bus bearing the line 'Hello to all our readers in high office', in 1988, to a pair of posters at Heathrow Airport reading 'Nothing to declare' in green and '*Economist* readers' in red, in 1999.

The selection process is rigorous, with the agency working alongside Kean to whittle down some 200 ideas to 15 or so finalists. The small but important group that makes the final decision comprises Helen Alexander, CEO of The Economist Group, editor-in-chief Bill Emmott, and publisher David Hanger. Kean says: 'When it gets to that stage, not many ads are rejected – it's more that some are preferred to others. The team realizes that the campaign is a precious commodity, so there is no desire to undermine it. They are merely ensuring that the ads show some evolution and are of the kind of quality that readers of *The Economist* have come to expect.'

So what about the future? Is the white-out-of-red campaign in danger of running out of steam? Is it time for something different? The answer seems to be 'no'. Kean says the relationship between *The Economist* and AMV.BBDO is safe, because the agency's deep understanding of the brand is pure gold to a marketing director. And each burst of *Economist* ads remains as witty as the last.

In 2001, an ad appeared that seemed to cap everything AMV.BBDO had been striving for over the previous decade and a half. It was an entirely red poster, with a white jigsaw-shaped piece missing from the lower right-hand corner. No text, no branding, but instantly recognizable as an *Economist* ad. Called 'The Missing Piece', the poster won a slew of awards at advertising competitions like Cannes, Eurobest and Epica. Its creator was none other than Matthew Abbott, the son of David Abbott. The next generation of *Economist* ads was under way.

A COLOURFUL FUTURE

Although the white-out-of-red campaign has been a superlative marketing tool, enviously spoofed by brands ranging from budget airline easyJet to tour operator Club 18–30, it is not *The Economist*'s only promotional weapon. The style of the ads has been carried over to direct marketing, an efficient way of generating and retaining subscriptions. One can detect a familiar tone in examples like 'Extra focus for the far-sighted', which was printed in tiny type on a red envelope, 'It's time to renegotiate your contract', and 'Covers the world every week'. Unlike its 'broadcast' outdoor campaign, *The Economist*'s direct marketing is heavy on detail and designed to encourage a response. Yet it remains true to the central brand proposition articulated by the posters.

That is also the case for point of sale material. Boxes of *Economist* magazines recently placed near cashiers' tills bore the legend 'Counter intelligence'. Branded merchandise has included an all-red disposable camera with the slogan 'For big cheeses', and a red box of matches sporting the word 'Illuminating'. Another innovation, with Virgin Airways, was an eye mask containing the words 'Don't stay in the dark for long.'

A somewhat more sophisticated form of promotion comes in the form of conferences and debates hosted by *Economist* journalists. They cover topical geo-political and business issues (one recent programme featured a debate on the usefulness or otherwise of the UN) and are designed to introduce the brand to new and different audiences.

The advertising has also helped *The Economist* extend its brand into other areas – its branded shop on London's Regent Street sells a number of business books and diaries carrying the familiar logo. Furthermore, *The Economist* has a successful Web site, Economist.com, funded by subscriptions as well as advertising revenue. A separate business, The Economist Intelligence Unit, provides business and industry with detailed reports and analyses of the economic status of countries in every corner of the globe.

Content and quality are also inextricably linked with marketing, and the product itself has moved with the times. In May 2001 *The Economist* appeared in full colour for the first time, with a redesigned format. The magazine became easier to navigate, the typography was sharpened, and colour photographs and tints gave it a contemporary look.

The revamp was felt to be particularly necessary for readers outside the United Kingdom, as *The Economist* is now undoubtedly an international publication. Its worldwide circulation grew by 79.4 per cent between 1992 and 2003, and 83 per cent of its sales are now outside the UK. This becomes even more impressive when you consider that since the campaign began in 1986, we have seen the rise of satellite and cable TV, digital radio, and the Internet.

Kean says: 'The success we have had in Europe is very gratifying as we don't do local language editions, but our research clearly shows that we are being read by locals, not just expatriates. I believe it's because we offer an overview, rather than just a purely French, German, Italian or indeed English notion of events. Plus, we offer a different perspective from the American newsweeklies *Time* and *Newsweek*.'

The Economist estimates that it has a potential readership of 1.7 million in continental Europe, and as the circulation there currently stands at 187,017, there is clearly huge growth potential. Marketing outside the UK tends to be a little different, as the white-out-of-red campaign only works in the mature UK market, where the target audience understands English wordplay. Kean says: 'At the same time, we don't want to sacrifice our principles and do a boring campaign. So we have gone down a visual route that uses the red and maintains the same level of wit and intelligence.'

For example, one recent poster wittily explained to European readers that *The Economist* is about much more than economics. A single image of an apple was shown alongside the names Sir Isaac Newton (who of course discovered gravity thanks to a falling apple); Rudy Giuliani (the former mayor of New York City, otherwise known as The Big Apple); and Steve Jobs (the founder of computer company Apple). These famous figures encapsulate the themes of science, politics, and technology. And of course, there was the implication that only potential *Economist* readers would get the joke.

Jacqui Kean says: 'The quality, wit, and depth of analysis provided by *The Economist* appeal to readers all over the world, no matter what other media are available.'

PROOF IN THE NUMBERS

Nearly 15 years after its launch, *The Economist* regards the white-out-of-red campaign as a superbly successful marketing tool. It targets not only readers, but also the agencies and advertisers who buy space in the magazine (which has never offered deals or discounted its rate-card). Kean points out that advertising revenue rose by 250 per cent between 1988 and 2000, and UK circulation grew from 94,916 in 1990 to 146,754 in 2003 (ABC). All this for a magazine whose circulation was originally said to have peaked at 70,000 in 1984, remember.

And according to independent econometric and tracking research, *The Economist*'s advertising has been spontaneously recalled by more than 40 per cent of its target audience for almost the whole of the period of the campaign. It has contributed to 2.4 per cent of newsstand sales and 5.7 per cent of subscription sales. Not only that, but the campaign is comparatively cheap, costing just over £1 million a year. This represents a return on investment of 1:1.8. Not bad for a two-colour poster with a nice line in puns.

The brand in brief

Media brand: The Economist

Founded: 1843

Owner: The Financial Times Ltd (50 per cent), The Economist Group (United Kingdom)

Circulation: 902,107 (Source: ABC)

Key marketing strategies: Outdoor advertising, direct mail, point-of-sale

Brand extensions: Sponsored conferences and debates, The Economist Intelligence Unit, *The Economist* shop, books and diaries

Web site: Economist.com

18

Vogue

'A universe of dreams'

I am sitting in the canteen at Condé Nast's headquarters in Times Square. This being Condé Nast, the publisher of *Vogue* (and *GQ*, *Vanity Fair*, *Glamour* and other glossy confections) it is no ordinary canteen. Über hip architect Frank Gehry designed the interior, which looks rather like his Guggenheim Museum in Bilbao, only turned inside out. The walls are of undulating titanium. The semi-circular banquettes are upholstered in what appears to be marmalade-coloured leather, divided by Venetian glass screens. Some staffers refer to the canteen as 'the catwalk', because it enables them to check out what everyone is wearing. Yes, Condé Nast is exactly the kind of place you might imagine.

I shouldn't really be here at all. A friend who works here has smuggled me in, so I can have a peek. It's a rather voyeuristic thrill.

By all accounts Condé Nast is a tough and demanding place to work. Even my friend talks about the place with a sort of affectionate exasperation.

Yet it is hard not to be impressed. The place reeks of influence. Trends are created and destroyed, right here. The people who work in this building may take themselves seriously, but why not? Luxury is a serious business. Fashion is a multi-billion dollar global concern. Just ask Donatella Versace, or Miuccia Prada, or François Pinault, the owner of Gucci, or his great rival Bernard Arnault of LVMH (Louis-Vuitton Moët Hennessy).

Fashion is another planet, a higher plane that mere mortals can only access through the pages of glossy magazines. *Vogue* has served exactly that purpose since 1892. The magazine has survived two world wars, the Wall Street Crash and numerous smaller recessions (not to mention fashion aberrations like flower power, disco and punk) with barely a chip in its nail varnish. Like all the best media brands, it is not so much a paper product as an icon, a symbol representing a particular lifestyle.

But an office block in New York can only tell me so much about all that. And so it is on the other side of the Atlantic, in Condé Nast's less ostentatious Paris offices (but with a stunning view of the Eiffel Tower – trust the French to get it right without trying) that I get my first real insight into the *Vogue* brand. A dapper individual by the suitably voguish name of Didier Suberbielle, the chief executive of Condé Nast France, says: '*Vogue* was built in the three great cultural capitals of the world: New York, London and Paris. Its readers would be hard-pressed to tell you in which one of these it began, so therefore it has a sense of internationalism. This gives it mystery. In terms of contents, it combines art, fashion, luxury, and sex – an explosive cocktail.'

But Suberbielle's next phrase sums up the brand best. '*Vogue* is a universe of dreams.'

THE BOY FROM ST. LOUIS

It should come as no surprise to learn that *Vogue* was started by a bunch of social climbers. Condé Nast admitted it himself, as recounted in Carole Seebohm's (1982) definitive biography, *The Man Who Was Vogue*. 'Here I was, just a boy from St. Louis, and Edna Chase [the editor of *Vogue*] a Quaker from New Jersey,' says Nast. 'Between us, we set the standards of the time. We showed America the meaning of style.'

But although Nast turned *Vogue* into the media monolith it remains today, he was not its founder. In fact, the magazine was created in 1892 to serve as an example to another group of social climbers – America's new rich. With steel and railway money knocking on the door of traditional 'society', two wealthy men about town realized there was a market for a magazine that codified the art of stylish living. Arthur B Turnure and Harry W McVickar released the first issue of *Vogue* on 17 December 1892, as a weekly magazine costing 10 cents. Its supporters were the aristocracy of the United States: the Astors, the Vanderbilts, the Jays and a handful of others.

But *Vogue* was never really a serious commercial proposition, and Turnure and McVickar were not real publishers. After a few years, McVickar lost interest in the project, and Turnure died suddenly at the age of 49. By that stage, the magazine had few readers and hardly any advertisers. It might well have disappeared forever, had it not attracted the attention of a young entrepreneur called Condé Nast. (He was named after Dr Auguste Condé, one of St. Louis's first physicians and his great-great-grandfather.)

Nast was an advertising sales whiz who had worked at an art and literary weekly called *Collier's* – run by his old school chum Robert Collier. Nast was blessed with dual gifts for promotional copywriting and number crunching: while telling advertisers what a chic, influential group of readers they would be reaching, he would pull out with a flourish a sworn audit of circulation figures. Although it seems obvious today, Nast was one of the first media marketing men to discern that advertisers did not require vast numbers of readers – they just wanted the 'right' readers, and solid proof that these existed.

Seebohm writes: 'He was claiming exclusivity, affordable luxury, and the highest quality. These three elements were to be the foundation stones of the marketing strategy for his own magazines.'

With Nast's help, the circulation of *Collier's* rose from 20,000 in 1897 to 568,000 ten years later – and its advertising income from US$5,600 to almost US$1 million. Having achieved that miracle, and despite Robert Collier's pleas that he stay on, Nast was ready for greater things. And so in 1909 he bought *Vogue*.

TEMPLATE FOR AN EDITOR

Nast took the controversial decision of installing Edna Chase as editor. Described by Seebohm as a 'small birdlike woman with prematurely grey hair', she had no formal journalistic training. But she was tough and stylish, and had worked at the magazine since its inception, when she had become editorial assistant at the age of 18.

In terms of her tastes and behaviour, Chase set the benchmark for *Vogue* editors to come. Seebohm writes: 'Mrs Chase made great demands on her staff. They had to wear black silk stockings, white gloves, and hats – and never, never open-toed shoes.'

There are other stories. Seebohm claims that Chase once said to a journalist: 'You have a very fine pen, my child, but we must do something about your clothes.' And to another, who had tried to commit suicide during a fit of depression: 'We at *Vogue* don't throw ourselves under subway trains, my dear. If we must, we take sleeping pills.'

Like Nast himself, Edna Chase came from a relatively humble background. Although less forthcoming about it than her publisher, she was equally aware of her precarious social status. This insecurity translated into an acid wit, an obsession with social graces, and an instinctive grasp of the importance of good taste. For both Nast and Chase, *Vogue* was an entrée to a section of society from which they would normally have been excluded.

Whatever it was, it worked. *Vogue* was transformed from a 'society' magazine into a style bible. The crucial difference was that, instead of reading like a who's who of the richest people in New York, the magazine depicted the clothes they might wear, the places they might visit, and the goods they might consume. As well as pleasing its direct target market, it appealed to those who aspired to such a life. *Vogue* – the universe of dreams.

Circulation grew steadily, and so did advertising revenue. Nast told his clients: '*Vogue* is the elimination of waste circulation for the advertiser of quality goods. [I can] lift out of the millions of Americans just the 100,000 cultivated people who can buy these quality goods.'

Vogue cruised through and indeed benefited from the First World War, which strengthened cultural and political ties between New York and Paris, the fashion Mecca. The need to economize eliminated the frills and lace of the early 1900s, and gave women the sleek and pared-down silhouette of the 1920s – a golden age for fashion and, of course, for *Vogue*.

CONDÉ DESCENDS

The Roaring Twenties began with expansion. With Paris occupying such an important position in the world of fashion, Nast realized that *Vogue* needed to launch a French edition – more to maintain its credibility than for any other reason. In 1920 he went into partnership with Lucien Vogel, the publisher of a fashion magazine called *La Gazette du Bon Ton*, to launch French *Vogue*. The magazine remained unprofitable for years, but Nast kept it going as a loss leader, conscious of its prestige.

Then, as now, French *Vogue* was occasionally embroiled in power struggles with the great fashion houses, most of which were on its doorstep. Designers would chastise editor Michel de Brunhoff for not writing about them when they bought advertising pages, or for running stories about rivals who did not support the magazine financially.

Didier Suberbielle, of today's Condé Nast France, makes it clear that the modern *Vogue* is not for sale, even to the richest and most influential designers. 'Obviously we like to support those who support us, but you can't "buy" this magazine. Those who ask don't necessarily get – quite the opposite, in fact.'

Suberbielle says the magazine got involved in such a debate with an advertiser three years ago, with the result that it has not carried their advertising since. 'No single fashion brand makes up more than 10 per cent of our revenue, and we can afford to lose 10 per cent. On the other hand, we often carry editorial about up-and-coming designers who can't afford to advertise.'

With French *Vogue* established, Nast's little empire was growing nicely – even if it wasn't adding to the bottom line. *Vogue*'s British edition (nicknamed 'Brogue') had been going since 1916, and although it did unexpectedly well during the First World War, it flagged throughout the 1920s and did not come into its own until the 1930s. An early attempt at a German *Vogue* fared even less well – launched in 1928, it was closed the following year.

But the 1920s were still a boom time for *Vogue*, and they defined the future positioning of the magazine. It was during this period that the title stopped using well-known women from high society as models, and began recruiting 'normal' girls for their faces and figures, thus creating the modelling industry. The three editions of *Vogue* employed legendary photographers like Edward Steichen, George Hoyningen-Huené and Cecil Beaton. Fashion had become an obsession for the newly liberated American woman, and as the advertising bucks rolled in, Condé Nast held increasingly extravagant parties at his huge Park Avenue apartment. This was America at its exuberant best.

Condé Nast Publications went public in March 1927, and that year its share price rose from US$32 to US$53. It continued to rise over the next two years, reaching a peak of US$93 in October 1929. When the stock market collapsed on 29 October, it plummeted to US$4.50. Condé Nast was ruined in the space of a day.

As Nast no longer held control of his stock, his company ended up in the hands of a shadowy group of financiers. He spent the next few years trying to get it back. In the meantime, he continued to run *Vogue*, and to live the debonair lifestyle that he had before the Crash. As Seebohm's book points out: 'One of the themes he had always stressed to his creditors was that his magazines stood for something more than the trivialities of momentary fame or fashion: that the name *Vogue* was synonymous with quality and style…'.

In the end, the British bailed him out. Ironically, the London and Paris editions of *Vogue* – which up to that point had been the poor cousins – began to make a slight profit during the mid-1930s. The success of the British edition under such adverse conditions attracted the attention of Lord Camrose – a friend of Nast and the owner of *The Daily Telegraph*. The pair came to a discreet arrangement in which Camrose provided Nast with the means to buy back the majority of his company from the moneymen, in return for a controlling stake. Although this did not allow Nast to regain control of his empire, it kept him in the game.

The British edition of *Vogue* continued to do well during the Second World War, but the French version was closed down for the duration of the conflict. The Nazis had offered editor Michel de Brunhoff the chance to continue publishing *Vogue* during the Occupation – if he provided a family history of all the staff with whom he intended to work. He refused, and the title did not appear again until after the liberation, with de Brunhoff back in the editor's chair.

Condé Nast died on 19 September 1942. His legacy was an ideal of class and sophistication that he had practically spun out of thin air. *Vogue* now had a life of its own.

REFASHIONING *VOGUE*

When Condé Nast Publications came up for sale in 1959, following the death of Lord Camrose, American newspaper mogul Sam Newhouse took a controlling stake. Newhouse had started out as an assistant at a small but battered New Jersey weekly called the *Bayonne Times*, which he later acquired and turned into a thriving business. On this foundation he built a mini-empire of local newspapers. Legend has it that he bought Condé Nast as a birthday present for his wife, Mitzi – but that may just be one of those delicious myths that swirl around the company. Whatever his motivations, Newhouse eventually bought all the stock and turned it back into a privately held concern.

By that stage *Vogue* was under the editorial direction of the brilliant Alexander Liberman, who had joined the art department back in 1941. Born in Kiev in 1912, he had been forced to run twice: first to Europe with his mother in the wake of the Russian revolution, and then to New York to escape occupied Paris. He was introduced to Condé Nast himself, who was impressed by Liberman's experience on the French newsmagazine *Vu* and a prize he had won for magazine design.

Above all, Liberman wanted *Vogue* to be a work of art – a notion that is less pretentious than it sounds, as he was a genuine artist; his paintings and sculptures can be seen in museums around the world. With Liberman at the helm *Vogue* became more than ever a trendsetter rather than a follower. His theory was that fashion should be something personal and creative, rather than slavishly imitative. He used cutting-edge photographers like Irving Penn, William Klein and Helmut Newton, and combined fashion spreads with art by the likes of Jackson Pollock. Even when he moved up in 1962 to become editorial director of all Condé Nast magazines, to a certain extent Alexander Liberman 'was' *Vogue*. (He retired in 1994 and died in 1999.)

Vogue's editors have always been exotic creatures. The 1960s was the era of Diana Vreeland, who had previously been the fashion editor at *Harper's Bazaar*. Vreeland's *Vogue* was free-spirited and revolutionary, the magazine of the jet set rather than high society. She is said to have invented the term 'beautiful people'. Grace Mirabella was brought in when Vreeland's tenure was inelegantly ended in 1971. Mirabella made the magazine more democratic but no less stylish, staying on until 1988, when it was her turn to be deposed – leaving the way clear for current editor Anna Wintour.

These days Wintour is almost a brand in her own right, awed and envied in equal measure. British *Vogue*'s Web site (Vogue.co.uk) describes her thus: 'With her razor sharp bob, slim build and sunglasses – which she reportedly wears to shield her eyes from the fashion shows' flashbulbs – Anna Wintour is the fashion industry's ultimate icon.' The profile adds: 'Like her image, Wintour's daily regime is legendary… She wakes up at 5.45 am every morning, to go to play tennis, before being professionally made up, coiffed and chauffeured to the offices of American *Vogue*.'

This again is *Vogue* as dream factory, offering us glimpses of lives we couldn't possibly hope to emulate (unless of course we happen to be Wintour's tennis instructor).

S I 'Si' Newhouse Jr now runs Condé Nast Publications, having taken over after the death of his father in 1979. Over the past 20 years he has consolidated the company's position as the world's most glamorous publishing house – with *Vogue* as its flagship publication.

GLOBAL GLAMOUR

The *Vogue* brand has expanded a little since Condé Nast's day. There are now 15 editions around the world (with a Chinese version on the starting blocks at the time of going to press). But those in the know say that only four are truly influential: the editions in the United States, Italy, France and the United Kingdom. These have a wide circulation within the international fashion trade. Editions in new markets such as Australia, Brazil, Greece, Korea, Portugal, Poland and South Africa are run as franchises and don't have the same prestige.

Stephen Quinn, the publishing director of British *Vogue*, comments: 'Condé Nast International monitors all editions outside the US to ensure quality control. The European editions are 100 per cent owned and quality standards are already well entrenched. We protect our status and our heritage by paying attention to detail.'

Quinn says that the brand identity of *Vogue* is more or less set in stone worldwide: 'Fashion, beautiful models, stunning photography, upmarket advertisements, and an air of easy luxury. The magazine is positioned to look expensive and stylish… to command admiration and regard.'

The British and American editions of *Vogue* are more mass market than the French and the Italian versions – largely because of the disproportionate importance of Paris and Milan in the fashion arena. The French *Vogue* is perhaps the most decadently luxurious of them all, especially since the appointment of Fabien Baron as artistic director at the end of 2003. Before Baron's arrival there were signs that the magazine was unsure of its future direction, having already been revamped in April 2002 by hip graphic design team M/M (Mathias Augustyniak and Michael Amzalag). M/M's vision for the magazine was quirky and cutting edge, with typefaces that ranged from spidery neo-Gothic to bold schoolbook style. But fashion is an ephemeral business, and *Vogue* soon decided that a more classical approach was preferable. Under Baron (who made his name at *Harper's Bazaar* in New York), the magazine has regained its sheen of Parisian elegance.

Says Suberbielle: 'Paris is still the fashion capital of the world. Many of the greatest designers are here, and our annual shows are the most important. There was a time when we began to lose our edge, but over the last 10 years we have regained our central position, which has been reinforced by media coverage of the competition between [the luxury brand empires] of Monsieur Pinault and Monsieur Arnault. That prominence has made *Vogue* even more influential.'

Vogue Paris (as it is known) has a suitably fabulous editor in Carine Roitfeld, who is instantly recognizable from the fringe of hair that veils most of her face. In the French advertising trade journal *Stratégies* (20 November 2003), Roitfeld muses: 'If [*Vogue* has] managed to stay contemporary, it's partly due to our name, a word as French as it is English, which is difficult to define but which sums us up perfectly.'

While *Vogue* has survived numerous incarnations, its international masthead (in extravagant Bodoni, for typeface fans) has remained virtually unchanged. In all other respects, Roitfeld suggests, *Vogue* stands still at its peril. 'We've always known how to challenge ourselves so that we don't become an institution. [We must] stay at the avant-garde, within a hair's breadth of indecency but always chic.'

But how trendy is *Vogue*, in fact? The shoppers buying Dior and Versace in the fashion emporia on the rue du Faubourg St. Honoré – where Condé Nast France is based – look old enough to be my parents. And the issue of *Vogue* that appears on the day I interview Didier Suberbielle features Catherine Deneuve on the cover.

Suberbielle sounds a little offended by the suggestion that *Vogue* might be read by wrinklies. 'Half of our readers are under 35, and a third are under 25,' he insists. 'Although the clothes we feature are not accessible to everyone, many young people shop at department stores, which allow them to pay in instalments. Others read the magazine to daydream, or to seek inspiration, or to devise ways of recreating a certain look. After all, what is in *Vogue* is in fashion.'

With a circulation of around 110,000, *Vogue* Paris has a fraction of the sales of its American big sister, which sells over a million copies a month. But it is still the biggest seller in France's crowded fashion market. Indeed, Condé Nast says that *Vogue* has managed to retain the top slot in most of its territories (although in a characteristically blasé fashion, it was unable to provide a figure for worldwide circulation).

'It depends on how you look at the market,' observes Suberbielle. 'As an international magazine brand, *Vogue* has four global competitors: *Marie-Claire*, *Elle*, *Cosmopolitan* and *Glamour* [which is also owned by Condé Nast]. But the other titles are very different to *Vogue*, in that they cover lifestyle, health, entertainment, travel, and so on. *Vogue* is the only pure fashion magazine. That is all we are interested in. And in that respect we are the leader in our category, worldwide, by a comfortable margin.'

A BRAND THAT SELLS ITSELF

If 'old' is a dirty word at *Vogue*, 'marketing' is apparently almost as distasteful. In Britain, Stephen Quinn's response to my query about brand extensions is unequivocal: 'Condé Nast does not encourage brand extensions... they are likely to cheapen the image and take away the mystery.'

Didier Suberbielle is more philosophical. 'Although our logo is highly recognizable, we don't do a lot of branded products. The only reason we are tempted to do them is to protect the brand, because we know that if we don't, others will do it for us.'

A quick look on the French *Vogue* Web site (*Vogue*paris.com) reveals an online boutique where visitors can buy a *Vogue*-branded bag, headscarf, t-shirt, towelling robe, manicure kit, makeup mirror and watch (the latter a snip at only €30).

And then of course there are the spin-off magazines: *Vogue Hommes International* in France, *Teen Vogue* in the United States, even *Vogue Business* in Germany. Italy has no fewer than five *Vogue* spin-off titles, from *Vogue Bambini* (kids) to *Vogue Sposa* (weddings), while Spain has six *Vogue*-branded magazines. Australians can buy *Vogue Living* and *Vogue Entertainment & Travel*. In Brazil there is an interiors magazine, *Casa Vogue*. (There are other examples around the world, too.) If these aren't brand extensions, I certainly don't know how else to describe them.

Back in France, Suberbielle says the magazine avoids 'mass advertising'. 'We tend to use the magazine itself as an advertising tool, by placing it prominently at the point of sale. We do some kiosk and poster advertising, but generally we believe the product should convey the image we want to project.'

Quite reasonably, he says that he would prefer to spend the money other magazines set aside for advertising on hiring the best editorial staff. 'Our reputation rests on our ability to continue producing a great magazine each month.'

And producing *Vogue* is a costly business. Unlike the franchise editions, which frequently borrow and recycle material, the Big Four develop their own exclusive content. This means that the *Vogue* offices in New York, London, Paris and Milan must have access to the best photographers, the most beautiful models, and the sharpest writers.

'It is only due to the power of the *Vogue* brand that we can afford the best,' says Suberbielle. 'The magazine is self-perpetuating – because it looks beautiful, the best people want to work with us. We don't pay famous photographers the rates they charge for advertising campaigns – we can't, otherwise each issue of *Vogue* would cost hundreds of euros. We can only pay their expenses. But they want to work for us because it's a showcase for them.'

Suberbielle says the strategy of keeping marketing to the minimum in order to preserve a product's mystique is nothing new – it is often used in the luxury sector. 'That's how we see the magazine, in a way. It is a very refined and elegant product.'

The brand in brief

Media brand: Vogue

Founded: 1892

Owner: Condé Nast Publications

Circulation: 1,174,677 in USA (Source: ABC); worldwide not supplied

Key marketing strategies: Point of sale, posters

Brand extensions: Branded accessories, spin-off magazines, books

Web site: Vogue.com (plus country-specific sites)

PART 4

THE INFORMATION
PROVIDERS

19

Reuters

*'People are almost unconsciously impressed by a brand
that has stood the test of time'*

If *The Matrix* really existed, Times Square in New York would be at its heart. The place is a multiple pile-up of media: billboards, giant video screens, rolling electronic news banners, neon signs, lurid shop-fronts, and touts with flyers. It is one of the global epicentres of information dissemination – located in and around this chaotic triangle are the headquarters of *The New York Times*, Condé Nast, and Viacom, to name but three. Whether you get your communication rush from TV, magazines, newspapers, the Internet, or 24-hour news services, you can plug yourself in right here. On this torrid afternoon in June, with big silver raindrops tumbling slowly between the skyscrapers, and the streets thick with black umbrellas, it is as though science fiction has already happened.

Even in this sense-scrambling environment, Reuters has managed to make its mark. Its US base at number 3 Times Square sports the tallest electronic sign in the world. You can see it from the middle of Central Park, way uptown. It is made up of a number of synchronized panels, so the news bulletins whoosh down the side of the building and cascade into the lobby. When a major story breaks, people gather around outside, staring up at the electronic oracle.

Compared to the pandemonium on the streets, the lobby is eerily calm. A security guard sees you to the elevator, and you ride smoothly up to the international marketing department. You feel as though you are at the centre of a vast web that stretches out across the world, its glittering strands designed to trap and transmit nuggets of intelligence to newspapers, TV stations, financial traders, and the public. Everything seems taut, efficient and ultramodern.

It's hard to believe that the whole thing began with carrier pigeons.

THE MAN BEHIND THE BRAND

Ironically, Reuter was not his original surname. Paul Julius Reuter was born in Cassel, Germany, on 21 July 1816, under the name Israel Beer Josephat. He changed it in 1845 after converting to Christianity, and just prior to marrying an English woman at St George's Lutheran chapel in London. (German novelist Fritz Reuter may have inspired his new identity.)

Although it was some time before he was able to put his theories into practice, Reuter had become interested in the possibilities of transmitting information at an early age. When he was 13, and working as a clerk at his uncle's bank in Gottingen, he made the acquaintance of mathematician and physicist Carl Freidrich Gauss, who was experimenting with an early version of telegraph.

Reuter was also something of a journalist. In 1847 he became a partner in a small publishing concern in Berlin called Reuter & Stargardt. But after publishing a number of political pamphlets that aroused the hostility of the authorities, he was forced to flee to Paris, a city that had always welcomed revolutionaries. Working as a translator for the news agency Havas, he extracted articles from French newspapers and sent them to newspapers in Germany.

By now news was regularly being transmitted by telegraph, but there were gaps in the network, notably betweens the ends of the German and Franco-Belgian lines at Aachen and Brussels. Reuter got permission to set up a carrier pigeon service to bridge the gap. Although this seems primitive, Reuter was a great believer in getting the news out as quickly as possible, and pigeons were four times faster than the train.

When the Aachen to Brussels telegraph link was completed, effectively ending his business, Reuter tried to set up his own news agency in Paris – but he found French government regulations too restrictive and moved to London. The first undersea telegraph cable had recently been laid between Dover and Calais, and Reuter used it to transmit share prices and other intelligence to business contacts on the continent. The maxim 'follow the cable' would drive the expansion of his business for years to come.

At first his service was limited to the transmission of private commercial telegrams to places not connected to the telegraph system. Reuter appointed agents at the telegraph termini, who would then forward the messages to their recipients by rail or carrier pigeon. At the same time, he tried to sell news items dug up by his agents to the English newspapers. The service was greeted with little enthusiasm until 1858, when an exclusive report of an important speech by Napoleon III, provided by Reuter's Paris agent, appeared in *The Times*. The agency had its first scoop.

Reuter's network now began to expand apace. He got permission to base reporters at the headquarters of the Austrian and French armies, and obtained a cable concession between Cork in Ireland and the English coast at Crookhaven, which enabled him to circulate news of the American civil war hours before the mail boat could reach Liverpool. Reuters Telegram Company was registered as a public limited company in 1865. In April that year, in its greatest marketing and promotional coup up to that point, Reuter's service broke the news of the assassination of Abraham Lincoln. Reuter had arranged to row out to the mail boat before it reached the coast of Ireland, in order to intercept the news and telegraph it to London.

Also in 1865, the first Reuters office outside Europe opened – in Alexandria, Egypt. Worldwide expansion continued throughout the 1870s. In 1871 Reuter was granted a baronetcy, but with his health failing, he retired to a villa in Nice a few years later. His son Herbert succeeded him at the head of the agency. Baron de Reuter died in Nice in 1899.

FAMOUS FOR FACTS AND FIGURES

The modern world began with the end of the First World War, and Reuters, typically, was first with the news of the Armistice.

Proudly bearing the name of its founder, the pioneering agency continued to establish itself as the leading brand in the field of information provision. Although it had been using printers to send news electronically to newsrooms since 1888, in 1927 it introduced the much faster teleprinter, which was to remain a vital resource for newspaper editors until the birth of the computer decades later.

At the same time, Reuters was also developing its financial information arm. In 1923 it became the first agency to use radio to deliver financial news, sending quotations and exchange rates by Morse code to Europe.

During both world wars, Reuters came under pressure to serve British opinion and interests. In 1941 it deflected this pressure by restructuring itself as a private company owned by the national and provincial press (later joined by the Australian and New Zealand press associations). The new owners formed the Reuters Trust to safeguard the organisation's independence and neutrality. The principles of the Trust were maintained and the power to enforce them strengthened when Reuters became a public company in 1984.

The agency's commitment to using new technology was maintained throughout the late 20th century. Reuters journalists began using VDUs instead of typewriters as early as 1971. The agency also pioneered the use of computers to transmit financial data, with the launch of Stockmaster in 1964. This quickly evolved into Videomaster, a screen-based display of stock and commodity prices. And in 1973 the financial markets were revolutionized with the launch of Reuter Monitor Money Rates Services, an electronic foreign exchange market. This technology eventually led many countries to abandon fixed exchange rates. By the 1980s it had evolved into a service enabling brokers to trade directly on their screens.

The 1980s and early 90s were periods of expansion and acquisition, with Reuters snapping up Instinet, the world's largest electronic brokerage firm, in 1986, and acquiring TV news agency Visnews in 1992, renaming it Reuters Television. It launched its Reuters Television Financial Service – giving traders live news on their screens – in 1994. In 1995, foreseeing the dotcom boom, Reuters established its Greenhouse Fund to take minority stakes in start-up technology companies – a move that would later provide as many financial headaches as it did profits.

From 2000 onwards, Reuters strived to make the most of the rise of the Internet, launching a range of initiatives designed to transfer its core business on to the Web. In October 2001 it completed the largest acquisition in its history, buying most of the assets of Bridge Information

Systems, and in March 2003 it snapped up global financial information provider Multex.com.

Today, through a bewildering range of electronic tools, Reuters supplies real-time quotes on equities, bonds and derivates from 244 exchanges and markets. The agency provides historical information on over 40,000 companies. And an average of 30,000 headlines and 8 million words by Reuters journalists are published in 26 languages every day. Through Reuters.com, the agency claims to be the most widely read source on the Internet, with up to 10 million unique users a month, and it can even reach subscribers on their palmtop computers.

THE VALUE OF CONFIDENCE

One of the people responsible for Reuters' global brand image is chief marketing officer Alexander Hungate (a good, strong surname), and his office is perched high above Times Square. Hungate believes that no matter what other kind of marketing a media brand does, it should develop a dialogue with its customers.

'I am here to ensure the voice of the customer is heard within the organization,' he explains. 'We measure very carefully the customers' perception of Reuters, so that we can confront the organization with their opinions about the improvements we need to make in order to stay ahead. Being quantitative about the views of the customer is one of the best ways of protecting your brand.'

It is no coincidence that, alongside his marketing role, Hungate is responsible for managing the company's relationships with its biggest financial services clients worldwide. 'There are various definitions of marketing, but this is one we truly value – the ability to respond in real time to the most demanding of our customers. The likes of Citigroup, Deutsche Bank and HSBC, among others, are driving financial services, and listening to them gives us a powerful insight into the direction we should be moving in.'

While Hungate can help Reuters tailor its services to suit its customers, he believes it is more important to be proactive – to antici-pate their next move. 'We try to understand their business strategies, to determine where they want to be in a few years. That gives us a much longer lead-time for innovation. Rather than asking them to comment on our existing services, we prefer to work in partnership with them on new projects, so we arrive at the same place, technologically speaking, at the same time.'

Hungate points out that this policy connects back to Paul Julius Reuter's original strategy – which was to use technology to give customers what they wanted, before they even realized they needed it. Indeed, all of Reuter's original precepts continue to drive the brand today. Take speed, for example.

'The swift delivery of information was the reason for the company's existence,' points out Hungate. 'And today, when you look at the customer satisfaction data that I was just describing to you, our financial services customers perceive us as being by far the fastest information service – and they are the customers who are the most sensitive to that characteristic. To them, the time it takes to receive a piece of intelligence can mean millions of dollars one way or the other.'

Accuracy also remains at the heart of the Reuters brand. 'We are fiercely proud of our long-held reputation for providing accurate information. In China, the word Reuters is a slang expression for "truth". For years, the BBC would require a second source for any piece of information it broadcast, unless that information came from Reuters. And we know that many intelligence agencies around the world subscribe to Reuters, because they trust it to be accurate. Once again, this is a hugely important attribute, not just for our news customers but for those in financial services too.'

As with so many media brands, Reuters depends on its customers' confidence in the information they receive. Hungate says: 'If there is one emotion we want to stand for, it is "confidence". Whether you are a financial trader, or a member of the public trying to decide whether it is safe to go to a foreign trouble spot, you should feel that you can turn to Reuters with total confidence that you will get the right information. Reuters should enable you to make a decision based on undisputed fact.'

(David Ure, a former Reuters journalist and now one of its most respected executives, tells an anecdote that many of the company's employees are fond of repeating. As a small boy, he once pointed to the word 'Reuters' beside a story in his father's newspaper, and asked what it meant. His father replied: 'It means it's true.')

Lack of bias is another customer perception that Hungate is keen to stress. 'As well as our written news service, we have the biggest photo news service in the world. On certain days, the same Reuters photograph appears on the front cover of every newspaper you pick up. And you will often see an American newspaper and an Arabic newspaper carrying the same shot. Perhaps more than any other medium, we are seen as neutral, independent, and not associated with any nationality or government. Every newspaper has a target readership with a particular political viewpoint. But we supply media on the left and right ends of the spectrum, and everything in between. That is unique.'

These three brand attributes – speed, accuracy, and freedom from bias – run through every aspect of the business, says Hungate. 'We have a consistent view of who we are and what the brand stands for. Everyone in the company understands these values, whether it is the engineer who has been sent to install a screen, the sales person calling on a newspaper, or the person who picks up the phone on our help desk. We want our customers to share our understanding of the brand's identity.'

NEWS AS MARKETING TOOL

Even accounting for the recent job cuts, Reuters employs some 2,200 full-time journalists around the world. Its media clients can subscribe to its entire service – which provides a constantly rolling stream of words, pictures and video images – or take packages tailored to their needs. Made-to-measure online services are available to clients that want to add Reuters' news bulletins to their Web sites. Investment in editorial training and technology is 'immense', according to Hungate. 'Our reputation depends on our ability to deliver the news in real time. When we covered the Olympics, for instance, we had photographers with digital cameras linked to their laptops sending photos back to our subscribers as soon as they were taken.'

But Reuters receives only 10 per cent of its revenue from media customers, with a whopping 90 per cent coming from financial services companies. It is almost as if the news service, brilliant though it is, now exists largely as a marketing device to attract higher-paying financial services customers.

Hungate concedes: 'It is fair to say that the average person on the street, while they undoubtedly know our brand, probably don't realize how much of our revenue comes from the financial services sector. But that has happened simply because our key brand attributes – speed, accuracy, freedom from bias – allow those customers to make a great deal of money. That was the case 150 years ago and it still is today. When Kuwait was invaded in 1991, sparking off the first Gulf War, we had news of the invasion half an hour before any other service. That doesn't sound like a long time, but if you were trading energy commodities, you could have lost a fortune without that information.'

It was perhaps inevitable that one of Reuters' most recent advertising campaigns focused on its coverage of the war in Iraq.

'We felt that our approach to Iraq illustrated the difference between ourselves and other news organizations. We actually have Iraqi journalists on our payroll – five people who have spent their entire careers in Iraq. They are locals and completely understand the way Iraq works, which gave us a local insight that nobody else had. In addition, we have dozens of reporters in the Middle East who are Arabic speakers and are in touch with the culture, and we were able to move them into Iraq and the surrounding countries very rapidly. On top of that we brought in various specialists in warfare and regional politics. In total we had about 150 people covering that conflict, one of the largest news operations on the ground. In contrast, Bloomberg had no one in Iraq. Even CNN does not have a team in Iraq full-time. As a result, on the night the conflict broke out, if you were watching TV here in the United States you could switch from channel to channel and see the same pictures. The Reuters feed was going directly to all the networks, and for the first hour and a half of the war, all the pictures you saw came from us.'

After the conflict, Reuters ran a campaign carrying the slogan: 'When Saddam fell, we caught him.' The target demographic was traders and financial professionals, as well as the group Hungate calls 'global influencers' – the chief executives and high-ranking management of multinational companies. The ad ran in the *Financial Times*, *The Wall Street Journal*, *The Economist*, and local upmarket media such as *Frankfurter Allgemeine Zeitung* in Germany. Outdoor sites in major financial centres like the City of London and Frankfurt were also used. A television version was carried on CNBC.

Although Reuters believes in targeted rather than mass advertising, Hungate points out that the Reuters building in New York, with its vast electronic sign, is effectively an outdoor advertisement. 'We are in the centre of what is arguably the media capital of the world, and this building is designed to make a statement.'

Reuters is traditionally regarded as a London-based organization, but it is quoted on both the London and New York stock exchanges, and its senior executives are spread fairly evenly between both capitals, with significant posts in Geneva, Hong Kong and Tokyo.

'The international aspect of the company is another part of our brand identity, and it helps us to remain free from bias,' Hungate points out. 'After all, Reuter himself was a German who worked in Paris and ended up in London.'

It is no coincidence that the marketing department is based in New York, the home of Reuters' most aggressive rival – Bloomberg.

A LEGEND UNDER PRESSURE

Like many successful media brands, Reuters has successfully exploited its own mythology. You don't have to look far on its Web site to find the names of some of the famous journalists who have worked there, including John Buchan, Edgar Wallace, Ian Fleming and Frederick Forsyth.

Fleming, who of course went on to create James Bond, joined Reuters in October 1931. He is quoted as saying: 'It was at Reuters that I learnt to write fast, and above all to be accurate because in Reuters if you weren't accurate you were fired.'

But the media aren't always kind to other media, and over the past couple of years the legend has taken a pasting. This is not without justification – its conversion to the new world of the Internet has been turbulent, and it has faced heavy competition in the financial information sector from Bloomberg, which has usurped its position as market leader. Not only has the recession led to a slump in trading screen sales, but Reuters' devices are said to be less user-friendly than Bloomberg's, and its huge range of products – numbering some 750 different systems at the time of writing – reportedly baffles customers.

In 2002, Reuters announced a loss of £493 million before tax – the first loss in its history. This followed news of extensive cost cutting and the shedding of about 2,250 jobs. But chief executive Tom Glocer – the enthusiastic 43-year-old American appointed in 2001 to shake up the company – remained confident that the brand's global strength would enable it to weather the storm.

Under Glocer, the company embarked on a major regeneration process called Fast Forward. It promised to clarify its offering by junking obsolete products and dividing the rest into clearly delineated segments, spearheaded by three new products called Reuters Trader, Reuters Knowledge and Reuters Intelligent Advisor. It laid plans for a global branding campaign, and introduced a beefy new slogan: 'Know. Now.' The downside was that more jobs would be cut, with total staff falling to 13,000 from 16,000 by the end of 2005. ('Reuters "bumping along the bottom"', *The Guardian*, 22 July 2003.) In London, Reuters was forced to give up its Fleet Street headquarters, as well as several other offices across the capital, when it moved most of its 3,000 UK staff under one roof in Docklands. (This echoed a similar move in New York two years earlier, when workers scattered across Manhattan were moved under one roof in Times Square.)

Although the media continued to focus on the company's seemingly brutal staff cuts, the efficiency drive seemed to be achieving the desired results by September 2003, when Reuters announced that it was back in the black with a £16 million pre-tax profit for the first half of the year. It looked as though the brand was groping its way back to recovery.

Hungate admits that protecting the brand's status in the face of media criticism has been a challenge. 'The most important thing to do was to make sure people understood the reasons behind [the job losses]. It is no secret that the number of people on the payroll in financial services – in other words the number of people out there looking at screens – has fallen by 20 per cent in the last two years [until mid-2003], so the absolute market size has shrunk. We were forced to adjust our cost base accordingly.'

And he adds that the job cuts were only partially a result of economic pressure. As at so many other media companies, new technology has allowed Reuters to streamline its operation. 'Technological advances now allow us to operate with fewer staff, while at the same time providing a higher level of service to our customers. For example, by implementing electronic commerce techniques, which allow customers to commission additional services and receive bills at the touch of a button – services that would have previously been handled manually by support staff – we have been able to take a lot of people out of our back office operations.'

Hungate believes the brand was insulated from harm partly by the nature of its customers. 'Our clients are clearly highly sophisticated in terms of their assessment of a company's financial health. They know that we have one of the most robust balance sheets of any media company you have been talking to during the course of researching this book. They realize that by taking these opportunities to improve efficiency, we've succeeded in reducing our operating cost faster than our revenue has fallen. When the financial services market picks up and revenues begin to rise again, we will be in a highly advantageous position.'

THE ARMOUR OF HERITAGE

Branding consultancy Interbrand consistently lists Reuters in its ranking of the world's 100 most valuable brands – it stood at number 76 in 2003, with an estimated brand value of US$3.30 billion, higher than the likes of Levi's, Shell, Heineken, and Starbucks. It may have fallen a few points in recent years, but with a heritage that stretches back more than a century and a half, it is difficult (although not impossible) to imagine it going out of business.

'Our customers certainly can't imagine that,' Hungate agrees, 'which is crucial from a marketing point of view, because it makes them confident when they sign a long-term contract with us. If a younger, smaller and less robust company offers them a competing service, even at a lower price, they may not feel so comfortable.'

He believes that an impressive heritage is one of the most valuable attributes a media brand can call upon. 'One of the things that protects Reuters against market fluctuations is the sense that it has been around forever, and that it will continue to be around. If you are a 10-year-old brand, no matter how much money you spend, you'll never be able to create that level of trust. People are almost unconsciously impressed by a brand that has stood the test of time.'

This is the case even though most Reuters clients – and certainly the general public – would be hard-pushed to say exactly when the brand was founded. 'Media brands like Reuters have become part of folklore. It's enough that customers simply have the impression that these brands have been around during the whole of their lifetime, and probably the whole of their parents' lifetime.'

Iconic media brands cannot afford to stand still, however. 'The trick is to maintain your relevance – there is a big difference between being viewed as an elderly brand, as opposed to a current brand with a long history. We stay relevant by using new technology to continually reinvigorate our reputation as the fastest, most accurate provider of information. We constantly strive to maintain our leadership in those areas, just as our competitors constantly monitor them for signs of weakness. That is the one danger with being an iconic brand: you are vulnerable to attack, and as soon as you lose your paranoia about staying ahead, you risk becoming a historical artefact.'

The brand in brief

Media brand: Reuters

Founded: 1851

Owner: Reuters Group PLC

Number of clients: 458,000 professional users of Reuters products worldwide (Source: Reuters)

Key marketing strategies: Customer relations, global advertising in international media

Brand extensions: None as such – Reuters provides a comprehensive range of news and financial information services across all media

Web site: Reuters.com

20

Bloomberg

'I was Bloomberg – Bloomberg was money – and money talked'

Bloomberg does not have a formal marketing department, and it does not spend money on traditional advertising or promotional campaigns. And yet it has more right to be here than many of the brands I've written about. Why? Because Bloomberg's success is almost entirely down to its founder's instinctive grasp of strategic marketing – in fact, the company may well provide one of the best examples of branding principles in the history of the media.

Even the reception of its New York headquarters is a marketing tool of genius. Everything about this buzzing space above Park Avenue is designed to make you feel as if you are at the centre of something urgent, exciting, and ruthlessly cool.

The area is dominated by a snack bar dispensing coffee, juice, cereals and fast food to the harassed staff. A giant tank of tropical fish should add a note of calm, but their lurid colours merely contribute to the sensory overload. TV screens blaze everywhere, and as you try to relax on one of the bulky leather sofas, intense young people criss-cross in front of you as if marching to a constant pulse of information. To your right, you can see directly into a glassed-off TV studio, where a presenter scowls into her hand-held mirror, making a last-second adjustment to her fringe before she goes on air. This is a pop video version of finance news, and the atmosphere has much more in common with MTV than it has with its great rival, Reuters. 'Make no mistake,' the reception area is telling you, 'Bloomberg rocks.'

TERMINAL VELOCITY

'For us, the medium really is the message,' says David Wachtel, who like everyone else at Bloomberg has no official title, although he admits that it should probably be something like 'director of media and marketing'. We're sitting in a glass office next to the TV studio – nothing at Bloomberg is enclosed, everything is on display, and everyone knows everyone's business. It's part of the ethos of the company, as laid down by Mike Bloomberg himself.

Wachtel gestures at the PC screen in the corner of the room, which is spouting strings of – to me, at least – incomprehensible financial data. 'That's our core product, the Bloomberg terminal for financial professionals. We see selling those terminals as our main business, and everything else is just an outgrowth of that.'

At the time of writing, there were 174,000 Bloomberg terminals around the world (although the word 'terminal' is now somewhat misleading, as the original Bloomberg box has largely been replaced by software). The subscription price is US$1,350 a month, and the company claims that it never gives discounts. To this day, 95 per cent of its revenues come from this side of the business.

Wachtel insists: 'We're not really a media company in the traditional sense of the term. That's to say, our business is based on a medium of sorts, but it's a very narrowcast one.'

But that is only a fraction of the story. As well as its data terminals, Bloomberg has a 24-hour satellite television operation reaching 178 million households worldwide, a news wire service with more than 1,200 reporters in 85 bureaus, a radio station, magazines, a book publishing arm, and a Web site that gets more than 180 million hits a month. Oh, and an electronic trading service that enables investors to trade stocks through the Bloomberg terminal, with an average of around 90 million shares traded per day.

So is Wachtel seriously trying to tell me that all of these are just marketing tools designed to help the company sell more terminals?

He nods: 'That's about right. Take our news service, for instance. The two pillars of our service are data analytics and financial news.

Ten years ago, we realized that we had become one of the largest third-party resellers of financial news. So we went into the news business. We began to syndicate to newspapers all around the world – and today we are probably the biggest supplier of business news to non-financial newspapers. *The New York Times* relies on us for the bulk of the financial coverage not provided by its own reporters. And each story has our name on it – can you imagine what a potent branding tool that is? It all contributes to the success of our main business.'

OUT OF THE BOX

To understand the true genius behind Bloomberg, it's necessary to go back to the beginning – and to Mike Bloomberg himself. Back in 1981, Bloomberg was a 39-year-old partner at Salomon Brothers, one of the most successful securities trading firms in the United States. This was the high-pressure, high rewards Wall Street of Tom Wolfe's novel *The Bonfire of the Vanities* – and Bloomberg was one of the masters of that universe. Then, following a merger and political infighting, he was fired – and given a US$10 million payoff.

Bloomberg was not the kind of guy to sit around counting his money, however. With a four-man team and a small office, he set out to create the self-contained data analysis device he knew Wall Street traders sorely needed. As he puts it in his book, *Bloomberg by Bloomberg* (1997), 'they were practically relying on abacuses and slide rules'. The box he had in mind would track the prices of stocks, bonds and commodities, while providing detailed analyses of thousands of different companies, industries and markets, with a few touches of a user-friendly keypad. With typical panache, Bloomberg sold the product to Merrill Lynch before it even existed, promising to deliver it in six months. (Merrill Lynch still retains a 20 per cent stake in the company.)

Bloomberg delivered his box on time, and just as he had predicted, it became indispensable – not just to Wall Street, but to anyone interested in the fluctuations of global finance. Legend has it that even the Vatican leases a Bloomberg terminal.

A great deal of this success sprang from Bloomberg's natural talent for branding. His terminal was originally called the Market Master, but he noticed that customers had begun to refer to it as The Bloomberg. This was not surprising, as he was constantly travelling around the world promoting and selling the device. So he changed its name, and willingly stepped into the media spotlight.

'I would become the Colonel Sanders of financial information services,' he explains in his book, 'the target for clever barbs from acerbic journalists, but simultaneously the one whose company and product would be on everyone's lips… And to make good copy, I gave the press a colourful personality to focus on. I was Bloomberg – Bloomberg was money – and money talked. Perfect!'

The step from providing financial data to supplying business news was not large, but it was astute. Dow Jones (the publisher of *The Wall Street Journal*) and Reuters were already competing with Bloomberg in the data terminal business, so why shouldn't he challenge their news services? He hired Matthew Winkler, a Wall Street Journal reporter who had written an unusually perceptive article about his company, to run the operation. They launched Bloomberg News into the teeth of the early 1990s recession – meaning that there were plenty of recently laid-off journalists who couldn't wait to come and work for them.

Writes Bloomberg: 'Our timing was right. When the Berlin Wall came down in 1989, there was no question who had won the Cold War. Capitalism had triumphed. The… battle of the superpowers had ended – and gone, too, was journalism's top tale. Money, in contrast, was emerging as the big story that needed telling at the end of the century.'

Bloomberg felt that few general-interest newspapers were covering business properly. At that time, not many journalists understood the complexities of the stock markets, and most papers had more reporters devoted to sport than to finance. The kind of journalism that won prizes focused on war and famine, human interest and crime – not share prices. Bloomberg realized that he could give these newspapers a means of covering the financial world cheaply and accurately, in words they understood.

Not surprisingly, Bloomberg News is one of the facets of the brand that intrigues journalists the most. Stacks of articles characterize editor-in-chief Winkler as a growling perfectionist, while at the same time failing to hide their admiration for his insistence on accuracy and precise prose. There is nothing anecdotal or descriptive about a Bloomberg news wire story – everything is explained in solid facts and figures, devoid of commentary. Adjectives and adverbs are banned. In fact, all the rules are laid out in a 360-page style guide called *The Bloomberg Way*, created by Winkler. Needless to say, this emphasis on getting the facts right meant that Bloomberg News quickly went from nowhere to becoming one of the most widely used wire services in the world.

But Bloomberg News was not created to raise the standards of financial journalism. Bloomberg writes: 'Our purpose was to do more than just collect and relay news; it should also, ethically, advertise the analytical and computational powers of the Bloomberg terminal by highlighting its capabilities in each news story. This would make each story better and, at the same time, make it easier to rent out more terminals.'

Marketing, pure and simple. Bloomberg moved into radio and television for much the same reason, as he explains. 'To reach potential customers who don't yet subscribe to our print products, radio and TV are the only practical ways to get our message through. The people who lease our terminals... need news while jogging, showering, driving, or sitting at home, and we've got to give them what they need.'

He needed a little prodding at first, though. The catalyst was Jon Fram, an employee at an ailing television channel called the Financial News Network (FNN). Fram contacted Bloomberg to suggest that he buy FNN, as it made perfect sense for the business information brand to have its own television channel. Bloomberg wasn't convinced, because he preferred to build businesses from the ground up, rather than trying to rebrand existing organizations.

A day later, Fram called again – this time suggesting that instead of buying FNN, Bloomberg should hire him and a couple of his colleagues to set up a broadcast operation from scratch. Once more, Bloomberg failed to bite. After a short interval, Fram called him with a detailed pitch explaining exactly why broadcast was the perfect promotional platform for the Bloomberg brand. Bloomberg thought: 'One of us is stupid – and it isn't him!' So he hired Fram and two other key employees from FNN, and charged them with getting the company into the broadcasting game.

First, Bloomberg bought an ailing New York radio station called WNEW and transformed it into an information service. Using a groundbreaking production method in which journalists recorded their reports onto computer files (a bit like MP3 files), the company was able to cut and paste its programming at the push of a button, and sell its stories to other independent radio stations.

When it branched into television, Bloomberg worked in exactly the same way – pre-recording shows and then putting them on a computer, so they could be assembled in the order required. From a daily 30-minute syndicated show called *Bloomberg Business News*, Bloomberg Television expanded into a global service that now broadcasts in seven different languages. Its killer application is the widely emulated multi-format screen, which displays rolling bulletins of breaking news, stock market shifts, weather reports and sports scores alongside conventional TV pictures. All this keeps viewers hooked, much to the appreciation of advertisers.

David Wachtel says: 'The format is familiar now, but when we launched it, people thought we were crazy. To us it made perfect sense, because our core audience were the people who used our terminals. They were used to studying screens and taking in different pieces of information at the same time. These days, everyone has adjusted to that way of looking at data. At the time, it was considered revolutionary.'

By the end of the 1990s, the company Mike Bloomberg had set up to market his data terminals had evolved into a multimedia business information empire. In his autobiography, he states: 'Some companies declare themselves to be "in radio" or "in television" or "in newspapers" and so on... Bloomberg is in the business of giving its customers the information they need – no matter what that information is – where and when they need it, in whatever form is appropriate.'

The Bloomberg brand was so well established that when the company launched its Web site in 1995, it went straight into the top five financial information sites with no marketing whatsoever.

FLOUTING CONVENTION

As a multifaceted media brand, Bloomberg had achieved by the end of the 1990s what many of its rivals are still struggling to accomplish today. The name Bloomberg simply meant 'business information' – not 'newspaper', 'magazine', or 'TV channel' – giving it the flexibility to stamp its brand on any number of related products.

David Wachtel comments: 'All our media products are designed for financial professionals. We focus single-mindedly on that narrow audience, and on providing the services they need. In that way we can move across platforms much more convincingly than other media owners. The big media conglomerates that are the result of various mergers are trying to convince advertisers that a TV brand here can link with a magazine brand over there, but it doesn't really work. At Bloomberg, the multiple platform structure actually makes sense.'

But Bloomberg also has a number of other attributes that distinguish it from its old-school rivals. For a start, it has never forgotten that the customer is king. Indeed, to use an unwieldy marketing expression, the company is extremely 'customer-facing'. The early data terminals featured a prominent message urging customers to e-mail Bloomberg himself if they had a problem with the service. Bloomberg employees sit down at their desks at 7.30 am – the same time as the majority of their customers. The company's 24-hour telephone help line is known to be fast and efficient, as is its online equivalent. Bloomberg sales people constantly visit customers to ensure that they are happy with their terminals. And Bloomberg TV and radio news bulletins are available on demand via the Web for people who have missed them. Right from the very start, Bloomberg has been about selling – and that means cuddling up to its customers.

Bloomberg's promotional efforts are similarly unconventional. Although the company has no time for traditional advertising, it excels at what might be called 'asymmetrical marketing'.

For instance, the company has let movie studios know that if they need a set for a film about high finance, Bloomberg will build them an entire trading floor – for nothing. (Of course, it will feature lots of flashing and blinking Bloomberg terminals.) In 2000, Bloomberg arranged for its TV presenters to record the passenger announcements for the New York transport authority's new subway trains. The company also has teams of people doing what it calls 'ancillary distribution': putting screens showing Bloomberg Television into banks, bars favoured by brokers, and other suitable environments. (This works because Bloomberg's multi-format screen enables viewers to glean plenty of information even when the volume is turned down.) In Hong Kong, where Bloomberg had trouble finding a distributor for its TV channel, it did deals with real estate companies to get its images pumped into the lobbies and elevators of landmark buildings.

The company has always understood the value of press coverage: the Bloomberg party that follows the White House Correspondents' Association dinner in Washington every spring is regarded as one of the year's most prestigious events, and generates reams of clippings. (Bloomberg once stated: 'Journalists are just like you and me… they try to do their jobs and get home to the kids. If you make filling inches and minutes easier for them, they'll help you every time.') And while it is overly cynical to consider charitable donations a marketing tool, it is worth noting that Mike Bloomberg has given millions of dollars to his old university, John Hopkins. The school's Bloomberg Center for Physics & Astronomy opened in 1990.

Conversely, the intense working conditions at Bloomberg have occasionally attracted negative press coverage. An article in *BusinessWeek* quoted a former Bloomberg News reporter who described the wire service as 'a journalistic sweatshop' ('The Bloomberg Machine, *BusinessWeek*, 23 April 2001). The company's founder seems to have wanted to re-create the frenetic, macho environment of a Wall Street trading floor. An emphasis on equality and productivity means that everyone works at small slab-like desks with little or no division between them. The day begins early and finishes late. Lunch, presumably, is for wimps.

David Wachtel, referring to the company's in-your-face reception area, tells me: 'This is just for fun, to give visitors like you a bit of a thrill. We bring a lot of our customers in here, which is the entire reason for its existence. The real stuff happens in the rest of the building – floors and floors of thousands of people working away at narrow desks.'

Journalists from rival news organizations may criticize this set-up, but it is doubtful that Mike Bloomberg believes there is such a thing as bad publicity.

And now, of course, he is mayor of New York.

BLOOMBERG SANS BLOOMBERG

It is fair to say that Bloomberg LP, to give the company its full name, is at a turning point. Although Bloomberg himself still owns 72 per cent of the privately held business, his mayoral duties mean that he can no longer run it. And the brand somehow feels diminished without him. When I visit the headquarters, the company's official spokeswoman Chris Taylor shows me his empty desk and a series of framed press clippings charting the rise of the company. Her voice is tinged with something very like nostalgia, and I can't help thinking that Mayor Mike's old workspace resembles a shrine. Can Bloomberg continue to thrive without Bloomberg? Is it now a brand in its own right, like Reuters?

Lex Fenwick, who used to run the London office, filled Bloomberg's shoes as chief executive. But while Fenwick has an impressive reputation as a manager, he is unlikely to equal his former boss's high profile as a brand spokesman. And Bloomberg left at the worst possible time for the company, which has seen its customer base shrivel as thousands of traders lose their jobs in the dismal economic climate.

Reuters has not been vanquished either, despite its own economy-linked problems. Bloomberg may have more firepower in the United States, but Reuters remains the leading financial information brand in Europe. And its new, youthful American chief executive, Tom Glocer, is determined to streamline the old warhorse and shake it out of its malaise.

Bloomberg's revenues are up – estimated at more than US$3 billion in 2003. It is still selling terminals – but the growth rate of sales has slowed from 21 per cent in 1998 to 6 per cent in 2002, according to an article in *The New York Times* ('Bloomberg, Without Bloomberg, Faces an Industry in Retreat', 8 September 2002). This could present a morale problem for the company, whose employees' annual bonuses are linked to the growth of its terminal business. In several reports, Reuters has accused Bloomberg of offering discounts for the first time to boost sales – a charge the American company hotly denies.

There is even a danger that Bloomberg's role as New York mayor may dent the image of the brand. An unpopular smoking ban, raised taxes, and pressure on the city's police force to enforce obscure local laws (at the time of my visit, a man was fined for sitting on a milk crate) in the hope of reaping revenue from fines have created an aura of negativity around his name. Yet that name is still emblazoned on a valuable array of media properties.

David Wachtel does not believe the company's image has been affected by its founder's status. 'I really don't think it has made any difference. Perhaps people outside our core target market are now a little more curious about Bloomberg the company, but that won't have any impact on our profits. We provide a professional product and the people who buy into our brand are more interested in what it can do for them than whatever the mayor of New York's policies might be. We have kept a lower marketing profile in the city, for legal as well as branding reasons, but otherwise it's business as usual. The company is running in the same way that it always has.'

Wachtel points out that Bloomberg is now a global brand. 'Half of our employees and half of our customers are outside the United States. Our sales are run out of New York, London and Tokyo. And of course we have news bureaux in every major city. It's unlikely that what happens in Manhattan is going to have a great influence on that.'

Finally, Wachtel stresses that the company's key advantage is its almost obsessive focus on its target market. 'Our strategy of concentrating on our core customers means that our products now market themselves. It's almost like viral marketing – they all feed off of one another. For instance, we bring somebody in because they are looking for some financial information on the Web, and they discover our Web site. But once they go on the site, it extremely aggressively promotes all our other media. After all, if you're already there, the chances are you are in our target market. Our marketing is successful because our message is totally clear – no surprises, no ambiguity. Wherever you are, if you are looking for quality financial information, you can get it from Bloomberg.'

So while Mike Bloomberg is busy being mayor, his brand hums away like a supercomputer in a science fiction movie, marketing itself, generating new customers, and perhaps awaiting his return. After all, there's no reason why Bloomberg shouldn't come back to his desk after his stint in politics. F Scott Fitzgerald (a Bloomberg newsroom favourite) famously wrote that there were no second acts in American lives. But Mike Bloomberg is currently on his third act, and is likely to have plenty of energy left for a fourth.

The brand in brief

Media brand: Bloomberg

Founded: 1981

Owner: Bloomberg LP (Michael Bloomberg – 72%)

Customers: Terminals leased by 174,000 clients (Source: Bloomberg)

Key marketing strategies: Multiple media promote one another to the same narrow target audience. Plus – product placement, public relations

Brand extensions: News wire, TV, radio, books, magazines

Web site: Bloomberg.com

Conclusion: how to build a media monolith

'The medium is no longer the message'

In 1987 I got my first job in journalism, at a medium-sized daily newspaper in Wiltshire. It was never going to be a cutting-edge environment – but by today's standards it was positively prehistoric.

We would bash out our stories on towering ancient typewriters, making two copies (one for the news editor and one for the sub-editors) by placing purple sheets of glossy carbon between the leaves of cheap, grainy paper. Typing errors were corrected by hand, and if we made a real hash of it we'd impale the sandwich of paper on a metal spike and start all over again.

There was one fax machine in the building, and it belonged to the advertising department. If a PR agency wanted to fax us a press release ('How exotic,' we mused) we had to trudge upstairs and fetch it. Similarly, we had only one mobile phone. I use the word 'mobile' with hesitation, because it came in a suitcase.

In the office, phones rang – actually rang, not chirruped politely – all the time. What with that and the insistent clacking of typewriters and the tinkle and slash of carriage returns and everybody shouting and smoking, it was a chaotic, unhealthy environment. (I dread to think what it must have been like at a paper like *The Times*.) We all loved it, naturally. The first thing we noticed when 'new technology' arrived – in the form of glaring green screens – was the clinical silence that pervaded the newsroom.

To me, 1987 does not seem so very long ago. And yet the world has changed utterly since then – for everyone, of course, but particularly for the media. Less than 20 years ago there were no computers, no mobile phones, no satellite TV. As for e-mail and the Internet, they have only become mass communication tools over the past seven or eight years.

During the few months that I spent researching this book, I got the impression that some of the media monoliths – particularly the print media – had been taken unawares by the pace of evolution. The ease with which audiences had adapted to new technology, utterly changing their media consumption habits, seemed to have left the older brands flummoxed – as if they had emerged from suspended animation in a science fiction movie, to find their world radically altered. Since then, after taking a good look around and scratching their heads, they have made concerted efforts to adjust.

Meanwhile, the newer brands caught the wave of change and rode it, growing very quickly from rebellious outsiders to members of the media aristocracy: I'm thinking of Bloomberg, MTV and CNN. Now they, too, must defend their brand equity in the face of competition from the next generation.

And yet they will survive. If I've learnt one thing during my journey through the media bazaar, it is that a good media brand is hard to destroy. Will *Vogue* cease to exist as a brand next month, next year, in 10 years? I doubt it.

So how did the 20 media brands in this book get it so right? How do you get from a scrappy project on a sheet of paper to an MTV? Well, I don't claim to have the definitive answer – but I reckon I've got a pretty good idea. For your information and amusement, here are my keys to creating a media monolith.

HAVE A VISION

It's incredible how few of the media monoliths grew out of a team effort. When you probe into the history of the world's greatest media brands, you realize that, more often than not, a single individual created them, as well as putting in place the values that still drive them today. James Gordon Bennett Jr, Condé Nast, Paul Julius Reuter,

Adolph Ochs, Ted Turner, Mike Bloomberg – all fascinating personalities who had the spark of an idea and took it through to its logical conclusion, paying little heed to their critics.

The growth of the media monoliths has not been steady – on a chart plotting their progress, there would be a helter-skelter of peaks and troughs. But the secret is not to give up, to fight tooth and nail to stay in the game. Do deals, make sacrifices, and play dirty if you have to. And remember that some of the best ideas spring from necessity – I particularly appreciate the fact that the *Financial Times* was printed on pink paper not just because it would stand out, but also because it was cheaper.

PICK A TARGET

Few great media brands are aimed at everyone. The gentlemen above had very specific targets in mind. *Vogue*'s Condé Nast and the *IHT*'s Gordon Bennett targeted the new elite – the 'jet set' of their day – that had been created by turn-of-the-century industrialization. Today their products continue to serve well-heeled globetrotters, whether interested in international news or in high fashion.

Paul Julius Reuter and Mike Bloomberg targeted those who worked in the financial markets. The creators of the French newspaper *Libération* aimed their product at the emerging generation of post-1968 rebels. Ted Turner was a well-travelled news fiend looking for an international perspective, and he correctly assumed there were others like him. MTV was created for a tribe of music fans that knew no geographic or linguistic boundaries.

A magazine like *Paris Match*, with its wide demographic appeal, may be the exception that proves the rule. Remember Olivier Royant, the publication's deputy editor? He said: 'If you launched *Paris Match* tomorrow, you might not be able to get it off the ground.' But even Royant accepts that *Paris Match* is at the end of the day a French newsmagazine, and thus has a self-defining market.

CREATE A CLUB

Once you've identified your audience, it's essential to make them feel part of your project. This strategy is perhaps best illustrated by two utterly different but enormously successful media brands: MTV and *The Economist*. MTV became compulsive viewing largely because its audience felt as if they owned it. They had the impression that it had been created by people who understood them – were, in fact, very much like them. 'I want my MTV', ran the channel's first advertising slogan – a jewel of inclusive marketing.

The Economist's famous poster campaign plays a similar trick. Witty, intellectual, a bit elitist – those who get the joke feel as if they are in on something, as if this has been written with them in mind. For me, the execution that sums it up is this one: 'A poster should contain no more than eight words, which is the maximum the average reader can take in at a single glance. This, however, is a poster for *Economist* readers.'

These are just two examples, of course, but there are plenty of others dotted throughout the book. Almost every newspaper and magazine editor I interviewed felt that readers did not buy their products as mere sources of information, but as lifestyle statements.

GO WIDE – YET NARROW

'Aggressive, creative, relentless distribution.' Bill Roedy, the president of MTV Networks International, said that this was the company's key marketing strategy.

It is practically impossible to become a true media monolith without some kind of international status, even if that means getting your paper or magazine on selected newsstands around the world. It's far better, though, to have print sites in every corner of the globe. Better still to have regional foreign-language editions. (If you can't afford that, try thinking asymmetrically, like the *International Herald Tribune* and its strategy of placing branded supplements inside prestigious domestic newspapers.) For broadcast media, it means getting your brand on to as many screens as possible – not just in homes, but in hotel rooms, bars, airports, planes, buses, taxis ….

As well as going wide, you have to go narrow. The world is not as homogenized as the anti-globalization paranoiacs think. The other strand of MTV's marketing strategy is localization. At the time of writing it has 42 different channels. These are tailored not only to reflect cultural and linguistic differences, but increasingly, variations in musical taste. The wonders of digital technology are allowing MTV to create channels for those who like rock, rap, techno, and so on.

But remember – although you can adjust the content, it is essential that you maintain the brand's values. MTV means 'irreverent', *Vogue* means 'elegant', the *FT* means 'business'. Lose sight of your core message and you could lose control of your brand. Mark Wright, the creative director of CNN International, told me: 'The number one component for successful branding is consistency.'

BE FLEXIBLE – AND BE QUICK ABOUT IT

When I was reading Mike Bloomberg's biography, *Bloomberg by Bloomberg*, it became apparent that his company had an important edge on its competitors. Bloomberg realized quicker than most that a brand limited to a single medium was at a disadvantage in a world where audiences synthesized information from a rapidly widening pool of sources. He sensed that, once you had a brand people trusted, you could put it on as many media platforms as you liked – print, TV, radio, the Web, mobile phones – and still attract eyeballs.

But Bloomberg was not alone. One of the oldest brands in this book – *The Wall Street Journal*, founded in 1889 – was also one of the quickest off the mark, charging a subscription fee for WSJ.com almost as soon as it had the site up on the Web. The others were slower to catch on. All of them are now desperate to become cross-media brands, having launched various TV, Web and mobile phone offerings. But sometimes their efforts have an unseemly haste about them, as if they are running for an accelerating bus.

BUT MAINTAIN QUALITY

It's a long time since I've read any Marshall McLuhan – but if the medium was ever the message, it doesn't seem to me to be the case any longer. Consumers feel comfortable accessing their preferred brands via a wide variety of media, as long as the quality is consistent. It's no use having a cultivated newspaper and a primitive Web site, for instance, or a sumptuous magazine that lends its name to a trashy TV show.

It brings us back to trust, which nearly every single one of my interviewees mentioned, and which I touched on in the Introduction. When you move across media platforms, make sure you're not tempted to cut corners and undermine your reputation. To deliver consistently high quality is to protect your brand. The message, in other words, is the message.

Quality also plays a crucial role in marketing strategies. For example, although branded accessories are an acceptable way of raising awareness and generating revenue, not many media monoliths – with the notable exceptions of *Playboy*, *National Geographic* and (despite its denials) *Vogue* – are keen on the 'bags-and-t-shirts' style of promotion. Books and CDs seem to be about as far as they are willing to go.

Even classical marketing techniques are given short shrift. *The Economist* has built a superlative brand through an equally inspired advertising campaign, but I was surprised by how many media companies told me: 'Our product is our best marketing tool.' Everyone from CNN to *Vogue* said they preferred to spend their money on content and distribution rather than advertising. Those that could get away with running branding initiatives as cheaply as possible did so: think of BBC World and its barter deals with other channels, or CNN and *Time* magazine using cheap (perhaps even free?) advertising space at other media brands in the Time Warner group.

It's worth noting that the smallest brands are often the most inventive when it comes to marketing. I particularly admired the daily radio and TV 'news bulletins' run by *El País* – which combined creativity, coordination and teamwork. And *Die Zeit*'s decision to position itself as the exact opposite of the Internet – presenting the newspaper as a luxurious, time-consuming product in which one wallows like a hot bath – was inspired.

FINALLY, STAY RELEVANT

A heritage is a wonderful thing – but it doesn't make you invulnerable. There are plenty of historic brands that have been reduced to mere shadows of their former selves by various economic and strategic mishaps – I'm thinking of *Life* magazine in the United States, and the satirical publication *Punch* in the UK. The older media monoliths

I visited were almost as paranoid about relevance as they were trust, and rightly so.

The recession has alerted big media to the danger of complacency. Reuters is currently going through a painful modernization process, and over the past few years both *The Times* and the *Financial Times* have revamped to pull in younger readers. The *IHT* – possibly the most fragile of all the media brands I've covered – may have acted just in time with its 2004 relaunch.

Yet the events of the past few years, from the Twin Towers to Iraq and beyond, have proved that veteran brands have a certain advantage. Both *Time* magazine and *The Times* told me that their readership figures soared after 11 September 2001, and have yet to sink back to their previous levels. CNN – always a safe bet in a war – undoubtedly benefited from events in Iraq. In times of uncertainty, people embrace the familiar. The trick is to make sure you deliver what these returning audiences expect, but in a fresh and surprising way. Then they'll stick around for more when the smoke clears.

So that's it – seven tips for survival. Reading through my notes once again, I was struck by how similar the business and marketing strategies of the media monoliths were. There is never an exact template for success, but it does seem that – almost by accident – these great media brands have established efficient formulae for maintaining their pre-eminent status, no matter what is thrown at them.

At the beginning, I said that the media landscape had changed utterly since I started out as a journalist. In another 10 years it will have transformed again. But I'm willing to bet that the brands in this book will still be around – and that they will be more powerful than ever.

References

BOOKS

Bloomberg, Michael (1997) *Bloomberg by Bloomberg*, John Wiley & Sons Inc, New York

Flournoy, Don M and Stewart, Robert K (1997) *CNN – Making News in the Global Market*, John Libbey Media, Luton

Kynaston, David (1988) *The Financial Times – A Centenary History*, Viking, London

Marcantonio, Alfredo (2002) *Well-written and Red – The Story of the Economist Poster Campaign*, Dakini Books Ltd, London

Robertson, Charles L (1987) *The International Herald Tribune – The First Hundred Years*, Columbia University Press, New York

Sante, Luc (1991) *Low Life – Lures and Snares of Old New York*, Farrar, Straus and Giroux Inc, New York

Seebohm, Carole (1982) *The Man Who Was Vogue – The Life and Times of Condé Nast*, Weidenfeld & Nicholson, London

ONLINE RESOURCES

BBCi (www.bbc.co.uk/thenandnow/history)

CNN/Money (money.cnn.com)

Museum of Hamburg History (www.hamburgmuseum.de)

National Geographic Online (www.nationalgeographic.com/birth/)

Reuters.com (http://about.reuters.com/aboutus/history/)

Timesonline (www.newsint-archive.co.uk)

Vogue.com (www.vogueparis.com)

OTHERS

Paris Match 'Le Film', 2003, issued by Hachette Filipacchi

Index